MY NAME'S KENNY I CAN'T TALK

Lynda Holler

My Name is Kenny

I Can't Talk

Life is precious
Over 200 people voice the impact of one man on their lives

ISBN 978-1-7338879-0-8

A word is accepted or rejected for three reasons: because of the person who speaks it, because of the word that is spoken, because of those who hear it. For this word to be honored and accepted, the one who is speaking it must be a good man, a virtuous man, one worthy of being believed. Otherwise, rather than being accepted, it will be rejected, despised. Further, what is said must be good and true. Finally, those who hear it must be good, prepared to receive it; if not, it will be neither accepted, honored, nor kept...

Saint Frances de Sales

TABLE OF CONTENTS

PRANKING   65

LISTENING   89

COACHING 139

Acknowledgements

My heartfelt appreciation goes out to all the people that enthusiastically agreed to meet with me to talk about their relationship and impressions of Kenny.

I have to admit that I never anticipated how much I would enjoy the interview process. I got to sit and really talk with 207 people that are very important in our lives. We shared a pot of tea with cookies, or dinner, a glass of wine or a beer, or lunch. We met singly and in groups; some gatherings turned into parties like the one at the McCormick house where I sat in an upstairs bedroom with eight Astoria friends taking turns coming up to what they called, "the principal's office." Or reunions, like at the FDNY's Special Operation Command, where firefighters, active and retired, gathered to sit with me one at a time at the iconic kitchen table. Kenny's medical professionals set time aside from their busy schedules and our talks routinely ran overtime. They enjoyed our time together as much as I did.

Each interview was done one-on-one. I wanted to make sure that every contributor's perspective was kept pure and not influenced by anyone else. These friends took time that no one seems to have any more and I am grateful. Not just for the stories and the memories, but they opened up to me and shared very heartfelt sentiments and personal experiences. Of course we cried, but we laughed too and I came to love each of these people even more than I had before. Some were still really hurting two years after Kenny's death. By sitting together, looking into each other's eyes and hearts, we all were able to heal a little more.

Of course the recordings were impactful for our sons Colin and Tim. They knew their dad from one perspective, now they heard the impact that he made on so many different people, in so many different ways. And they heard what people admire in other people; that is sure to influence their behavior and interactions for the rest of their lives.

I want to acknowledge and specifically thank Chris Moore for the important role he played in transforming scores of pages of vernacular dialog into the book I envisioned. He recognized that I had a story that needed to be told and his expert synthesis of publishing experience and moral insight supported and complimented my inexperience and vision. Chris never knew Kenny, but as he read, edited, and formatted this unique volume of stories, we bonded in the unified purpose of extending Kenny's reach a bit further with the hopes of making the world a bit better.

Additionally, I want to thank Anne Nevin, Louisa Bisogno, and Ellen Farley for the encouragement, mentoring, and detailed proof-reading that they did throughout the four years this book journeyed from conception to completion.

I know that my life and the lives of Colin and Tim have been enriched by the investment that these loving contributors made to this project. I pray that yours will be too.

Introduction

The format of this book may be different from any you have ever read before. It is comprised entirely of direct quotes from the 207 people that I interviewed, a few outside quotes that I thought enhanced the message, and some of my thoughts interspersed to fill in the blanks. Some of the quotes are longer and formatted as chapters, while others are short and positioned to enhance and ratify the longer messages.

It is also important to understand from the beginning that I never intended this book to just be a memoir or eulogy of Kenny Holler's life. Even though he was a colorful figure and well-loved in his communities, that wasn't enough of a reason for me to spend hundreds of hours compiling these words. I knew that the process would reveal a story that was much bigger than Kenny. Love, friendship, suffering, and death are all part of the human condition that we struggle with every day. I recognized that although our family's experiences were not unique, how we handled them was. I saw that it was impacting people very profoundly and I wanted to dig deeper.

I could not have written Kenny's story alone. I spent sixty percent of my adult life with that man, almost twenty-four/seven over his last thirteen years, but I didn't know him well enough. I didn't know him through the hearts and minds of the other people in his life, which was a huge perspective. But Brian or Steve or Big Dave didn't know him well enough either. I learned so much about Kenny in those interviews and I know that every single contributor will be amazed at the perspectives of the others.

It was enlightening to recognize that people did not usually say what I expected them to say. Before the interviews, I sent my participants a letter explaining the book, including some questions to ponder before we met, but the interview was not in a question and answer format. I asked everyone to just speak freely. They did and the results were unexpected and wonderful.

Many of our conversations ran for twenty minutes or longer, with some logging over an hour of recording time. It was astounding how diverse the reflections were and how much material I had to work with when I finally decided to stop collecting. I wanted this book to contain thoughts from every interview; thereby much wonderful material has temporarily ended up on the digital cutting room floor.

My intention is to keep this conversation going and to inspire readers to reflect on the wisdom and insight of other people like them, people traveling the same joyful, disappointing, fulfilling, and complicated roads. In the months ahead, I will be building a platform for people to read and share stories that will allow us to ponder the big questions and find encouragement in diverse perspectives. Watch for it at www.speakforkenny.com.

Lynda Holler
Brewster, New York
Spring, 2019

PROLOGUE

Two women walk into a crowded bar. A Friday-night-after-work-in-Queens kind of crowd. A local place, like Cheers, but no one knows their names. They order a drink, chat alone, and then start for the door. A man wearing an FDNY hat cuts them off, holds out his hand to one woman, and says, "Hi, my name is Kenny. How do you like me so far?"

People
Sister Edwin: Rosary Hill Home for the terminally ill

Beginning the very same day Kenny was admitted, people came. Some from his childhood neighborhood, a lot from the Church, there were all these different groups and they were from different places. Men and women.

I didn't have a personal relationship with Kenny. By the time he came to us he was pretty unresponsive. I couldn't talk to him; he couldn't communicate with us really. At first he would open his eyes, but he was barely conscious. He was here less than three days.

Kenny not being able to talk didn't deter friends from visiting. That is what I was impressed by and that is what I remember. It has been almost two and a half years since he was here; sometimes we don't even remember people after two days, but we all were impacted by this.

Why did people come?

Who was this man?

Eulogy

Father Jack: St. Lawrence O'Toole Church, August 5, 2014

Please join me in singing an old time favorite:

> *East Side, West Side, all around the town.*
> *The tots play ring-a-round rosie,*
> *London Bridge is falling down.*
> *Boys and girls together:*
> *me and Mamie O'Rourke.*
> *We tripped the light fantastic*
> *on the sidewalks of New York.*

I have no idea how I learned that song, but I have known it all my life. It was written in 1925 as Al Smith's theme song in his run as the first Catholic candidate for the presidency of the United States.

There are so many other songs from our childhood that we just remember: songs that were sung at family gatherings throughout our youth and most of them were about living in New York City.

There's just a spirit in all of us who grew up in the city. Whenever I'm asked to speak to couples preparing for marriage or at Pre-Cana Conferences, I use the same example. Our minds are like high-tech video recorders: not just recording what they see and hear, but more importantly, what we feel. Our video recorders are programmed to go on rewind and play—but keep in mind there is no erase button. Truly to understand yourself or another, you must understand and appreciate what's on the recorder.

Kenny Holler, as we all know, had a ton of experiences on his recorder. It made him the man he was. Kenny's video recorder was taking in all of the experiences throughout his life and the lessons were well taught and accepted. The importance of family was a value that Kenny never failed to live. His devotion to his parents and brother, Gerard, was absolute. To be loved by Kenny Holler was a true blessing, and boy, did he love a lot of people!

Commitment to the service of others is something he internalized. I have been surrounded by the NYC Fire Department all my life. Tim and Colin, there is something very special when your father is a firefighter. It brings a real pride knowing your father, each and every day, was part of New York's Bravest. As Jesus said, "We are here to serve, not to be served."

Kenny was very popular when he was a kid and that popularity continued all his life. He was accepting, welcoming, and very funny. My brother, Kerry, told me that Kenny was the first friend he made in Astoria and that was because Kenny extended his hand of welcome first.

Your father played basketball for Power Memorial High School. This great Manhattan school was named after Bishop John Power, the Irish bishop who encouraged Edmund Rice to found the Irish Christian Brothers, who taught at Power, Rice, All Hollows, and Iona. In our day, every New York City kid believed otherwise. We all thought Power received the name because it was a basketball Powerhouse; the school of Kareem Abdul-Jabbar. Kenny played for Power. For all of us, it made our friend a superstar.

Lynda, you are and always have been a class act. I celebrated your wedding and baptized your boys in this very church. You chose the Gospel for this Mass as one of the Stations of the Cross: Simon helps Jesus to carry His cross. Your husband received his cross of serious illness twenty-one years ago. Lynda, you are Simon to us, but you do know you are not the only one who helped Kenny to carry his cross. This church is filled with assignments, a testimony to the loyalty of your families and especially Kenny's friends who honor us with their presence today: Hut, Stove, McCormick, Pete R, Shorty, Pete and Sue, and the super faithful Steve. Steve and my sister Carole helped Kenny carry his cross at the very end.

Colin and Timmy, my father died when I was very young like yourselves. My personal dream was at that time and remains to this day the same: to grow up to be a man like my father. May you two wonderful sons have the same dream.

Lynda, the cross has been lifted, but its weight still remains. You have the loyalty of everyone here in this church. This Kenny taught us all.

St. Paul, at the end of his ministry, writes in his letter to Timothy: "The time has come for me to be sacrificed. I must leave this life. I have fought the good fight. I have run the race. I have kept the faith."

Kenny you have done the same and we who love you are better for it.

BASKETBALL

Believe it or not, you can tell a lot about somebody on the basketball court. Kenny was always looking for somebody else to be open. He probably should have shot a lot more than he did, because he was certainly capable of scoring, but he just didn't play that way. Somehow, all of that figures in to the kind of person you are, because there are guys that never give up the ball. They are always shooting; they don't care if the team wins, as long as they get to shoot. Kenny was the opposite.[1]

Many people can play, but don't know the game. Kenny knew the game. I don't know where he got that. I'll see these days, when I watch my grandson Thomas play, some kids get the ball and dribble, dribble, dribble. Put their heads down and they are oblivious to everybody else on the court. But Kenny had that feel. I think it is a special feel; maybe he would just do it innately. He got the ball, saw the defense, he knew he didn't have a shot, so he would drive and kick it to the open man. He did it naturally. He was the type of guy that people would like to play with, because he was not selfish.[2]

---

1   Kerry, Astoria Friend
2   Brendan, Basketball Coach

1
Admirable
Johnny: Astoria Friend

I lived on Thirty-Eighth Street in Astoria, Queens and that was one block away from where Kenny lived on Steinway Street. As a young boy living on a family street, where each family had at least five or six kids—my family had eight—we had a block that was chock-full of people to play with. So, for the first maybe eight years of my life, I never remember going off that block, but the one time I did, one of the first friends that I met was Kenny Holler.

We met through the CYO, Catholic Youth Organization, basketball program, and then started playing basketball together all the time in Steinway Park. The circle of friends started to grow from Steinway Street, Thirty-Eighth Street, and on out as we got involved in the school and CYO sports programs. We were probably nine or ten years old and we used to play basketball almost every day in the summer. We did a bunch of stuff together including hockey in the street and ping pong in Kenny's basement. Kenny didn't come to my house very often, because it was a small house with ten people; it was always chaos. One thing I remember about his house was that it was always quiet. Mr. Holler was a very quiet man.

Kenny was a quiet kid in school. I don't remember him ever being in trouble or anything like that. I can remember him going to church all the time. When I would go to Mass on Sunday, I would see him there and we'd meet outside.

Kenny's father's presence was always around him and I think that he had a healthy fear of his father. I think his dad really taught him a good sense of self-control, not to follow the crowd, and how to be a man. As we went into our teenage years, in those days it was very rough, and the one thing I always admired about Kenny was that he was always in control of himself. His father poked his head in Steinway Park a lot, but I think that Kenny seemed to know who he was and what was expected of him.

Even when we were playing basketball, he never seemed to lose his temper, never got into a fight, was a super athlete. When we were in grammar school, at the end of the CYO season, they had a big CYO awards presentation. They went over the season and had congratulatory speeches for teams and players that did well. They handed out MVPs for each team and they also had a new award dedicated to Bill Delheimer who was popular in the CYO program. He had died suddenly in a sleigh riding accident, so they created a *Sportsman of the Year* award for the best athlete and sportsman of the whole CYO program. You have to understand that it wasn't a hundred or two hundred kids; there were probably four or five hundred kids in this program. I remember sitting in the chair and thinking, "Well, maybe I'll get it, I don't know." I was one of the better players on the team, so I had hope. When they called Kenny's name, I understood that it was perfect for him, because he was a total sportsman.

Eventually there were so many kids around the neighborhood that it was like corporate movement. You didn't have your one buddy; you had a whole bunch of people just moving together. One summer, we had a friend group of like fifty guys, from all over the place, hanging out in Steinway Park. It was not a good environment. Even though he hung out with us, Kenny was a kid that knew what to do, what not to do, and what the limits were on things. That's what I admired in him, because I didn't. I was a totally out of control teenager and he was never like that, yet we hung out together.

After that there was high school, college, jobs, Kenny joined the FDNY, I married Annie; our lives went in different directions, so I might have seen Kenny only once or twice a year as time went on. One thing I can say is that he did not change, even when he was sick, from the way he carried himself when he was younger. I thought that was so admirable that he had challenges that you could physically see, yet his personality remained intact. And when I saw him, he never talked about his illness; whereas, I've had other friends who have had issues and they couldn't get off the subject of talking about what was happening to them. That says something about a man.

I know what it is like not to be able to talk, because I wasn't able to talk for a whole year in 1985. It is debilitating. I know what it is like going into public places and trying to communicate with people that are looking at me strangely. One time I went into a deli and the guy said, "You are going to have to speak up." I told him I couldn't. Then some lady said, "What's wrong with you?" I said, "I can't talk." She said, "Get away from me!" Yah, they thought they were going to catch something from me. So I understand how hard it was for Kenny not to be able to communicate.

Luckily, I got my voice back, but seeing Kenny and his attitude that nothing had changed with him, shows that he chose not to let this illness destroy him as a person. That is something that I keep in my mind: if something happens to you, you still are the person you are. You are still the person that you were when you were a child.

As far as Kenny is concerned, for all the suffering he endured and all the friendships he developed on earth, I am sure God has rewarded him. That's the one comforting thing; I feel that when people suffer on this earth, when they suffer like Kenny did, you can be happy for them that they are in heaven. I always tell my wife, "When you die, I am going to get up and say, 'I am happy for her!'" I can honestly say that I am happy for Kenny too.

***

This reminds me of the book, The Five People You Meet in Heaven, *in that as much as Lynda knows many people that Kenny impacted, there are so many people out there that Kenny impacted in his daily life that we'll never know. The reach is beyond what we can really know. She'll get stories later on where people will tell her, "Your husband was Kenny? I remember him..." and she won't even know that person.*

Pat, Astoria Friend

2
Family
Gail: Kenny's Cousin

Kenny and I were first cousins; Kenny's dad and my dad were brothers. They both served in the Navy in World War II. Our fathers grew up in Hell's Kitchen with their two other brothers and sister Eileen, Brian's and Tim's mom. The boy Hollers were always out on the street playing hockey; my grandfather Walter coached his sons' teams. We have pictures of them. If they weren't playing, they were in line down at the original Madison Square Garden to get tickets for the Ranger games. I know Kenny loved the Rangers and his boys do too. Four generations of Ranger fans in the Holler family!

Growing up, Kenny and I were very close. We spent almost every day in the summer down at Far Rockaway Beach. It was just such a wonderful place to be, whether we were jumping off the jetties into the ocean or watching the fishermen bringing their fish in. Kenny's dad, Rod, loved to fish and I remember Aunt Eileen telling me that Walter was a big fisherman too. He used to go fishing all the time and I know that was big for Kenny, and now Tim.

Do you know what? We didn't have a lot, we didn't come from a lot, but we always had a great time together. We were just simple kids growing up in a very simple time.

***

I would have liked Kenny to be my brother. He was someone I looked up to, somebody that I wanted to be like.

Dr. Herrera, Primary Physician

3
Showin'-up
Kerry: Astoria Friend

I guess I should start with where we met, which I have always thought was an interesting story. I was around twelve and it was a tough time for me. We were living on the east side of Manhattan. My father was a city fireman and he came home one day and said, "We are moving to Astoria, Queens." I said, "Where's that?"

I was uncomfortable with it, because my only world was the city. We had a boys club on the East Side called Kips Bay Boys Club on Fifty-Second Street. When we moved to Astoria, I was feeling really shaky. My mother said, "You have to go out and make some friends. I was thinking, "It's not that easy." Right?

So my first venture out, I walked one block and I saw a face that I knew in front of Heineman's Drug Store on Steinway Street and Ditmars. Kenny lived right across the street. I thought, "I know this guy. Where do I know this guy from?" Then I realized that I saw him at "Kips," of all places, fairly recently, but didn't know his name, didn't know anything about him. Kids that age, at least us, we didn't say much, but I gave him one of those head bobs. Then I walked up to him and he said, "So what's going on? Did I see you at Kip's?" I said, "Yeah, yeah, I have been going to Kips for years. I just moved here." He said, "I am going up to the park to play basketball. Do you want to come with me?"

That was the beginning of Kenny's and my relationship. I remember walking up the block to Steinway Park just throwing the basketball back and forth like kids might. Dribble a little and throw it back and forth, which is kind of like a getting-to-know-you kind of thing, if you know what I mean. It is saying, "I accept you; you accept me." It made me feel good at the time. We went to Steinway Park and the rest is history.

Back in those days, our world revolved around Steinway Park. In the summertime, all we would do is play basketball. Kenny of course was very good at it. He was faster than anybody; he could jump higher than anybody. He could shoot. So when we chose teams, Kenny was always the first picked. We played a lot together and when kids are growing up like that, there are friendships and conflicts that go along on the court, but I remember Kenny staying in the middle. He would back us up, but he was not one to instigate things. He would say, "Let it go. Let's move on." I always found him to be very safe that way.

Our parents were very good friends. They became friends because of us. Mr. and Mrs. Holler would come over to our house all the time and have a couple of beers.

One big thing for Kenny and me happened in 1966. We knew each other for a year or two. My mother let me go to the beach by myself with my friends; first day I was allowed to get on the Triboro Bus and go out to Rockaway totally unsupervised. It was a big day for me, but what I didn't know while I was enjoying my day, was my father had died at ten o'clock that morning. Everybody had made it to the apartment, but there were no cell phones back then, so they had to wait until I came home around five at night.

There was no warning. He had a major heart attack on the job where they train city firemen. Totally unexpected, so a big trauma for a thirteen year old kid. The reason I bring that up here is Kenny was on board with that. He was there before my Dad died, so he knew him, but he also knew that I was hurting.

The thing is this: kids don't say a lot of words. There was not a lot of conversation like, "Hey, how are you doing? How are you doing with losing your father?" Not a lot of that, because with kids that age, when something like that happens, they'll say, "Oh, Kerry's father died," but then before you know it, we are all playing basketball and no one ever mentions it again. Adults don't say much either, for that matter. They generally don't know what to say. But I always had the sense that Kenny was very supportive of me in my loss. Not so much by anything he might have said, but I could tell by his actions. I found out myself through life that it is all about people showin' up, rather than what they say. I always felt that he was very aware of that, more so than others. So, that was big to me.

Kenny's mother was always, always a pleasure. And she loved to laugh. She spent a lot of time before and after my father died, just coming around and spending time with my mother. Just showin' up, as we talked about. I think she had a profound effect on who Kenny Holler was. His sense of humor; that laugh that he had, she had that laugh. That quick wit, she was like that. She was a good woman. Even as a kid, we knew it. And Kenny's grandmother lived across the street. Mrs. Bridger, great lady and she loved her grandkids. You can see where Kenny's mother got it from.

My recollection of Rod Holler... When my father was alive, the two of them would hang around together. We would be in the park with a couple of beers and holy cow, here they came: Mr. Holler and my father taking a walk up to the park. Mr. Holler would have his green utility pants on from IBM, always in great shape.

I was a year ahead of Kenny, so I went to Power Memorial a year before he did. Every morning for three years we would meet on the corner and travel together. Kenny and I had some laughs on that train going back and forth. Just stupid kid stuff. There were a couple other guys that were involved in that travel. Big Gary liked to mess with people. He would create some situations with strangers that we didn't necessarily want to be in. Gary didn't care; Gary would fight anybody. Kenny would have no part of it. He would just sit there with his books on his lap and he never got included in all that ugly stuff. We smoked cigarettes; Kenny never smoked. We would ride between the cars; Kenny wasn't interested.

So, Kenny did well in Power; he was somewhat of a star. He was coached by Brendan Malone who later became an NBA coach and has seen a lot of stars over the years.

Back in those days, the neighborhood around Power was not good. They changed the hours of dismissal of Power from Harran High School; Harran was an inner city school and there was a lot of conflict when we were getting out at the same time. I remember Brother Noone reportedly had a .38 and he would stand on Fifty-Ninth Street so the kids could safely get to the subway, but you still would not want to walk from Power to the subway by yourself.

But when I had detention, which was fairly often, I had the same issue getting to the subway that Kenny had. He would practice until six o'clock or whatever and the neighborhood definitely was an issue. Now the Lincoln Center effect has grown around the neighborhood. There are forty-five story, high-rise, co-ops on that block. It is not like it was back in those days when it was just a lot of beat-up buildings.

My opinion on Kenny's suffering? My son passed away in 2006 and I started a grief recovery group out here in Malverne for people who have lost loved ones to substance abuse. I have also been involved in some other grief recovery groups over the years. So, I agree that the grief journey can lead to personal growth, because people seek out spiritual direction, counseling, get involved in self-awareness, yoga, or whatever and grow in their understanding of what is really important in life. Not to let a day go by without letting their loved ones know they love them.

I think of Kenny's kids. After my father died, not much was said; it was just too painful, I guess. Nobody talked much about it and that wasn't good. As they say, you can internalize things and they can come out sideways if you don't do anything about it. It is going to come out. So something like this book is such a healthy thing for Kenny's kids. I wish there might have been something for me back in those days, because two weeks after my father died I went right into Power and I was off to the races. My father was not around, my mother couldn't control me, and I struggled for years.

There is a bench down in Long Beach that reads something like: "For as long as we live, you too shall live, for you will always be with us." It is sending the message that as long as I keep you in my life, as long as I talk about you, you will be alive in me. Kenny is around. There is no question about it. Maybe not in the way that we want it, but that spirit is still very strong and doesn't go anywhere, unless we make the mistake of not talking about him. People will be talking about Kenny Holler for years.

***

Over the years, the Hollers became another family to me and Kenny exemplified that fatherly figure. I always felt included there, no matter what was going on. When I was there to hang out with Colin or Tim, Kenny would always make sure his presence was felt; always make sure to ask how I was doing, simple questions like that to show he cared.

Eric, Colin's Friend, Age 18

4
Mellow
Mike: High School Friend

What you need to understand about our high school, is that it was not like a typical local high school, where all the kids went through grammar school and middle school together and then wound up in the same high school. We went to Power Memorial, an all-boys Catholic school run by the Christian Brothers, on Sixty-First Street and Amsterdam Avenue in Manhattan, which is about as far west as you can get in the city, two more blocks and you were in the Hudson River. There were kids from the Bronx, from Astoria, from other parts of Queens, from Brooklyn; they all merged into this one school.

Our high school, like many other parochial high schools in the city, was very strict. If we did something wrong like talking in line, or chewing gum, or if our hair was down to our collar, we would have to visit Brother Boyle, the Dean of Discipline. Since it was a parochial school, our families paid tuition. I still remember that the tuition was $35/month. I think in our senior year it was raised to $40.

Kenny came to Power because he wanted to play basketball there. It had the reputation. Lou Alcinder (Kareem Abdul-Jabbar) graduated from Power six or seven years ahead of us. At the time Power was like the UCLA of high schools.

I watched Kenny play every year. In our junior year, Kenny played Varsity B and the Varsity A team was the best team in the country. That 1969/70 Varsity A team had some super talented guys. Lenny Elmore, the center for the team, went to Maryland which was a big basketball college. He then played in the NBA and is an announcer now on television. Ed Searcy went to St. John's. The best guy on the team was Japeth Trimble, he went to Maryland with Elmore.

His senior year on the Varsity A team, Kenny was coached by Brendan Malone, who went on to coach in the NBA. Kenny was a point guard and I guess I would say he was cerebral; he didn't do anything flashy. He just did everything steady. He wasn't prone to turnovers, you couldn't really pressure him, and he was smart enough to get rid of the ball. He had a nice jump shot and when I complimented him once on it, he told me with a little smirk that he "tickled the twine." I never heard that phrase from anyone before or since.

To pick one word that describes Kenny, I would choose "Mellow." In all the games I saw him play, no matter what kind of pressure he was under, I never saw him sweat. He never panicked; he was even-keel. So "Even-keel," and "Mellow" are the words I think of to describe him. He didn't fluctuate; he was a steady, steady presence.

Lynda mentioned that Kenny had told her that the neighborhood was bad and that he used to get jumped going to or from school. Power was on the northern border of Hell's Kitchen and many of the schools that we played against weren't in good areas either. In our division were Rice High School which was in the middle of Harlem, Cardinal Hayes which was in the South Bronx, Cardinal Spellman was in the North Bronx, and Stepinac was in Yonkers. Riding home on the subways after the games would have taken Kenny through some tough areas, so I am not surprised that he would have problems then too. After games, all the players headed in different directions, so they often took trains home alone late at night. It is ironic, because none of us ever had money. I am sure that he didn't have anything for them to steal.

Kenny was a great guy and I invited him to our home in the Bronx. My sister Ann had a crush on him, big time. My little sister Maureen remembered him too. Even though I was not a close, intimate friend with Kenny, I knew him and liked him a lot. Kenny was just one of those All-American kids. There is no other way to describe him, he was an All-American kid.

***

I wanted to share my thoughts on Kenny because I loved the guy and I want Lynda and his kids to know it.

Fred, Brewster Baseball Friend

5
Cool
Brendan Malone: Basketball Coach

I started coaching CYO basketball at Precious Blood Grammar School in Astoria. I don't know if it was in a tournament or whatever, but Kenny caught my eye right away. He knew how to play. He got people involved; he was a good passer. He wasn't selfish; he didn't take bad shots. He was athletic, he could run, he could jump. And it stuck with me. That would have been somewhere in the mid-sixties. That was the first time I saw Kenny.

The second time I saw him, I was up in the gym at Power. Brother Jenson, the freshman coach, had a tryout and there were a lot of guys on the floor. And that was when I saw Kenny. I said, "I know that guy. I saw him play for St. Francis of Assisi." He was getting lost in the crowd and Brother Jenson didn't have him on the list. I said, "Brother, I have seen this kid play and he is a good player." To his credit, he picked him and the rest is history. Kenny played four years at Power.

Great demeanor. Never got rattled. Was a team player. He could run. He could shoot and, for a white kid, he could jump. He was a good all-around player; a smart player. The biggest thing was that he never got rattled. If people tried to press, he was able to maintain his poise and make the good play or dribble through the press and make the right play.

I liked him as much as a person as I did a ball player. Always smiling. Quiet, he wasn't boastful. He went out and played and he was easy to be around. If I had to describe Kenny in one word, it was "Cool." He was unflappable. He never got too excited. As a basketball player he was always under control.

Then I lost contact with him after Power, because in 1976, the coach at Fordham saw me and I went from there to Fordham. Then I went to Yale and then Syracuse University for seven years. Then I was the head coach at Rhode Island, then from there Hubie Brown hired me for the Knicks. From there I went to Detroit; won two championships. I was just lucky; the timing was right and we had a great team. I have coached all over the NBA: New York, Detroit, Toronto, Cleveland, Indiana, Orlando, Seattle.

I hadn't seen or spoken with Kenny since he graduated from Power in 1971, but I still remember him well. Like I told you, the first time I saw him, I liked him. When I found out that he died, I said, "What a sad story that is." Because everybody that knew him benefited from knowing him. He had so much more to give. I wish his boys a lot of luck. They have a great person to follow in his footsteps.

6
Young Kenny

The Baby Picture

Mary with her sons Gerard and Kenny

The Holler Cousins at Rockaway
Beach - Kenny in the middle

Rod with Kenny and Gerard
1966

Kenny the young fisherman
1963

Kenny, age 11, playing baseball
for St. Francis of Assisi - 1964

Power Memorial High School Varsity A Team
Kenny #23 - 1970-71

7
Friend
Tommy: *College Friend, FDNY Firefighter*

I met Kenny in '72, that's a lot of years, a long time.

Kenny got a basketball scholarship to the Junior College of Albany. His parents didn't drive him to school, like we do these days. Kenny just got on the subway to Port Authority and took the bus up there with whatever he could carry. I did the same thing. Being a couple of city kids, getting on the subway was no problem; getting on a bus, that was what we did every day going to high school, so it wasn't a big challenge to us.

So, I met Kenny at JCA by the second or third day of school when I started playing some pickup basketball in the gym. Kenny said, "We're all living in a big barracks in the gym here, maybe you can stay with us." He talked to the coach, Bill Kirsch, who told me, "Well, if you want to help out the team, then you can stay here, no charge." So choosing between paying rent and not paying rent, I took him up on the opportunity and I became the manager of the team. I travelled with them to all the games. There was a tournament for junior colleges, NCAA nationwide, and Kirsch got his team into the Final Four every year. He was a really good coach and Kenny was probably the best player on the team.

Kenny had tendinitis in the knee and his knee would swell up. He would get frustrated with his knee, when he couldn't play. It was kind of a dark time for Kenny. When he couldn't play basketball, he would want to get away, go for a walk somewhere away from everybody, and think things out. He was by far the best player up there and the team was doing well. It was getting to be time for the tournament and it was going to be at JCA that year. Kenny couldn't play and we ended up losing the championship of our section. Kenny realized that he couldn't play college ball anymore and he didn't want to go to school without being able to play, so he dropped out after one year and went to work with his father at IBM in New York City.

We still kept in touch back and forth. I had met some of Kenny's Astoria friends when we were up in Albany; so, over the years when Kenny would be out on Long Island in the summertime, I'd go out on his boat and stay there with all his buddies. Then we lost touch for about a year or two, until I called him one day; I had an extra ticket to a Yankee game. We went to the game and he told me that he was on the Fire Department. I said, "Oh, man! I'm on the list. I'm waiting to get on!" He said, "Ahh, you're going to love it. It's a great job, a great job."

So about six months later, I got appointed to 50 Engine in the Bronx. I started playing the basketball leagues and low and behold, who is playing basketball, but Kenny Holler with 116 Truck in Long Island City, Queens. We started playing against each other and the guys from my house and the guys from his house hit it off. We would get together different times of the year too and have some fun. Of course, everyone in my house fell in love with Kenny. That's for sure, his personality, his sense of humor...

When our houses played basketball against each other, Kenny would come down with the ball and the guys on my team would start yelling, "Shoot, shoot!" because he was so far out. I would tell everybody, "Don't tell him to shoot! He doesn't miss!" Kenny would stop, look at the guys, and say, "From here?" They'd say, "Ya!" He'd throw up a shot and "Swish!" Never missed. I would tell my guys, "Stop telling him to shoot!" So after that, whenever he would come up over the line with the ball, they would start chanting, "Don't shoot Holler, don't shoot!" It was fun. That was Kenny, always had everybody laughing, everybody smiling.

He told me once that they were playing another firehouse in a basketball game and they were real serious guys. The game was like ten o'clock in the morning, so Kenny and the guys from 116 got some whiskey, gargled with it, then spit it out. When they went up for a jump ball, they breathed on the guys they were playing against. Those guys looked at Kenny's team like they were nuts, thinking, "They are drinking already?!" That was Kenny, a sense of humor, always getting these crazy ideas to screw with somebody's head. We miss him, that's for sure.

***

To watch Kenny play basketball was always a joy. He tried every trick in the book. Every time a guy would try to take a shot, he would be in his face. He would yell and stick his hand up, "Ya! Yaa!!" He would try every trick he knew when the team would go to inbound the ball. He would stay by the sideline and make believe he was tying his shoe, so when the guy would take the ball down court, Kenny would come up behind the guy and steal it. He was a heck of a ball player.

Bobby, FDNY Engine 261/Ladder 116

8
Laughter
Hut: *Astoria Friend*

When I first met Kenny, it was early on in grammar school. We ran track for St. Francis of Assisi in Astoria and I just remember Kenny being so fast! I always wanted to be on his relay team, because he would be the anchor and every time I was on his team, we earned a gold medal. After that, we didn't hang around much together, because he was fourteen months younger and two grades below me.

Later on, after he came home from college, we played basketball a lot together on the Zoo, a local team that played through the adult CYO and YMCA leagues. It was a pretty good team. Kenny was a really good basketball player. He was somebody that you always wanted to play with; he was a great team player and he had this far outside shot that never missed. I always say that if we had the three-point circle when he played, he probably would have led the league, definitely our team, in scoring every year.

Another thing, that impressed me about his playing, was that he could always leave the game behind. If we had a loss, a tough loss, it didn't bother him. Everybody would be down, but he would pick us up by doing some goof-ball thing and we'd end up forgetting about it. He never took the losses to heart. He was the hardest player on the team with intensity and toughness, but after the game, he could just let it go. I always admired that, because a lot of people, including myself, were kind of hot heads back then. Not him; he always found some way to bring everybody's spirits up again.

I started bartending in a neighborhood bar, McGivney's, which was a mix of older people and younger people. It was really a great mix, because we got along so well with the older people and they got along with us. It made for a fantastic bar. It really did. Kenny would come in basically every night, not that he was a big drinker; he may have had a glass of beer, maybe two beers, but he would always do some goof-ball thing and just make our day. We'd just smile and laugh.

The bar stools were round with four legs and a red cover over the seat. One night, I thought, "Where'd Kenny go?" He was back in the kitchen. He had taken off two of the covers, brought them into the back, put on an apron, put one of the covers on his head, and the other he started twirling around, coming out like he was a pizza maker: Giuseppe the Pizza Maker! Things like that, he was just spur of the moment. His whole focus was making people laugh by doing stupid cornball things.

I tell you, I'm glad he did what he did, because it made my life a lot happier. That is one of the greatest gifts that one person can give to another, the gift of laughter. That's what he gave me. Anytime I'd see him, even before he did anything, I'd have a smile on my face, because I knew eventually he was going to do something that would make me laugh.

At election time one year, they had a poster hung up in McGivney's of a candidate who was running for assemblyman or councilman or whatever. Kenny cut the face out of the poster, put it back in the window and stood with his face in it, looking out at the street. Two mothers and two kids walked by. The mothers were yapping away, but the kids looked up and all of a sudden Kenny stuck out his tongue or made some stupid face. One of the kids was startled and grabbed his mother and, of course, his mother turned around and Kenny just showed a stoic face. The mother said to her son, "What, what? Keep going!" They started walking again and of course the kid looked back and Kenny did the same thing, stuck his tongue out. The boy pulled his mother's arm and the mother again said, "What, what?" Kenny did that for like an hour. He just kept his face in that stupid poster. People kept passing by, Kenny would knock on the window, so people would look at him, and he'd make faces to startle them. These are just stupid, ridiculous things that he did, but they made us laugh and they brightened up our night. He was so good at doing things like that.

Kenny's chops-breaking started early in life. His brother, Gerard, told me a couple stories.

His brother was probably about seven years old and Kenny, I guess, was five. Gerard heard a dirty joke and told it to Kenny, something about Marilyn Monroe and her breasts. That night during dinner with their parents, Kenny goes, "Hey, Gerard, tell Mom and Dad that joke you heard today!" Gerard's face turned all red and all he could say was, "A humina, humina, humina…!" That is when all the kidding and chops-breaking started, at an early age, and it just kept up until his passing. Funny stuff.

Another time, he was a little bit older now; their mother and father were both sleeping. Gerard came home and the phone rang. Kenny picked it up and Gerard heard him say, "Hello?...Yes…. Oh, okay, yeah…What?…. Okay, hold on a sec." Kenny turned to Gerard and asked, "Gerard, who was that actor that was in the commercial, that said, 'What a chunk of chocolate?'" So Gerard responded, "Arnold Stang." Kenny got back on the phone and said, "Arnold Stang." He continued: "I won what?... How much?! … Holy!… Wow! That's great!... Okay you'll call me tomorrow?... Yah, all right. Goodbye." Kenny hung up and Gerard anxiously asked, "How much did you win, how much did you win?!" Kenny responded, "It was the wrong number."

There were some periods in our lives when we didn't see that much of each other. We had our own families; we were raising kids, although mine are older. We liked to play golf together and before he got really sick, I'd invite him down to play with me; he didn't miss a beat. He'd come up on Little Murph or Steve and break their chops. He really didn't break mine too much. I think I was more like the audience, because I would always laugh at anything he said. So, he would pick on them, knowing he could count on me to laugh at it.

I couldn't believe his mental toughness. I mean to endure that stuff for so long, you have to have a mental toughness about you. I don't think that I could have done it for twenty-one years and still maintained that personality. Not being able to eat solid food for such a long period of time, it still breaks my heart. But that is where that mental toughness came in, it just carried him through.

I had a bad accident, I broke my femur, plus I have had a bad knee for a long, long time and now it is arthritic. Anytime that I feel down, I just think of Kenny, how he didn't complain and he had it a lot worse than me. I think, "Get a grip on yourself, Hut, things could be ten times worse. There is somebody out there, one of your friends, that has had it a lot tougher than you, so man-up." That got me through a lot of feeling-sorry-for-myself times, knowing that Kenny had it worse than me.

Even when he was sick, we would go to golf tournaments and we'd all be eating normally and he'd bring his quart of homemade soup because he couldn't eat solid food. We'd feel a little bad, but you could see that it didn't bother him; he was always still upbeat. Even over all those years, living with that disease, he still had the bright light, that enthusiasm, that jokester, it was still there. It was just outstanding to see somebody that was sick and was still so wonderful.

As much as I loved him from the start, my opinion of Kenny increased greatly over the years. Somebody who has endured more than twenty years of horrific cancer and still maintained his dignity, his optimism, and his sense of humor, how can you not feel even more love for him?

***

I still think about Coach Kenny and there are two things that stand out. I still play a lot of sports. I don't play baseball anymore, but I play hockey and lacrosse. He taught me to have a fun time when I play, at all times. Maybe more importantly, now that I am older and I know what he was going through and was still able to keep a good attitude, it makes me feel like whatever I am going through I can keep a good attitude too.

Anthony, Tim's Teammate, age 16

9
Oak
Stove/Bobby: *Astoria Friend*

It goes back fifty-plus years to when I met Kenny.

One thing that I was reflecting on was that Kenny had a certain innocence about him, not that he was naïve, far from it, but I always felt that about him.

Kenny was like a brother to me. As a matter of fact, I saved a clipping from when he was playing grammar school CYO basketball. It has been in that scrapbook all along, not just because Kenny passed. Raymond Sabounghi, Gene, Johnny, and Kenny are in the clip from the Long Island Star. Mr. Sabounghi was their coach and he had competed with the Egyptian Olympic Basketball Team.

It is funny how our lives developed together: we lived near each other; we played basketball together in Steinway Park as kids; and then we played basketball together again in our twenties with the "Zoo."

We hung out together in McGivney's and one of the funny stories involved a friend named Louie Cessa. You'd have to know Louie; he'd walk down the avenue pumping his arms a mile a minute, so we'd call him Louie Arms. One day, we were looking out the window and here comes Louie Arms and his arms are pumping away. He came into McGivney's. He had to go to the bathroom, so he took off his coat and went to the back. Kenny put on Louie's coat—if you can visualize this—it was short on him because Louie was a small guy. Louie came out of the bathroom and Kenny was pumping his arms saying, "How do you make this stop!" We just cried!

Kenny went on the Fire Department about two years before me. He always said, "After your probationary year, transfer to my house." I said, "Are you kidding me?" He used to tell me all of the pranks that he pulled in the house, like the cheese in the sock under the pillow… I said, "Do you think that I am going to spend twenty years, with you as my senior, and take twenty years of that?" In a way, I wish I would have. But he started giggling. That's another thing. We both went into the Fire Department; we both loved the Fire Department; and we both were on for twenty-two years.

I knew how sick Kenny was and I would just pray that this thing would stop. I would pray to God and tell Him, "Enough is enough!" I know that everything has to be according to His plan, but it's hard to understand. A person like Kenny, for him to have to go through that… But at the same time, I thank God that he married Lynda. Oh yea. I would tell all of my friends, "Kenny married the right girl. Absolutely. Thank God for that." Two beautiful children, he had a good life with them; aside from the suffering, he was happy.

Kenny is constantly on my mind now. There are so many ways that we are intertwined. Somebody mentions a song, somebody mentions a name, the Fire Department and right away he comes to mind.

There are not many people that come through your life like Kenny. I couldn't even count them on one hand—maybe three fingers. Really extraordinary. I saved a card he sent me several years ago entitled, *The Oak Tree*. I was going through a hard time, but with him going through his thing, I didn't want to divulge my problems. But somehow he knew and he bought this perfect card and wrote a perfect message that is a treasure for me. Part of his message read, "Hang tough, we're from Steinway and Ditmars, we're the Bravest, we're all made of oak."

Like I said, he is the toughest guy I ever knew. I tell all my friends that. I knew some pretty tough guys in my day, tough guys from the neighborhood, nobody could stand up to him; he was the toughest, like oak. Yet, like I also said, he had that innocence; I always look at him like that.

The Oak Tree

A mighty wind blew night and day.
It stole the oak tree's leaves away,
Then snapped its boughs and pulled its bark
Until the Oak was tired and stark.
But still the oak tree held its ground
While other trees fell all around.

The weary wind gave up and spoke,
"How can you still be standing, Oak?"
The oak tree said, "I know that you
Can break each branch of mine in two,
Carry every leaf away,
Shake my limbs, and make me sway.
But I have roots stretched in the earth,
Growing stronger since my birth.
You'll never touch them, for you see,
They are the deepest part of me.
Until today, I wasn't sure
Of just how much I could endure.
But now I've found, with thanks to you,
I'm stronger than I ever knew."

***

Kenny was powerful; he went through all that treatment and used the power inside him to make himself stronger than the disease.

Joe, Lynda's Cousin's Husband

22

10
Character
Big Dave: *FDNY Ladder 116*

I first met Kenny late 1980, early 1981. I was at a bar-restaurant near St. John's University, The Sly Fox Inn. I was there with a couple of friends and he was there with a couple of friends. He recognized me as a fireman that worked in the next battalion, so he came over and introduced himself. My engine company, 262, was a little slow and I was looking to go someplace that was a little busier. Kenny recommended his company and I ended up putting in a transfer paper to Ladder 116. Kenny told a fellow in the house who actually helped move the papers; I transferred in about two days, which was unheard of. It usually takes a period of time. As soon as I got there, I became friends with Kenny and we started hanging out.

At that time, we had a house full of young single guys. We had a lot of guys that got along together right away and we had a lot of city kids, a lot of kids from Kenny's neighborhood either in our house or 260 Engine which was close by.

Right away, we had good sports teams. Kenny, who was a starting guard at Power Memorial, was the only guy in the firehouse who really knew how to play structured team basketball and so he was the leader on the court. He was also a terrific softball player. He was our lead-off guy and he was a left fielder.

When I first got to 116, Kenny handed me a decal of a flaming skull. He explained that when he was out on building inspection one day, up front, on the counter, he saw a rack of decals of flaming skulls, so he bought a whole bunch of them. He said, "All of the single guys in the firehouse are going to put these on their helmets and we'll call ourselves the 'Skulls.' We'll have a Boys Night Out once in a while together."

So, he put one on my helmet and it is on my helmet to this day. It was just supposed to be the single guys; there were thirteen of us. It really didn't mean anything, it was just silliness, but it eventually became the firehouse nickname. We were the Hellgaters when I got there, because we used to go up on the Hell Gate Bridge when there was a fire there; but then we became the Flaming Skulls. I said that we should call it "Holler House." I remind the guys, and I tell all the new guys, the story of how that name came about, and that it was Kenny Holler that was the founder of the Skulls.

Kenny could do a little of everything and he was just a very friendly, trustworthy guy to know. Kenny had principles. Old fashioned type of conservative principles, as far as how to carry himself, and how to behave. He lived in a cold water flat in Manhattan for his early years and he grew up with next to nothing. Myself too, although not quite to that extent, but we were lower middle class, old-school, city kids, so our values were just very basic and very simple. When the cops said, "Get off the corner," we didn't question it, we got off the corner. We didn't make any wise-cracks. The worst thing in the world was if the cop put us in the car and took us home and we had to face our fathers. There were kids that would tell a cop, "I don't care what you do to me, just don't take me home to my father!"

23

We started hanging out together and it wasn't too long before we became roommates. Kenny lost his apartment for whatever reason: the lease ran out, the rent was too high, the parking situation was terrible over there in Astoria. He kept getting alternate side parking tickets; a good part of his salary was going toward paying those tickets, because he couldn't remember to get up on time in the morning and move his car.

I grew up in Woodhaven, Queens, and I had an apartment there. My roommate had gotten married and moved out and I had an opening, so Kenny moved in.

Kenny was one of the greatest characters you could have in a firehouse. If there were ten empty seconds with nothing to do, Kenny was thinking of something to do to somebody. It goes in line with this old joke:

"A kid walks up to a fireman in front of a firehouse and says, 'Mr. Fireman, when I grow up I want to be a fireman also.' And the fireman tells him, 'I am sorry Kid, you can't do both.'"

Kenny falls in line with that. You leave a bunch of guys in a building and give them the slightest bit of downtime, they do things to each other. It's just silly stuff. Kenny was a specialist at this stuff.

One time, Warren was outside trying to vacuum out his car. He had the vacuum with the electrical cord going into the window of the firehouse, because we only had outlets on the apparatus floor. Patty the old timer at the firehouse said to me, "Come in here. You have to see this." Kenny was inside looking out the window at Warren. Warren crawled in his car and was all the way in trying to vacuum it. Kenny would pull the plug out, just gently, so the vacuum would just about go off. Warren would start to back out of the car and Kenny would plug it back in again. So Warren would go back in the car. Kenny had already been doing this for a couple of minutes, but Warren wasn't wise to it. He thought something was wrong with the vacuum. So he came in and out of the car as Kenny was working the outlet. Finally Warren got out of the car and you see a big grin on his face and he realizes he is working with Kenny. He runs in the door; he knew exactly who it was, but he didn't realize it for like five minutes.

Kenny would do this stuff all the time.

It was constant, just little stuff. He would pay attention to every little thing that guys did and he would do something to louse us up. Like in the early days of the VCR, the VCR was in the kitchen, in the Commissary Closet. Paul was crazy about watching movies at the House Watch. He'd get everything set up, run out to watch the beginning of it, and before he got there Kenny would hit the Pause button. Paul wouldn't even know that Kenny was in the kitchen; Kenny would go to the back room and peek out. Paul would run back in the kitchen, set it all up again, go back out, and Kenny would sneak out and hit the Pause button again. Or he'd hit the Reverse… It was just constant.

Have you heard any fishing stories yet? I have a couple.

Our Company 116 was called over to Roosevelt Island, because bridge crews were working on the Roosevelt Island Bridge. It is the only road on or off the island, so they had to put regular fire companies on the island, which they didn't normally have, to provide fire coverage. Another 116 firefighter named Ken brought a fishing pole with him. He grew up in Astoria also. He had it ready just in case the company ever went over there. That day he had the chance to drop the line in the water and see if he could catch something. He wasn't catching anything and he got up and went inside the firehouse to go to the bathroom or something.

Our Kenny had known that Ken was bringing his fishing pole and bought a fish at the fish store, a flounder or whatever it was. It was a good sized fish. When Ken went to the bathroom,

Kenny put it on his hook and threw it in the water. Ken had been there for a couple of hours trying to catch something and he had had no luck. So, when he came out of the building, our Kenny was hauling this big fish out of the water, yelling, "Whoa! Whoa!" He got other guys out there yelling and screaming too. Ken was cursing and saying, "I knew when I went inside and went to the bathroom something would happen!" He was going crazy and this dead fish was on the line, which he didn't notice for a couple minutes.

We went on a couple firehouse charter trips in the spring just for flounder. Most of the fish we pulled up were undersized and we had to throw them back again. We weren't doing much, but we had a couple fish in the cooler. Kenny put one of them on a fishing line, lowered it down and yelled out, "Whoa!" and pulled out the fish. Once he pulled it out of the water he made like he was going to put it in the cooler, but he would just put it on somebody else's pole. Then that person would drop it into the water when nobody was looking. Next we'd hear, "Whoa!" and that guy would pull the same fish up!

Other boats have a tendency to gravitate around the party boats, because the charter boats have electronic fish finders. They have radios and communicate with each other and they keep moving around looking for fish. It was hilarious to watch, because we weren't catching fish anyway. We were just drinking beer all day and it was great to see the boats start their engines and come over, like a dozen boats at a time. I'm not kidding. By the time the day was done, that fish was in bad shape, because we had already pulled it out of the water about twenty-nine times. Kenny was great for the fish prank

The officers loved Kenny. Everybody did. I don't know anybody that didn't like Kenny. It's not even possible, because he never carried any grudges or any bitterness. And he was very into the well-being of his parents.

I remember that Kenny would always be in a couple of expensive football pools that he really couldn't afford. Kenny would run through cash pretty fast, like a lot of us did, but he would run through all of it and we would say, "Kenny is broke again. Oh gee." I'd lend him fifty bucks or something until payday to carry him through. So he won like forty-five thousand dollars in a football pool. That was like thirty years ago. I know this was like a gift from Heaven for anybody to win that amount of money. Right away, he gave the majority of it to his parents and I thought that was great. That was Kenny.

We became good friends and could confide in each other about things like girlfriends. He had gone out with a girl on and off for years. They would only go out for a short period of time and they would get in an argument. Then, they wouldn't go out for the longest period of time; then they would get back together. It was like months at a time, one way or the other. This lasted four or five years or even longer. We were always hoping, at least I was, that Kenny would meet someone like Lynda. I said, "This guy needs a steady influence."

We would joke about the guys at the firehouse that grew up on the Island. There was a difference between us, the city kids, and them. It was like these guys were from Nebraska, from a different part of the country. They got married very early. Almost all of them married their high school sweethearts and had kids early. All of the city kids got married much later; we just couldn't get out of the partying mode, playing mode. "What's the next event coming up? The next basketball game, the next softball game?" We were all hoping for each other that we would meet a girl that was a steady influence, because we knew this couldn't last forever. We needed that type of woman to get us out of this. Lynda was a Godsend; when I met her I said, "This young lady is perfect." I was hoping so much that they would stay together and other guys were also. She was exactly what Kenny needed or any one of us would need. We had gone through our twenties and this was just going on and on.

When I heard of his first cancer diagnosis, I thought it was something that he would beat, because we were still relatively young. We had a couple of guys from the firehouse that had died that had paid absolutely no attention to their health; they died suddenly of heart attacks. We'd come in the next day and the guy was gone. We never had anyone until Kenny that had gotten a sickness that was going to linger, going to carry on.

Kenny had to go on light duty, of course, when it first happened, so he was separated from 116 and he went across the river to SOC Island. He ended up being there for seven years. I wouldn't see him for a while; then we would check in with him, "Hey, how are you doing?" He'd say, "I have to go in for a surgery and they have to clip out a little and it should be okay." We didn't take it that seriously right away. Then over the years it started to hit me that this thing was more serious than we originally thought.

I realized how serious it was when it started showing up physically. When you are young and happy-go-lucky it takes a while for something like this to sink in. Especially with a guy like Kenny; he was always full of life. He was always going to be there. It just didn't settle on us that maybe he was not always going to be there.

Kenny experienced such a slow torturous thing. I can't even imagine. Looking at Kenny's situation and looking at my situation sometimes, when everything goes wrong, I say, "This is nothing compared to what someone like Kenny has gone through." I have thought of him a lot in terms like that, if I run through a streak of bad luck; like now I am falling apart. I have to get my hips and my knees replaced. I have COPD; I had to get my shoulder joint replaced. I have had three knee surgeries. I'll think, "This is nothing. I can get through this and every day I am still here. Kenny is not here anymore. And the suffering that he went through was unbelievable." He was always the same when I saw him. He tried to keep a great positive attitude.

I think about Kenny quite a bit and I am not just saying that here. I quote him a lot, especially when I stop by 116. I say, "If Holler was here, what he would say right now…" Or I will talk about him in my current firehouse, mention Kenny's name and explain who he was. And there'll never be conversations amongst us where Kenny doesn't come up numerous times. "Remember when Kenny did this…? Remember Kenny did that…? Remember what Kenny said when this guy said this…?"

I chose the word "Character," because like I said, Kenny was one of the funniest characters I ever met and he was full of good character also. He was so consistently funny in the little things and so full of life. Always wanted to do something else: let's try this; let's try that. I'm going here; I'm going there. "Why don't you come along?" He invited everybody to everything. He wanted to take everybody along on this ride, this ride of life that he was on.

Make light of the world and of yourself and of all earthly pleasures… For you know well that life, health, wealth, honor, status, dominion—none of these belongs to you. If they did, you could own them in your own way. But just when we want to be healthy we are sick; just when we want to be alive we die; just when we want to be rich we are poor; just when we want to be in power we are made servants. And all this because these things are not ours, and we can keep them only as much and as long as it pleases the One who has lent them to us.

St. Catherine of Siena

***

We got along very well because we were both from that working class neighborhood. I wouldn't call it middle class; I'd say working class. We grew up in it. The biggest thing in my world and it was probably the same in Kenny's world was to get a civil service job—become a cop or fireman or garbage man. We're from the same blue collar mindset.

Paul, Brewster Friend

***

I was already married, so I was one of the Numb Skulls. The single guys were the Skulls; the married guys were the Numb Skulls and the older guys were the Flickering Skulls. But they were all nuts and they all got along; it was great. That was the greatest group of people I ever met in my life.

Mike, FDNY Ladder 116, Golf Partner

11
Providence
Lynda

It was Friday, January 13, 1990 and my friend Claire and I wanted to go to dinner somewhere new. Eleven months earlier, I had cut an ad out of a local paper promoting Queens' restaurants for Valentine's Day. I checked that list for the first time and we decided to try a place named Time Out in Astoria. We arrived, probably sevenish, but the restaurant was empty; not a good sign. The attached bar was crowded though, so we decided to check it out.

Claire doesn't drink, so we had no intention of spending a long time in a bar. She ordered a soda; I probably had a beer or a glass of wine. Although the place was crowded, everyone else seemed to know each other and we felt like outsiders. We talked alone, mostly about where we were going next for dinner.

As the story goes, we turn to leave and Kenny cuts us off on the way to the door with an outstretched hand and his now famous line, "My name is Kenny. How do you like me so far?"

It didn't take long before I realized that I liked him a lot. I had found a great guy. He was fun and very good to me. He had a huge circle of friends which was a testament to him as a friend. Everyone loved Kenny, so I knew that I was lucky that he loved me.

We were both in our thirties; Kenny was seven years older than me. We dated for two years and married in May 1992. All was well. We were both good people that were loved and respected by the family and friends we had accumulated over three decades. My family and friends loved him and his me.

Five months after our wedding, Kenny developed a sore on his tongue that wouldn't heal. His quack dentist rubbed ointment on it and sent him on his way. By Christmas, it bothered him so much that he saw a doctor when we were away visiting my family. He suggested that Kenny see an oral surgeon. By January, eight months into our newlywed year, we got the diagnosis that Kenny had tongue cancer. If I knew then, what I know now, I could never have borne the years ahead. I would also never have as intensely pondered, learned, and absorbed the richness of love, faith, sacrifice, and suffering.

Our life together did not unfold the way I imagined, but I believe it unfolded the way it was meant to be. When I think back on our courtship, a vivid instance has stayed with me, while many more colorful scenes have long vanished: One day Kenny was at my apartment and stood up to leave for work. As I watched him walk out, I got a powerful feeling. More than a thought or an idea. Maybe an intuition, maybe a message from God? I don't know, but the feeling clearly told me that Kenny would be a good husband to me and a good father to my children. It confirmed the more earthy feelings I had been having and gave me the confidence that I was moving forward in the right direction.

There are so many pieces of the puzzle that I didn't first recognize about that fateful night we met, but as I have pondered the coincidences that we experienced, I have to acknowledge that it could not have been just luck that Kenny and I came together the way we did.

What are the chances that:

- I would cut out that newspaper ad in February 1989 with Valentine Restaurant listings and never look at it again until January 1990? I am surprised I was able to find it.
- Out of all the restaurants on the list, we chose Time Out? I don't think we ever tried any of the others after that.
- I would meet Kenny in Suspenders? Time Out had new owners by then, but previously had been Suspenders, the bar/restaurant that Kenny convinced Pete to buy in Astoria.
- Kenny and I had both lived in Astoria, Queens at the same time years before we met. I could have been in line ahead of him at the grocery store, but he didn't notice me. Why did he notice me that fateful night in Astoria, years later when neither of us lived there?
- Kenny didn't live in Astoria at that time, but that bar was a long-time hangout for his crowd and it makes sense that he might be there, but he could have been working that night or in transit. Claire and I probably would have been in and out in twenty minutes.

God's timing is impeccable.

***

I was happy for the short time Kenny was here. He was able to find the love of his life and have children and in that short time he really accomplished a lot. He did things and accomplished things that people much older than him have not been able to accomplish. There is a lot to be said for that.

Joann, Astoria Friend

12
Faith-filled
Camille: *Astoria Friend*

The thing I remember the most about Kenny is when he first got sick. Many years earlier in 1976, I was Dr. Jatin Shah's first secretary at Memorial Sloan Kettering Cancer Center. I started with him when he had one patient. He went on to become the Chief Head and Neck Surgeon there. When Kenny got sick, I called Dr. Shah and told him, "I've got this great friend, we go way back." Dr. Shah said, "No problem, tell him to come in." We made the appointment and the rest is history. I was just so thankful. I feel that Kenny lived longer because of him. I really do believe that Dr. Shah is one of the best doctors. I know there are a lot of people with that kind of cancer that don't live very long at all, so I was grateful for that.

You see, I have known Kenny since I was fourteen years old. That's when I met him and Chuck and the whole gang at the park. What I also remember is that as a fella back then, he was very kind. I wasn't intimidated by him as I was by some others. He seemed to be easy to talk to and he always had a joke to tell.

We used to go to these parties at McGivneys; they had Italian Night, Irish Night. Kenny's mother and father were always there. I really loved his mother. Just a lovely, warm, inviting woman. You could see that she loved her family. Her boys were everything to her. Later on his father suffered tremendous pain from diabetic neuropathy. It was tough there for a while.

At twenty-two I married Chuck, so I was very young, had children, and we sort of got out of touch for a while. But if there was an event or something, Kenny was always there. No matter when he saw me, he always had a big smile, always a great hello, a hug.

From my experience in working with Dr. Shah, I recognized right away that Kenny's cancer was serious. So, when Kenny got that diagnosis I had a feeling of doom. I thought, "This is not good." I just knew what he was in store for, because cancer in soft tissue commonly comes back. I think it was a miracle that he lived as long as he did, because most patients do not. So it was prayers, it was the energy of all of his friends...

But I knew...

Chuck said, "You're so negative." I said, "I'm not negative, I'm realistic." I tried to be positive, but I always knew it would come to an end at some point.

Kenny had a tremendous support system. Everybody's support was keeping him going and I'm glad Lynda was the one to marry him. It was all meant to be that it was Lynda, because she stood by him. That doesn't always happen. I'll give you an example:

Dr. Shah had a patient, Natalie[3]. She was thirty-four years old, a beautiful girl, just beautiful. I remember some things vividly. She went to the dentist and they found a tumor in her gum line. Dr. Shah told her she needed surgery: she had to have her mandible removed; she had to have a neck dissection. She and her husband had not been married very long. He was a good-looking guy. He left her! After about six months! I remember her parents coming in as a support. I was thinking to myself, "You SOB!" How could he have just left her? She ended up

---

3   Name is changed

30

dying in nine months.

So I'm saying, there are reasons for everything. There are reasons why Lynda came into Kenny's life when she did. They got married, eight months later he got sick, but God knew that she was going to be the right wife for him.

I loved being in head and neck because they were amazing people. They needed that extra care because everything is open, visible. It's not a cancer you can hide. So people would look at them strange. Patients would be talking with their laryngectomy devices and maybe feeling insecure; I would tell them to be confident and look people straight in the eye. It was a very special time in my life. It's not easy, but being with those patients made me realize what's important.

We all suffer in our own little ways for different things and we don't know what is in store for us. There is a reason why every single one of us was born. We're born to make an impact on other people's lives. All of the stories that Lynda collected about Kenny are obviously a celebration of his life. God has His plan for us, whatever that is; it might not seem fair, but again, what is fair? We don't know the outcome, but if we trust in God and have faith, I trust that our burdens will be easier to bear.

***

I think part of why some people can endure suffering and others can't is faith. I guess some people don't know what is going to happen to them after death. The Hollers were very faithful and that helped them.

Mary, Tim's Friend, Age 15

13

Endurance

Dr. Shah: Former Chief of Head and Neck Service, MSK Cancer Center

My first contact with Kenny was through Camille, my former secretary. She called, and I said, "Of course I will see him."

When I saw him in the office, he had early stage cancer of the tongue on the left-hand side. We proposed surgery as the method of treatment. He was very stoic. He wasn't shocked by the proposition of the need for surgery, wasn't emotional or sensitive about it. His response was, "Doc, you have to do what you have to do." That makes the doctor's job much easier. When a patient understands his problem and is very realistic about it, then I would say that half of my work is already done. It dumps off addressing the issues which many patients are emotional about. So that is where we started.

Then it was a long story over a number of years and, as luck would have it, he required more surgery, radiation, and developed complications from surgery and radiation. It was not just the cancer, but the whole process that goes along with it, in terms of the long term cycle of treatment. But over all those years, every time he came to the office, he never complained, never had an emotional outburst. He took the bull by the horns as it came. He left an indelible mark on the memory as a person who is a solid citizen and a guy who was totally realistic about his own illness.

In general, patients who have a negative attitude about their illness—negative meaning: "Why me?" and the attitude that everything that happens to them is someone else's fault—those people do not do well. There are also the people that come with a completely broken attitude of a defeatist: "I'm done. I'm just dragging." Those patients don't do well. Patients that have a positive attitude clearly receive their treatment well, recover well from their treatment, and have a better outcome. There is data on that in the literature on psychological studies of how patients handle their sickness. Stage for stage, there is enough data to show that patients with positive attitudes do well.

Family support is an important and integral part of oral cancer care. The same comment I made about patients with positive attitudes: patients with good family support will do well. Psychologically they are well supported and they are solid, in deference to people that live a solitary life, or have a family and no family support, or a friction between the next of kin, spouse, partner, or whoever. Rejection by the family or the partner, because of illness, truly breaks down the patient, the psyche. The feeling that develops is, "I am losing two battles. I am losing my life to cancer and I am losing my life due to lack of support." Those patients truly do not do well. Some of them want to commit suicide before the treatment is finished, because they find that everything is coming at them from every side of the world and there is no escape.

Surgically Kenny came through every procedure that we ever did without any complexity or difficulties, but over the years, his morale started deteriorating a bit in terms of the long-term picture. I could see physically that he had started losing weight a little bit. Towards the later part of his sickness, he had come to grips with the issue that eventually he would probably lose the battle. I could see that transition in his personality, in his stance, in interacting, and in response to questions, to discussions.

Kenny had gone five years with no incidents, so in 2011, I transferred him to my new partner, Dr. Morris and Kenny was under his care when the cancer recurred in 2012.

This book is a nice project and Kenny is indirectly helping others through Lynda and all the people that are contributing. It will be a nice recital for people who may have somebody suffering in their family. A nice support instrument. That is what we are doing. We are basically fulfilling Kenny's desire to be of help to others.

***

But with respect to his cancer, I got the impression that he saw this as something that he was going to be stoic about, because being upset about it or being consumed with the unfairness of it all, was not going to help him do what was important.

Dr. Morris, Head and Neck Cancer Surgeon, MSKCC

14
True-grit
Jill: Dr. Shah's Clinical Nurse

I was probably the first nurse that Kenny met when he came to see Dr. Shah. My initial impression was that I was taken by his charm, his wit; he had a very endearing personality. There was a softness and a gentleness about him that drew me to him. Then, as time went on, and I got to know Kenny better, I was taken by his courage and his ability to accept very difficult situations. He was tried over and over again, with having these recurrences, and each time he just embraced it with great courage and was determined to always do the best that he could do. Lynda asked me to think of a word that describes Kenny and I would say, "True-grit." Just true grit. I think that was true all along from the beginning to the end.

He was someone that had a love of his family, had a great love for Lynda. When I met Kenny he didn't have any children, then the children came along and he was on cloud nine. Besides loving his family, Kenny loved his friends and his friends were part of his family. He made us feel like we were part of his family and for me, it was an honor. He was very private, but he would let me in and share certain things about his life. It was an honor to take care of him. He was someone of such depth, substance, and beauty throughout; he never lost that.

I have been a nurse for a very long time and there are certain people that have left their mark with me and they will never leave me. Sometimes I see a patient that is going through a difficult time and I can't help but think, "How would Kenny handle this?" Everyone does it a bit differently, but he was remarkable. He had an ability to embrace whatever he was given and he tried to play his cards with grace and dignity. Certainly, he played them with great courage, because he confronted some very frightening situations. I could see in his eyes that he was frightened, but he would say, "Okay, here we go." He never complained; I never remember him, "Woe is me," or feeling sorry for himself. Over time, he certainly had many situations where he could have done that, but he never did. I admired that about him.

I am getting flooded with all sorts of feelings and emotions about Kenny ... I really loved him. That twinkle in his eye, you know....

It gave me great comfort that he had Lynda. She was a great support to him. I admired him, but I also admired her, because she was able to be his rock, but quietly. She let him feel what he was feeling, but there was never a doubt that she was there for him. She gave him space, whereas sometimes I find that the anxiety that the partner is feeling will suffocate or not allow the patient to be in the place that they need to be. Lynda never did that. She was one of Kenny's blessings for sure. When she wasn't there, I would always ask about her and he'd have a little twinkle in his eye; it was really nice.

Support is absolutely critical in helping patients be successful. When people have love around them and support, that allows them to have the courage and the will to want to stay around, even in the most adverse physical situations. I myself had cancer and I had friends that did also, but their husbands and partners left them, because they couldn't handle their illnesses.

Fortunately, I had a partner, like Lynda was for Kenny, who was my rock. It brought us closer, but that doesn't always happen. Some people need a lot of help if they cannot deal with the emotions of the illness of their spouse, of someone they love.

I also felt that Kenny had faith in something greater than himself. I think when people have that, it is something that gives them strength and the will to endure very difficult situations, physically and emotionally. That never dwindled and I know he was in situations where if his hope was going to leave, it would have left, but it didn't.

I absolutely see good that comes out of suffering. Hard times make us stronger, more determined and aware that life is precious. When we suffer, we have to reach very, very deep in our souls and try to understand that dark place we are in and be determined to go towards the light and get out of the darkness. Kenny had the ability to do that over and over again, but I think each time that he had to do it, the light wasn't as bright. He got out of the darkness, but the light was dimming for him.

In spite of Kenny's many recurrences, and the cancer advancing, he had this ability to rebound, so Lynda was kind of conditioned to think, "Okay, he's going through this difficult time, but he's going to rebound. He's not going to die. He's going to get beyond this, because he always has." For them it was more about getting beyond, continuing on; Lynda didn't think about Kenny dying. She was focusing on what they had to do next, how they had to adapt their lives to the new changes, not thinking that it was going to end. It was a long, long time with many recurrences. I have seen it, but it is not common. Kenny really lived, I think, beyond what we thought he would, but we did not think about him dying; he was all about living. With someone like that you wouldn't have the conversation of end of life, because that was not part of his conversation.

Kenny always felt that he could contribute to his family; he never felt that he was a burden, even when it got really hard and there was a lot of maintenance. He was never at that point that he said, "I am ready for this to just all be over," because he saw meaning in his life to the very, very end. Even when his body said, "Enough," his mind wasn't ready to accept that. It doesn't always go hand in hand. He felt that he contributed and he did. He has two wonderful boys that love him. He left his mark and they are going to be ok, because Kenny and Lynda did a great job at parenting and caring for their boys and loving them, and love is forever. Isn't it?

***

Our culture is so afraid to discuss suffering and death; it is taboo. I think that is wrong. Suffering gives growth and allows us to see the world from a different perspective.

Tara, Palliative Care Home Care Nurse

15
Hunger

Saint Teresa of Calcutta: *Foundress of the Missionaries of Charity*

In Haiti just as in England, Spain, Italy, or India—there are unhappy people everywhere. Not only because they don't have any bread to eat. No, they hunger for love, understanding, and companionship. They suffer from loneliness, the feeling of being unwanted and rejected, a poverty of the soul. These are the things that can be far worse than being hungry or not having enough material goods....

Sometimes we see how joy returns to the lives of the most destitute when they realize that many among us are concerned about them and show them our love. Even their health improves when they are sick. After all, was it not Christ himself who said, "Every time you did it to the least of my brethren, you did it to me?" You are not to be indifferent to the suffering of others, but it is meant to affect you deeply.

FISHING

Kenny was one of the most colorful people that I ever knew or ever will know. He enjoyed life to the fullest and he enjoyed so many different things. He loved sports: baseball, basketball, hockey, golf, any sport you could play and he was good at them. He was a team player and he gave it his all. Very talented man. But of all of the sports, including horses, all of the things that he liked, I think the most important thing to remember is that Kenny's true passion, through his whole life, was fishing. As a little kid fishing in the pond by my house in Queens, to fishing down at Rockaway, to fishing the lakes and the reservoirs, and then moving it into the high gear that he knew only out at Montauk with Pete catching huge striped bass.

And so it was with his life. Kenny was a fisherman. He would cast his net and he would bring people in, always deeming them worthy to keep. He would work on them and bring out the best in them, then set them on their way, letting them know that he was their friend and they were great. Just like our Lord, he was forgiving, and funny, and he had all of the qualities of the fishermen that Christ collected for His mission. Kenny was a fisher of men and that was great for everyone who met him.[4]

---

4   Tim, Kenny's Cousin, FDNY Lieutenant

16
Generous

Pete: Queens Friend, Owner of Suspenders

I am here to talk about Kenny, my buddy Kenny. Where can I start?

Well, it started in the Hamptons in the '80s. I had Suspenders on Montauk Highway; it was like a disco. Tony and Kenny were two guys I met and they said, "Listen, we love Suspenders. You have to put a Suspenders in Astoria." They kept bugging me. I finally said, "Okay, let me go look." And believe it or not I found a great location, a place named Joe and Jack's on Steinway Street. They introduced me to the owner and I had an opportunity to buy it. I gave it a shot and it was a success.

Kenny and I became closer and closer and he was my bartender. He worked in the firehouse down the block and occasionally he had to make a meal for the firehouse. So, him and I used to cook in the kitchen. One time, we stuffed two turkeys and took them to the firehouse. They loved it. It was a sausage stuffing.

So, I got to know all of the guys from Astoria. They are a very tight bunch of guys; you very seldom see that. The neighborhood sticks together. Everybody that worked for me in the bar lived in the neighborhood; it was like a family. I liked living there. I loved Astoria. I found a whole new family of friends that I loved to hang out with and to this day I still do.

I used to take my boat out to Montauk. We fished in Montauk. We fished in the Hamptons. We fished in Fire Island. Kenny was a good fisherman, a natural fisherman. Just like anything else he did; he could play baseball, basketball, golf. The scary thing was when he played golf there would be all the guys with the fancy clubs and super deluxe bags. Kenny came out with a canvas bag and four clubs and would beat the hell out of them all. It was pretty cool.

Then I was dating this girl and we had a fight. I had scheduled to go to Puerto Rico with her. I had the tickets and a time share down there, so I said, "Kenny, I have tickets for Puerto Rico and it is on me. It is already paid for; you just have to go as Carol." At that time there was no identification check-in at the airport and he was available to go. It was perfect. It was the middle of the winter, the last two weeks of January; it was cold, and off we went to Puerto Rico. We really bonded then; now we were really tight. Buddy buddies. We were on our little honeymoon.

Schmidty, Shorty, Joey and a bunch of guys all owned at the same resort. We could actually stay there a month because they were large units and everybody had a week. We all had fun. Kenny wanted to come again the next year, so we became partners in the time share. Every year we knew we would go on vacation to Puerto Rico. I don't know if he had a lot of vacations as a kid, but Kenny really looked forward to that.

This is a good story: One year when we were in Puerto Rico, I was out swimming in the ocean and I saw Kenny close to the shore with two good-looking girls in bikinis. They were French girls. The next day we see the girls and they call me Jacques Too Tight. Kenny had told them my name was Jacques Too Tight, so every time we saw them in a restaurant or somewhere, they would call out "Jacques Too Tight!" Only Kenny could give me that name. That's how it started and he thought it was funny and I said, "You got me now." I couldn't tell the girls, "That's not my name." With Kenny and I, we would say, "I got you." I couldn't get upset about the name because he "got me." And I would get him at times. So it was a "Gotcha." That was a good "gotcha." Some guys would get upset, "Ohhh, that's not my name… My name is Pete!" I had to live with Jacques Too Tight and it stuck.

Little things like that stick in my memory over the years about Kenny and me. These are all good things.

There really weren't any bad things. What bugged a lot of guys from Astoria is Kenny would know their breaking point. A lot of guys don't have a sense of humor, can't take a joke. If Kenny picked that up, he would run it down them ten times. For instance, he had a mechanical bunny rabbit with a tambourine and he would put it on the bar. It would go up and down the bar and it would knock over drinks. Some guys would get upset, so he would send the rabbit back down. But if you didn't care, he wouldn't set up the rabbit. He would take you to your limit; he could pick you out. It was good in a way; he was just challenging us.

I was in the bar one day and Kenny told me to come into the restaurant in the back; he wanted me to meet his brother's ex-girlfriend, Sue. So to make a long story short, I started dating Sue and it is the best thing that ever happened to me. I married her. She is a wonderful woman. The ironic thing is that I met Sue in Suspenders in Astoria and guess what? Kenny and Lynda met in Suspenders too. I guess things work out for the better in Suspenders: I found Kenny, I found Sue, and then Lynda found Kenny. That is the bottom line. It is a happily-ever-after.

I got married; then Kenny got married, so we went to Puerto Rico with the girls. And guess what? The girls don't like Puerto Rico. Too many old stories and fun we had in Puerto Rico, so the girls transferred us to Aruba! We went there; we bought time shares, but prior to that we had to time-share shop. Have you ever gotten those promotions to go to a time share presentation? They would offer a $100 voucher for dinner or shopping; Kenny and I hated it.

One beautiful sunny day, the girls had us out looking at time shares. We were not supposed to know each other as couples, because then we wouldn't get two vouchers. We were in the elevator together and the salesman had no idea who we were. Kenny out of nowhere, he is so sharp, said to me, "You know, you look like some jerk I know in Astoria. As a matter of fact, you are that jerk!" I said, "Who are you calling a jerk!" and I grabbed him by the collar. They broke us up and we walked out of there with two vouchers and we didn't have to look at the units! It was a good move on his behalf.

One year, we went out night fishing in Aruba on an old, rinky-dink steel boat. It was scary, like our last voyage. The water was rough; it was windy. The crew couldn't make it around the point of the island by the lighthouse; I didn't think that clunker would make the point. Sue and Lynda wouldn't even know where to look for us if we didn't come back.

Then, we went out wahoo fishing in Aruba with Dave. We got a local fisherman and the three of us went out fishing around the lighthouse. Really rough, I am talking rough. The waves were busting over the bow and all of a sudden we got into fish and the captain just left the wheel. He would rather fish than drive the boat! I took over the wheel and told Kenny, "This guy is nuts!" I was driving the boat, keeping the bow of the boat into the waves, so we didn't capsize, but we went back with a lot of really nice big fish. That was good fishing.

When Kenny first got the cancer he said, "Pete, I have this pimple on my tongue. It is cancerous. I have to have it taken out." He went into the hospital. I got a phone call and I hear, "Ahhh ahh ah…" I said, "Who the hell is this?" and I hung up. I got another phone call, "Ah, it is Kehhn…" I said, "Geeze Kenny, you sound like Donald Duck!" I was so proud, I was the first phone call when he came out of the operation. I said, "Kenny, are you going to be all right?" He said they went in and it looked fine.

In the second operation, three months later, they did a lot of damage. And after the radiation, he couldn't taste things. We used to like to eat and that really set him back. From then on he had a will power. He was strong and he stuck with it. He loved his kids and the main reason that he fought as hard as he did was for the kids and for Lynda. I would talk to him one-on-one and say, "Kenny, I know you are doing this for the kids and all, but I'll tell you one thing: your kids had the quadruple father time that no one else has. That is something they will have for the rest of their lives."

After that operation, I thought, "This has got to stop now." Then we had five years with no recurrences and I thought, "This is what we will live with. This is good."

Then Kenny said, "Pete, guess what? I got it again. I have to go back in." That's when I realized this thing was nuts.

I am not much of a pray-er, but when I pray it is a big prayer. I don't pray all the time. I save my prayers for special occasions and Kenny happened to be one of those special occasions for a prayer. I dusted off all my prayers for Kenny.

He would still go fishing with me, but want to cut it short. In the old days, we would spend extra days in Montauk; we used to stay there about a week. Later, he would spend more and more time with the family. He'd say, "I have to be here." "I have to be there." "I have to do this for Lynda."

He kept coming out with me until he really couldn't with the trach; it was tough. But he stayed with it and I don't know how anybody could do what he did and with the pain he did it in. It was the love of the family. It was like he had a finish line and until that finish line he wanted to give as much of his life as he could for his family. And he did. He wasn't selfish. He did it for others.

I miss him and I think about him all the time. I do. When I am on the boat I can see where he used to sit. I had his fishing poles and his room downstairs. What are you going to do? Life goes on. He left a good legacy with his friends, family; his kids are always going to remember all the quality time he spent with them. An abundance of quality time.

Kenny wasn't wealthy, but he was always generous. Generous goes two ways. You can be generous with money; you can be generous with gifts. Kenny was generous with his life. He was very generous of himself for others. Generous with his time; he would go out of his way for you. Generous with love for the family to an extent that was more so than others. Whatever he had he was generous. There was not a selfish bone in his body and "Generous" is the best word for Kenny.

That was the part that I really loved about him. He was sincere. He was honest. He was funny and he went through a lot of pain that no person as nice and as loving as he should have went through, but he did it for a reason. The Lord said, this was his time to do it and he had to do it. It wasn't his call.

Kenny brought the balance of life to the kids through sports. He was there with his two boys and their teammates on the ball fields and he taught a lot of those young kids how to win and lose. That was a big step and the kids didn't know what Kenny was actually doing with them. If you get it in sports, you will be a much stronger person in life, because you accept the winning part of it and the losing part of it.

The most important thing is to learn how to lose and to accept it. Kenny played sports a lot and he knew how to lose, even though he was always striving to win. Kenny would laugh at guys when they lost to him, because he was such a natural athlete, but Kenny could accept losing. He would laugh if he lost. Kenny gave that to the kids. He guided them through it and he was the best at it, because he could add a little sense of humor. I can imagine him saying, "It's not bad to lose and the next time we play them we'll lose even more!" And the kids could laugh at that. They gave him a lot of respect and that is why they accepted him and they looked up to him.

Sue and I went up to see Kenny at Yale New Haven the weekend before he was transferred to hospice. I still remember his last smile. That was all he could do. He gave me a smile when I told him one of my stupid stories. He had every medical device known to man hooked up to him. It was a tough thing.

The following Friday morning, I knew I had to go see him. I hadn't talked to Lynda, but I called Sue, went into Manhattan, picked her up at work, and drove to Rosary Hill in Westchester.

Kenny wasn't awake, but I could touch him and say goodbye.

Kenny passed away that night, but I got the last goodbye, which is good. I had the first "Hello" with him in the Hamptons which was the beginning of a relationship that did a lot of good things for me. My parting words: "Goodbye Kenny, I love you." What else can we do? Life is tough, but it has to happen. Everybody is going there; some are hard and some are easy. You can't write the script. If you could, everyone would write an easy script.

***

Mr. Holler was always the coach that was the confidence booster. If anybody was freaking out after striking out or something, he'd always calm them down. He was really the only one that had that effect on people; he could change their emotions right away.

Mike, Tim's Friend, Age 15

17
Selfless
Trish: Astoria/Brewster Friend

I met Kenny, twenty-five or six years ago, through John at Suspenders. Right off the bat, he made me feel like I had known him forever. He felt like an older brother, somebody that I could trust.

At that time, that stupid song, *Don't Worry, Be Happy* was popular and that was his song. He sang it in the bar; he played it on the jukebox. To me, that kind of became the symbol of him. When I thought of Kenny, I thought of: "Don't worry be happy!" Even after he got sick, I kept thinking, "Here is a guy that was living his life with that happy attitude and now he is stuck with this horrible, horrible disease that has taken such a toll on him."

Kenny was known as the "Mayor of Astoria," because he knew so many people. I remember being out in Suspenders and he would come in and he had that booming voice and personality. I was thankful that I was in that group that got to be part of his circle of friends. I was happy for that. I like that.

I remember when we were all first dating. We met up with Kenny and Lynda on their first date in a Polynesian restaurant in Queens. John and I were on our first-date-again after having broken up for a while. It was nice that we had that in common and then we got married close together. Ultimately, we moved to Brewster because of Kenny and Lynda. I haven't thought about that for a long time.

Lynda and I became friends way back on those first dates. We went through the same amount of time being married, had our kids around the same time, and I think I have had it really, really easy compared to Lynda. She dealt with cancer from day one. The fact that Lynda was able to get through it speaks measures for who she is. It really does. I handled my dad's cancer hanging by a thread sometimes and that was a short period of time compared to what she dealt with.

I became sensitive to Kenny's challenges right away when I heard him speak after having his first surgery to remove a portion of his tongue; then shortly after, he had the radical neck dissection which changed how he looked. To hear him talk, and see him struggle, is when it became a reality. I realized that this had now taken a big chunk out of the man I first knew.

Lynda would tell me that he had a hard time sleeping, that his mouth was always dry. I would think about them when it was really hot and how they couldn't have air conditioning, because the dry air was damaging to him. I don't like the heat and I crank that baby up when it's hot, so I would often wonder how much Lynda had to sacrifice to do what she had to do to be there. How much the boys had to sacrifice.

I chose the word, "Selfless" to describe Kenny, because I think that even with everything that he was going through, he was more concerned about everybody else than himself. Lynda and the boys were at the top of his list. I could see him biting the bullet and doing whatever he needed to do to make sure they were okay.

In spite of all the suffering I saw, my memories of Kenny are always happy ones. Always.

Even after he was sick, he continued to live that motto: "Don't worry be happy." I will always think of him with a smile on my face and remember that when I was around him, he made my heart feel full. That was a good feeling.

***

Kenny was a person that didn't want anybody to worry about him, didn't want people to feel bad for him. So they don't remember him as the sick Kenny. Even after the funeral, after that talk that Lynda's niece Corinne read, we needed tissues, but then when you listened to everybody talk, everything everybody said had to do with laughter and happiness.

Karen, Kenny's Cousin, Steve M's wife

18

Young Adult Kenny

McCormick and Kenny on the boat

Kenny the Gondolier in a pool in the Hamptons

Kenny (aka Carol) and Pete (aka Jacques Too Tight)
in Puerto Rico

Kenny's stringer of fish caught with Mike in
Putnam County

Roommates: Big Dave and Bobby

Kenny and Brian fishing in Canada
(getting eaten alive by black flies)

19
Extraordinary
Brian: *Kenny's Cousin*

The first things I remember about Kenny is being about five years old down on the beach at Rockaway riding the waves and going for knishes at lunch. Kenny was four years older than me. We caught enough fish in the summer in Rockaway that my mother could cook fish every Friday through the whole winter. It was all Uncle Rod's fish: fluke, flounder, blowfish, striped bass.

When we grew up, Kenny, my brother Timmy, and I took the Fire Department test. I was in Ladder 107 in East New York, Brooklyn. We never ran in with each other in the Fire Department, but Kenny and I were able to get time off when we wanted, and we would hang out together down in Long Beach and on the Island.

We would go fishing a lot too. One time he said to me that he wanted to go to Canada fishing. I was married and that was right after my twins were born, so it was kind of tough in my house, but he talked me into going. That was the infamous plane trip…

So, Kenny talked me into going to Canada, Club Caesar in Northwest Montreal. There was supposed to be a bunch of firemen that met us there and we were all going to get on a fifteen person plane and take a half hour plane ride to the lake. The other option was to take a logging road for four hours in our car, but they said that there were cars that were broken down and we would have to move them out of the way to get around them. That was how bad the road was. I had a brand new Suburban and I told Kenny, "No way am I driving four hours on a logging road. I am getting on a plane."

Instead of us going on a fourteen or fifteen passenger plane, they put me and Kenny on a plane where the inside was like the inside of a Volkswagen; I was bumping shoulders with the pilot. Kenny was behind him. The pilot just about took off, because the plane was struggling with the weight of all the stuff we had. We got up in the sky; it was a beautiful day, but when we looked toward the horizon it looked like midnight. I said to myself, "Oh God, we are going to hit a storm!" Sure enough, five or ten minutes into the flight we started dropping from three thousand feet to five hundred feet. We were banging around inside this plane like we were in a beer can. I was hitting the pilot; Kenny was behind me banging around. I had a death grip on the handle next to me.

After one of the episodes, where we dropped like two thousand feet, Kenny said to the pilot, "Good job!" and smacked him on the back. Then he cracked open a beer and said to the pilot, "Do you want a beer?" I was looking at him and wanted to kill him. I was thinking, "He talked me into going on this trip and now I am going to die here today."

It continued to be rough and we were all shaken up; the pilot was not smiling anymore. He was pumping things and touching things. I was watching him saying, "Are we going down or what?" And Kenny was behind me playing with my ears and saying, "Look out the window. Do you see any moose?" I said, "When we land I am going to kill you!"

When we landed, I swear this is a true story, I couldn't open my fingers. My fingers went into a spasm and I couldn't let go of the handle. I said, "Kenny, I can't open my hand. I can't open my frigging hand." I was so scared. Finally I got my hand open and I just about fell out of the plane onto the dock. So Kenny said, "Get him a drink; get him a Jack Daniels or something." They gave me a shot of Jack Daniels right on the dock. It was a big laugh after that.

We stayed in a cabin and every time I went to roll up my sleeping bag and my pillow there were nuts and little twigs, acorns and stuff under my pillow. I told Kenny, "There is a frigging mouse in this cabin. It's building a nest in my bed every day." I would sweep the thing out; I would have all the cabinets open looking for the mouse. Nothing. I couldn't find anything. Then, after one of the times that I had cleaned my bed out, I was outside and looked in the window, and there Kenny was putting the stuff under my pillow! I wanted to brain him!

That all being said, it was the best trip of my life. We caught hundreds of pounds of rainbow trout. It was incredible.

When I found out that Kenny was sick, I sat down, said prayers, hoping it would work out and that it won't be that bad. That they could take the tumor out of the tongue and that would be it. Kenny told me that when the first doctor told him it was cancer, he walked into some bar and got a shot of Scotch. He said, "I don't drink Scotch." He was so beside himself. When he heard that word he thought, "What the hell!" Like everybody would.

I used to say to myself, "Just biting my tongue hurts so much. What is it like when he wakes up after they cut this thing and it is sore? The pain has to be phenomenal." I never asked him, "How is the pain?" because I didn't want to harp on the pain. I knew it had to be very painful. I can only imagine, really, the pain that goes with that. And if it was me, I would be in the bathroom every other day looking in my mouth with a flashlight, wondering, "Do I feel something here now?" Lynda said that Kenny had a lot of that too. You can't help it. You want to be on top of it.

Extraordinary is my word. He was extraordinary the way he dealt with being sick. He had an upbeat, positive attitude every time we saw him. He inspired me because he was so sick and he was able to handle it. I thought the world of him. I always did. Before sick, after sick, even now. I used to pray for him; now I pray to him and tell him to save me a seat.

***

I look back on it and say he lived every hour of his life as if he wasn't sick. I don't know if "envy" is the right word, but I always looked up to him, because if I wanted to be like somebody, he was definitely the person. He always looked after his family; he always looked after the kids and everybody around him; he would always give the shirt off his back. He would always do anything he possibly could to help people out. I guess envy is the word.

Bryan, Brewster Baseball Friend

20
Alma de Dios
Dr. Herrera: *Primary Physician*

Kenny and I had something very much in common: fishing. He used to go to Long Island with a buddy of his and they would go out in a little dingy that was twenty-four feet, which is quite dangerous if you have ever been out there fishing for stripers and whatnot. He used to catch massive fish and when he came in to the office, he would always show me pictures. Being a fisherman, I was always jealous, because his fish was bigger than mine! One time he told me about a really neat experience that he had; he was out in that little dingy and a giant whale shark came by the boat. He was a man that was part of nature.

I'm a general internist, cancer is not my forte, but I don't think there are many internists, in fact, I know there are very few, that have seen as many patients as I have. I am above the ninetieth percentile when they measure how much work I do. I never expected to see Kenny live as long as he did. He stayed alive and it wasn't because of his medical treatment. I believe there is a will to live. I think he had that will to live because of how he felt about people. Essentially, how he felt about his family and his responsibilities as a husband and a father.

I have known Kenny and Lynda for twenty-two years. The thing that killed me about him was, I'm a doctor and here's this guy that's really quite sick, but he never really complained, ever. He would sometimes have to come in for pain pills, but he would never complain that it was something that he couldn't bear. I knew he would only take medicine if he really needed it. One time he came in and he had gotten chemo and it had destroyed his fingernails. I said, "Kenny, does that hurt?" He said, "Na, doesn't bother me at all." It bothered me, because I couldn't believe how selfless he was. That he didn't care about the degree of suffering that he was going through, because he would do anything for his boys and his wife.

For most people, their world revolves around themselves and they don't "get" it. He was on the right side of the bell curve. His world revolved around the well-being of his friends and family, and it was like everybody was his friend. He had excellent values; he must have had great parents. I felt that he was like my family.

Lynda is very lucky, because she was his wife. While it is kind of horrible what happened, it is also very beautiful. Sometimes that is how life has to be. The good is so good, because the bad can be so bad.

I never really talked much about religion with him, but anybody that is that in tune with nature is a gift from God. In Spanish, we have a phrase for it: Alma y Arma de Dios, the Soul and Weapon of God. I was brought up very religious, very Catholic; my mother was a devout Catholic and my aunt still goes to church every day.

I was brought up to believe like Kenny. It is really true; God works through people and that's what kept Kenny alive, because statistically, he should have been dead within five years after I met him. He lived long enough to see that his children were fully developed and formed and I am sure that it was quite an experience for them to know how much he loved them. That is the problem with people; people don't always have somebody like that around for them. A lot of people, unfortunately, don't feel secure about themselves. Maybe that is what kept him going; maybe that is one of the reasons why he would never give up, why God kept him here as long as He did.

People that complain a lot, they get to us and they produce angst in us, but that wasn't the case with Kenny. Even though he suffered, I don't think he cared. He was willing to put up with it, because he was a fighter.

My father died from Alzheimer's. In my waiting room, I have a poem that was written hundreds of years ago by a Catholic theologian, John Donne. "Ask not for whom the bell tolls, it tolls for thee." It embodies what being a doctor is all about. No man is an island, but he's a piece of the main. I always pray for my patients and do you know what I also try to do? I also try to believe that no matter how crazy a person acts, that I know something good about them. And I do. I usually can see good in everyone.

It was a pleasure to have been Kenny's doctor, because now he is a piece of me. We incorporate people like him into our personalities and it makes us stronger and better people. It really does. We have to consider ourselves very lucky if we knew Kenny and cared for him.

I know that as much as I cared for him, and I cared for him as if he was my own family, he also cared about me. He made us all better people, because when he was suffering, he still cared about his family, his friends, me as a doctor. It makes everyone a better person then, because basically, that is the greatest good. The greatest good is to help other people and not really worry about ourselves. He lived it. He was truly what we would call a disciple.

***

Being sick never seemed to affect Kenny; it kind of came natural to him to a point. Or he didn't care, I guess. He didn't care that he was sick; he just wanted to live every moment making others happy and not worry about anything else for himself.

Declan, Marie's Son, Age 16

21
For Whom the Bell Tolls

John Donne: *17th Century Theologian*

No man is an island,
Entire of itself.
Each is a piece of the continent,
A part of the main.
If a clod be washed away by the sea,
Europe is the less.
As well as if a promontory were.
As well as if a manor of thine own
Or of thine friend's were.
Each man's death diminishes me,
For I am involved in mankind.
Therefore, send not to know
For whom the bell tolls,
It tolls for thee.

22
Self-deprecating
Andrea: Dr. Herrera's Secretary

I think about how I first met Kenny and Lynda in January of 1993, shortly after they moved to Brewster from Queens. We were all young back then. Kenny had just been diagnosed with tongue cancer and it was pretty shocking to me to hear Kenny's diagnosis, because we were all about the same age.

Their insurance company was brand new back then; it was the first round of HMOs. They were the first to make us write paper referrals. Patients had to request permission to go to another doctor and they had to stay within the approved doctor list. It wasn't like the old days where we had insurance, doctors accepted it, and we just went.

Kenny had just switched to this new insurance in the NYC open enrollment period the previous fall and it became effective January 1st. So when they learned he had cancer and needed surgery a week into their new policy, Kenny and Lynda didn't realize how complicated it would become. They wanted to go to Dr. Shah at Memorial Sloan Kettering, but the insurance company rejected it, because he was out of network. They got a quick course in navigating the system.

They started by staying in network and they spent the next two or three weeks consulting with at least three different Manhattan specialists that participated with this insurance, but they were shocked at how unprofessional those doctors were and they soon determined that there was no way that any of them were going to treat Kenny. So Lynda went straight to the top and faxed a long detailed letter to the president of the insurance company. She was outraged that those were the quality of doctors that this company found acceptable for their patients and she included specific details from each of their visits. She quickly got a response from a high level case nurse that was able to issue a non-participating referral for Kenny with Dr. Shah at Sloan.

From then on, I don't know how we did it, but we continued to get non-par referrals every year to Sloan for Kenny's continued follow-up and subsequent surgeries with Dr. Shah. It wasn't easy; I would call the insurance company and say, "He has been there. You cannot tell him he cannot follow up. That is his doctor. This is his life. He has a wife." They didn't have the kids yet.

I always expected Lynda's phone calls a certain time of the year, every six months or whatever it was. Sometimes Lynda would call at the last minute; they would forget that a referral had expired and Kenny was scheduled for an appointment tomorrow! But those are challenges that I like. That didn't bother me. We just did it. We got the job done.

One day, many years into this, Lynda said she was talking to a customer service rep from the insurance company and they were shocked that we had a non-par to Sloan. He told her, "No one gets non-par approvals for Sloan." That is pretty good. I am proud of that. I had to speak to a lot of people and spend a lot of time, but you know it was never a chore. Even though it is my job, there are some things that we do because we want to and I really wanted to make sure that Kenny was okay. I don't know what it was. I didn't have long conversations with Kenny and

Lynda; they were the patients and I was here to help them, but it was just something that they put out. Spiritually? I don't know.

Kenny was just very self-deprecating, always considering everybody else's needs, "Do you need anything? Can I do anything?" He even offered to get us coffee while he waited in the office. That left an impression on me. No matter how much pain, no matter how frustrated with the insurance company, he was patient, kind.

I don't know what my future holds, but I will always take that with me, because he is an example. I have seen people be very angry, very sad, very beaten. He never looked defeated. How did he do that? What did he have that he got up every day and just lived in the moment?

There have been a few people that I will never forget, that really meant something to us in the office and it isn't because they brought cookies. We were all very sad when we got the bad news about Kenny.

My husband is the local funeral director and one night, while we were in the cemetery, he told me that Kenny's stone had been delivered. I said "Let's just make sure that everything is perfect."

***

Even when you meet somebody like him for a short period, it is impactful, because it is such a rarity for somebody to be that genuine. It really is. So, you appreciate it when you find it. A lot of people have that gift, but they just don't want to let it out. It is a great hope of mine that this book will encourage people to use their gifts.

Ed, St. Lawrence O'Toole Friend

23
Reflection
Lynda

By 2014, Kenny had accumulated hundreds of days of inpatient stays on the seventeenth floor of Sloan Kettering over his twenty-one year battle and had come to know well many of the dedicated medical professionals that faithfully served their radically affected head and neck cancer patients. Bill was new to the floor and to Kenny's service. When I met him for the first time he said:

"The other nurses told me that I had better take good care of Mr. Holler or I will be hearing from them."

I said, "Yes, Kenny is well known here."

He looked at me sincerely and responded, "There is a big difference between being well known and being well loved."

***

I think we all want to make a difference in this world. We can't all be the president of a corporation or hold some kind of formal position where we impact hundreds or thousands of lives, but I think when you see the results of what Lynda is doing here with the book and when you think about the impact a guy like Kenny had, it is hundreds, if not thousands of lives, countless.

It can make us think about ourselves and all the people that we touch and how we can do that too. Speaking bluntly, we saw a guy like Kenny and how he could favorably touch everybody that he came in contact with. Then we saw the reaction and the love and support that his family received from countless people after everything happened, and we start to realize (if it's even possible) how Kenny's short life made a difference far beyond what any of us could imagine. Like me, I am just a normal guy that Kenny had a very significant impact on. I would like to emulate that impact and pass it on to others. It is the multiplier effect that surpasses our daily chores and worries and helps us focus on what is truly important in life.

Frank, Brewster Friend

24
Warrior

Norine: Nurse, Head and Neck Floor, MSK Cancer Center

I have known Kenny Holler since his first surgery in February 1993. Actually he was my favorite patient.

The first time I met him, I will never forget. I walked into work in the morning, got my assignment, and made the rounds. I can remember his room number; it was 926, on the ninth floor before we moved to the seventeenth floor. It was a Sunday morning and my husband, a fireman, had worked the night before. There was a big blizzard expected. I introduced myself to Kenny, took care of him, and right away we realized that we knew a lot of the same things. He knew my husband, I knew Suspenders in Astoria, and we just had a lot in common.

So we started talking, and the weather started getting bad, and he said to me, "You have to get out of here." He was looking out for me. So that was the first time I met Kenny and fell in love with him. We were like brother and sister and I always felt that I had to look out for him, make sure that he always had his pain meds on time. Make sure that everybody else looked out for him. That was the first bout.

The next was the neck dissection. Later he had surgeries on his mandible, and then they finally did the fibular free-flap. And that time, I think he was in 1731, and he was in the room with a Yonkers fireman that was going through the same thing. It was my husband's friend's brother-in-law. The guy lost his life anyway, but Kenny was so encouraging to him. He was taking care of him too. Giving him support.

He had a tough doctor. Dr. Shah was tough, but Kenny needed somebody that was a total surgeon that would give it to him in black and white with no fluff. It was hard seeing Kenny coming back and forth, but he was like a warrior. He would always be up walking around after his surgeries doing his laps around the floor. Keeping an eye on the territory; giving me the eyes.

During every admission we would catch up, "How is this one? How is that one?" He knew that we were adopting Ally. I'd show him the pictures. I'd tell him what was going on with my husband; we'd talk about him going through all the ranks. I think he called me after 9/11 to make sure my husband was okay. And we have been exchanging Christmas cards for years, watching each other's kids grow up.

As a nurse, I could see the writing on the wall and knew how aggressive that cancer was. Tongue cancer, for a man that young, usually has a very quick outcome, but at that time they started getting more advanced surgeries in, so they were getting a little better at controlling the speed of the cancer and getting a little better spin on it. And they were getting better with the surgical techniques. It is amazing that he lived as long as he did with that diagnosis.

He would take the one-two punch; he'd be down for five seconds, ten seconds, then he was up again. He would not give up. That is why I respect Kenny, because he wasn't going to let anybody take the fight away from him until he was ready. He was in control from 1993 and he stayed in control really, if you think about it. He managed it; on top of a cancer diagnosis he was a wonderful father, great husband, great friend and lived his life for every minute.

The pain issues were ridiculous. The bleeding… Towards the end with the bleeding, scary. I just wish that didn't have to happen for him. The doctors were very forthright; they would tell him what they were afraid could happen. For him to have that courage. He fought for Lynda and the kids. He fought for those Aruba vacations.

I prayed for my patients and I prayed for Kenny. I still do. When I was working, I started at 7:00 am. I used to get up at like 4:00, have my cup of coffee, and say a decade of the rosary. Then I would get in the car and start praying: "God bless… Let there be no codes… Bless all the people that are working today, that we have a good day. Bless all the patients and their family members…" because there is nothing worse than being a family member and going up to that floor.

There is nothing worse. Sometimes it is even harder for the family members, especially on that head and neck floor, because some of these things are beyond our wildest expectations. The surgeries can be very radical and leave people very disfigured. And I have seen aliens, almost, coming out of people's bodies. Tumors that are fungating and unbelievable, yet people still have the will to live.

When I think of what Kenny lived through; to live with that disease in his life at the caliber that he did, OMG. I think about Kenny all the time. When I hear of someone getting diagnosed, I think of Kenny immediately, because of the fight that he fought. And he fought it for so long. So long. And always stayed true to himself; he never lost his personality. Even when he wrote on his white board, he was as pleasant as he could be. And funny.

Kenny made me me. He and patients like him are big contributors to how I feel, my career. It is a tough go and you don't realize it until it is over. Now that I am retired and I look back, I amaze myself. They validated my life. It is total validation.

***

I only saw Kenny in Aruba and we saw that his health declined a little each year, but not his determination and inspiration. We heard about his suffering, but he had Lynda and the boys and that's all that mattered. You could see it on his face; he was totally devoted to the three of them. That was a beautiful thing. I think it kept him going for much longer than they expected. I don't know if he was conscious of it, but most of us that knew him for the short period of time we spend in Aruba each year, found him inspirational. He inspired me because I was dealing with a child that was sick for thirty years. He motivated me to be more positive with my daughter and her issues.

Carol, Aruba Friend

25
Fatherhood
Sandy: Lynda's Sister

In thinking about Kenny, I recognize that there were so many aspects to him. I think back first to before his kids were born, to when Rich, our kids, and I spent time with him and Lynda. He was always hospitable, always funny, always ready to laugh, always wanting to make us feel welcome and happy to be together.

But there was so much more. Sports: he was such an avid athlete and fan. Work: so dedicated to the FDNY—such a vibrant and respected part of his work community. Neighbor: to all from his old neighborhood to his new neighborhood. To these and all the other aspects of his life, he put such effort, such vibrancy, and such desire. He just wanted the most out of each experience.

That leads me to fatherhood. He was a very good father and we in our family have very good fathers. Lynda and I had a very good father. My husband, Rich, is a very good father. My son, Sean, and my son-in-law, Brad, are very good fathers. But that is not the norm; we kind of take it for granted, when it really, absolutely, should not be taken for granted.

Kenny, even though he was one of many good fathers in our family, he was not one of many in the community or the world. He was one of a kind, because it was always family first, it was always his children first, even over all those other aspects that were so important to him for the decades before his children came along. He could be watching his beloved Yankees, but when the kids walked in, he would totally divert himself from the game and give his full attention to the boys.

His genuine interest was such a good, authentic role model for his kids and mine. That is, I believe, how Sean learned to be a good father, by emulating his father and Kenny, watching and feeling how a man should be with his kids. And I believe that if he didn't have those constant male role models, he may not have grown up to be the good, devoted father that he is to his young daughters. I really believe that Kenny's dedication to life, work, friends, and especially fatherhood has gone on to inspire a whole other generation.

***

He taught many people what it was like to be a dad. He also showed us how to be a husband, a survivor, and how important it is to maintain one's humor.

Claire, Lynda's Queens Friend

55

26
Incredible

Dr. Wenick: *Colin & Tim's Pediatrician*

I didn't know Kenny that well, but because the sons are children of the father, his qualities are seen through them. So his strength is their strength. The boys also have devotion, diligence, and a touch with reality that is very nice to see. They had to learn it from somewhere, it had to come from the parents; therefore, in knowing Colin and Tim, those are qualities I see in Kenny.

That the boys are always thinking of someone else first, that is what a family does, isn't it? They think of other people around them, they do not think of themselves only. They think of how the community is affected. The boys have other people around them; they are on team sports, and the father is the same way, as with the Fire Department. The whole 9/11 thing; I don't know what he did exactly, but he was part of that effort. That is what the boys are going to do one day also for the same reasons. It speaks of his qualities as a person, what the boys will do with their lives.

Of course, I recognized his medical challenges. Incredibly, he would go out of the house. Incredible! Think about it for a moment. I am sure that he must have gotten comments and looks that were off-putting from other people, because it was a physical feature that you could easily recognize. But he still said, "I'm going out." The strength of his character said, "I am not going to be held back by this illness: I will go out of the house; I will be seen by other people. I will continue the best I can on my adventures for the day."

Oral cancer is awful. It is awful. You are reminded on a daily basis with everything that you do that is oral in nature, from speaking, eating, all of those functions are affected. I don't know how much he lost of his taste buds and sensations, but I am sure that is was an incredible amount of loss, yet he was still able to go forward. It is a very painful process. It means that it takes an incredible amount of force and character to do that.

As for suffering, over time we have forgotten our histories. A hundred years ago we didn't have medicines like we do today. People knew suffering; they knew life and death on a daily basis from their parents, grandparents, and great-grandparents. Nobody had the childhoods that we have today. They all suffered at some level. And because they knew suffering as children, they knew and expected suffering as adults. It was part of life. Pain is part of life. If we accept that, it makes pain and suffering easier to live with and teaches us the reality that we cannot expect life to be a bowl of cherries. The lesson learned is that we have to make it better for ourselves and for others around us. Pay it forward.

God's plan is beyond our understanding. If we knew what His plan was, we wouldn't be who we are. So, we do the best we can and we all suffer together. Kenny, Lynda, Colin, and Tim's pain was awful; it was awful. Terrible pain, but people can learn from their pain. Colin and Tim learned from the pain; the rest of their family and community learned from their pain. Maybe the community of people that learned from their pain are better off as people now. Some may have become different people because of it.

The value of suffering is to see what life can be without it. Without suffering you don't realize what comfort really is. You need… and it is hard because you don't want anybody to suffer, but for us to be stronger, and to hold on to who we are, we need that. Kenny's suffering inspired me. As much as I went through with my own cancer, Michael would say, "Look at everything that Kenny is going through, you can do this." He was my inspiration: if Kenny could do it, I knew I could do it too.

Suzanne, FDNY Wife

27
Markings

Jack: *Brewster Elks, Golf Partner*
Mac: *FDNY Ladder 116, Golf Partner*

I met Kenny in the Brewster Elks. It was a Friday night because Pete O. was working. This guy comes in, stands next to me, and Pete says' "Hello" to him. I turned around and he had these markings on his head. Kenny said, "What are you looking at? I am a marked man." They had him marked off with very obvious purple lines because he had to go to the hospital the next day to begin his radiation. That's when I first met him, June of 1993. Then we became good friends.

I worked with Kenny at Ladder 116, but I remember him coming into the bar that June and he had those purple markings all over his face and neck. He made it seem like it was nothing, just shrugging off the severity of it. Just the way he was. I've never seen anybody with cancer have that kind of thing done. The markings showed the technicians where they had to direct the radiation. He wore those marks on his face that whole summer, until the radiation was completed. I mean he had to walk around with that. People must have stared, kids must have stared. They had given him a choice of the purple markings or small permanent tattoos. He didn't want anything to permanently remind him of this.

***

There has to be good to come out of Kenny's suffering because it happened. I don't know God's plan, so there had to be a reason for it. I don't think it is given to everybody. Maybe in that way he was special.

Jo, Lynda's Friend

28
Influential
Cara: Colin's Girlfriend, Age 18

I remember Kenny from when my brother Brian was on Colin's basketball team in elementary school. I don't think I knew that he was Colin's dad; I didn't really know Colin that well. I remember that he always had a tissue and was putting it by his mouth, so I recognized that he was sick, or had an issue.

It's a different perspective for me, than anyone else doing this interview, because they all knew Kenny personally. I only know him by what people have told me. Colin and I started dating a couple months before Junior Prom. Kenny was very sick and went into the hospital about that time. It is so interesting to think that Kenny was such a huge part of all of their lives, but I don't know that part of their family. I know so much about Colin, and his life with his dad was such a huge part of his life, but I don't know any of it in person. They know where Kenny would sit on the couch or where he would sit at dinner, but I don't. I think about that all the time. When we sit down for dinner, I think about that.

Whenever we do stuff in the garage, like when Colin is sanding one of his wood projects, I think of Kenny. Colin is so good at that type of stuff, I feel that he wants to do things that his dad would do. When he is putting the tools together, it makes me think, "Those were probably Kenny's tools."

On the one-year anniversary of Kenny's death, when they had the gathering, friends and family were all sitting on the lawn telling stories and it made me realize how much Colin and Tim do stuff like their dad all the time. I see that. They are jokesters and some things that Colin does remind me of stories people told. I hear that Kenny was super funny, but also a really nice guy, genuine, a gentleman. I think that of Colin; Colin is funny and genuine too. I always hear stories about Kenny wanting other people to be happy and Colin wants me to be happy. When we are going out to eat or something, he'll always open the door for me. He will go around and open my car door to let me out and I think that could be something that Kenny would have done. He either learned from his father or heard about it and wants to be like that.

I have noticed that Colin not only treats me well, but is kind to everyone. And like his dad, Colin doesn't complain. He has had to do some things that are disappointing and unpleasant, but he just does them quietly and to the best of his ability.

As for me, hearing the stories about how Kenny never complained even through tough times, always makes me think twice when I am in an undesirable situation. It helps me step back, put my life in perspective, and realize that my situation could be worse and that if Kenny didn't complain and was grateful for all the other things in his life, then I can certainly manage to do the same.

I see Kenny in Colin and Tim. I think Colin is unassuming. He is a nice mellow kid; Kenny always seemed so mellow. I don't know if unassuming is an insult, but to me it is somebody that has a quiet strength to them.

John, Brewster Friend

29
Dad

Tim: *Kenny's Youngest Son, Age 15*

When I think about Dad now, it is never about bad memories. It is always good memories like him taking us to different restaurants or surprising us with special treats for no reason. Or watching us play sports.

Growing up, basically all Dad was about was making us happy and doing everything that he could for us. He would surprise us with bagels or doughnuts or breakfast sandwiches when he would go out in the morning. Or get us a toy when we were home sick. Or we would go to the gas station to get a gallon of milk or something and he would come back and in his pocket we'd hear, "Crinkle, crinkle." He'd have his hand in there and he'd be looking at us and smirking. We would say, "Oou! What is it? What is it?" Then he would pull out a pack of baseball cards or Pokémon cards or something for each of us. He always knew what we liked. It was all about making us happy, making us laugh. He would sing or clap or give us high-fives, little stuff to brighten our day up; not just when we were having a bad day, but just to make us happier all the time.

It was always the little things with Dad. Always the little things. And that is always what makes the biggest difference with people, little things. Obviously Dad wasn't a perfect person, no one is perfect and I don't want this book to seem like we are making him to out to be immortal or God-like. But he made the most out of his life and he made everyone happy with little things.

Now we are looking back and we hear all these interviews with people and that is what they talk about, little things. Like firm handshakes, Dad always said that one of the best traits you can have is having a firm handshake. I remember that and people always comment on my handshake. You hear about this and other stories and there are not very many big moments, it is all little things that impact people the most.

Dad made the best ribs, oh my gosh. They were so good! With his special sauce, his secret sauce. That was always the best part of the summer. Ribs night was always: drop everything, eat ribs, go through four hundred napkins. By the time we were done, the whole table, our hands, our drinking glasses, and our elbows were covered in sauce.

I remember going over to friends' houses and sitting down to dinner with them and their dads eating with us and I thought it was the strangest thing, because all my life my dad had never eaten with us. Eventually, he was able to progress into eating small pastas with a lot of sauce instead of just soups, but he had to give eating his full concentration, so he always had to eat by himself. I thought that the small pastas were a big turning point. I thought eventually he would be able to eat bigger foods, more solid foods, but that never happened.

Dad was my coach on and off the field. As a coach, Dad never really yelled at us. Even at home, he never really yelled that much, it was mostly little stuff about me and Colin bickering that would make him angry. He just wanted silence sometimes and I can understand that now. I couldn't before, because I couldn't understand why he wouldn't want a couple of little boys running around whistling and yelling and banging into stuff and throwing balls all the time.

But on the field, or on the court, he would never yell at us; he would never yell at anyone. First of all, he couldn't raise his voice, but getting the message across by yelling isn't always the best way, because then kids just get more upset. They didn't want to make the mistake in the first place. It was big that Dad didn't yell a lot because, who knows, if he yelled at us, I don't know if I would be the same player, same athlete, same person at all.

My teammates too. They always speak highly of Dad. He would come into the dugout when it was blistering hot; we would be working our tails off, sweating like crazy, drinking so much water. He would come over with his cooler and his big spray bottle that had been on ice, sneak up behind us and spray it on our necks. Kids would jump, shocked at first, then say, "That feels so good!" It was so refreshing.

I was used to Dad teaching me how to play every sport. He never played soccer, but he would be out there passing the ball with me and doing these little tricks with his feet. He'd say, "That's my move!" It was so funny. He always encouraged us to be outside and enjoy the outdoors. Mom and Dad wouldn't let us get video games when we were little. They thought it was better to go outside and enjoy the outdoors, to go fishing, play wiffle ball or basketball in the yard, instead of sitting inside all day. At the time, I was mad. I said, "Come on. Let us get video games. All our friends have them." Now I see a difference between me and so many other kids in our school. I have grown in my athleticism and it started at that young age.

I remember having catches with Dad and if I threw it too high, he would step back, so he could catch it further back, because he couldn't reach up all the way with his left arm after an early surgery. He would say, "Don't throw it too high. Hit me in the chest. Hit me in the chest." I remember accidentally hitting him in the chin a couple times and that was terrible. Not that he would get mad, but he would be in a lot of pain, so I would feel bad about it. I knew that Dad was different that he couldn't eat and I didn't know why, but I never really cared, because when you are little, you don't worry about anything. I didn't know about the cancer until I was like twelve.

Another thing Dad was all about was hustle. He would always say, "Once you make contact with the ball, put your head down and run, whether it is foul or not. The ump will tell you, but as long as you hustle you will have a much better chance of getting on base." I still do that. Nowadays, we see all the professional players and they are jogging it off, going through the motions, because they think that the defense is going to throw them out, but I have learned that if I hustle, I make the other team worried and there is a better chance of them messing up.

When I hit a ground ball, I get mad that I screwed up a good pitch. Getting mad just makes me want to run faster. They see me bolting down the line with my head down like I actually have a shot and then they make a lot of mistakes: they start to get flustered, they drop the ball, or they get it caught in their glove and they lose it, or they make a crazy throw to first and that baseman misses it. That has happened to me so many times. Countless times. I have gotten such cheap hits out of little things like that. I'll see other kids hit the ball and stare at it and pout and jog out of the box. I think, "You could have beat it out; there could have been a bad throw..."

Any sport, dad told us to give it our all, to hustle, because he experienced himself that he got an injury and couldn't continue playing. He could have had a full ride to Siena to play basketball after JCC. He always told us to play our hearts out, because you never know when you might get an injury. Dad fought through his cancer with hustle too; he didn't stop and let it take over or think, "I guess this is it." He fought through it so he could spend more time with us and Mom.

Dad taught me to go fishing. That was big too and I still remember the last time I went fishing with Dad. It was on a summer night and the sun was setting. We were right down the road from our house. Looking back at pictures with me with the fish, I was still young and chubby. It is sad that I didn't have any more chances after that. At the time, I didn't know. How was I supposed to know that that was the last time I was going to go fishing with Dad? He couldn't go for very long, because he would be hungry or he had to suction his trach or something. Or he wouldn't feel up to it; he was too tired. It was all of us there that night: Mom was there and Colin was there.

That memory will stay with me forever, as small as it was. Because from then on, when Dad was in the hospital, I always prayed every night that I could just go fishing with Dad one more time. That was always my thing, "I just want to go with him one more time. As long as I have that one more time, then that's fine." It never happened, but that was what I asked for then. I had been praying for Dad every single night, basically, for my entire life. He was the first request to come up in my prayers, that Dad's mouth would feel better and be able to eat again.

When I hit my first home run, Dad was in the hospital and it had been tough for Mom to get me to the game. I had been looking for it throughout the whole spring season. It was one of our first games for summer ball against Yorktown. I hit it and right after the game, I went running in the woods looking for it. Then I remember going to the hospital after the game, showing him the ball, and he said, "Ah, I can't believe I missed it!"

That is a tough memory that he missed that important game. I always still hoped for him to recover and come to one of my games, but it never ended up working out. He was in and out of the hospital a lot after that.

I always enjoyed when Dad's family would come over; they would tell funny stories, especially Uncle Brian. He would tell us about some of the stuff he and Dad used to do, like the trip to Canada, and how much fun they had. The Astoria friends and firemen have told so many great stories too. Dad never told us many of his stories. It was mostly other people that would tell us about where he lived, funny things he did, acts of kindness he had done. We will appreciate them for the rest of our lives.

I see good that came out of Dad's suffering for me. I saw how humble he was, how he had so much that he went through and he was still able to be tough, keep his head in the right place, and headed in the right direction. When I saw him suffer all the years, especially the last two, it was obviously very tough, but it has taught me to stay humble. I think about having a headache or jamming my finger and, yes, it hurts, but it is incomparable to anything that Dad went through. Incomparable to anyone with cancer or so many other things that people have gone through. How can I sit here complaining about my jammed thumb or something stupid, when some people would trade everything they have for a jammed thumb?

Once I found out about the Redemptive Suffering, I realized that Dad was suffering for something else, something bigger. I don't know if it was for me, or if it was for Colin, or if it was for Aunt Sandy, or for my young cousin Joie, or for anyone in our family. Or people all across the world whether they are living now or not. I don't know what it was for, but I trust that God put it in the right hands and that it is being used for something purposeful and not being wasted. God wouldn't put someone through all that for nothing.

There was one thing that Dad used to say that never really registered with me that much, but I kept it in the back of my mind. He said, "Life is too short." When Mom and Dad finally told us that Dad had cancer, I realized that he meant that he didn't know how long he was going

63

to keep living, so he wanted to make as big of an impact on people as he possibly could. And to show his affection for them in the short amount of time that he had left. He knew that in whatever amount of time we are given in our lives, we should be able to treat others well and make a good impact on them.

Not a day goes by that I don't think about him. I don't really think about the feeding tubes and the trach and all the suctioning that he had to do. I still remember it, but they aren't the memories in the foreground for me. Not anywhere near as much as the fishing trips in Lake George and the Hamptons with Pete and all the holidays that we spent together with family and friends.

***

I definitely see Mr. Holler in Tim: fishing. Everything about fishing. I learned so much about fishing from Tim, but Tim got the information from his dad, so I know most about fishing secondhand because of Kenny. Everything he told Tim, Tim told me. We've been fishing ever since.

And baseball, their love for baseball. And hustle, always going hard. I remember Tim beat out a ground ball to first base, to the base he was running to, so that was hustle! That reminds me of Kenny battling and beating cancer. He fought; he hustled, I see that.

Tino, Tim's Friend, Age 15

PRANKING

He was always a quiet guy with a real good sense of humor, but he would be the type that if there was a little kid someplace, would say, "Why don't you go take that ketchup bottle and pour it all over the flowers…" We'd say, "Don't tell the kid to do that!" He was always needling from behind, always with the practical jokes, stuff like that. He was never bombastic, never out in front, but if something was happening, we'd look around and say, "Where is Kenny? He's doing something." [5]

A lot of people used to say, "You can't fall asleep around Kenny, because you never know what is going to happen." I remember a funny story. All the guys rented a house in Huntington for the summer one year. Kenny was very friendly with Louie and Louie fell asleep on the couch. When he woke up Kenny had put shaving cream in his belly button and in his hat. You could never, ever fall asleep around Kenny. [6]

We would have eleven guys per shift, then we would have a change of tours and we could have fifteen, twenty guys in the firehouse at that time. If we had something good going on that day, guys didn't even want to go home, because they didn't want to miss anything. I would see Kenny light up. Twenty guys and there's Kenny in the middle. Or on the outside! I liked Kenny in the middle, because we all could watch him. When he was on the outside, we wouldn't see him and we would say, "Where is he? What is he up to?" [7]

I was known for being a clown too and I enjoyed that banter with Kenny. It really was what distinguished him. But it was not all smoke and mirrors there. He was very intelligent, very gifted, and very loving. To have your chops broken by Kenny was a sign that he loved you. And he broke everyone's. [8]

---

5   Jack, Astoria Friend

6   Joann, Astoria Friend

7   Richie, FDNY Ladder 116

8   Jim, FDNY Lieutenant, Ladder 116

30
Ambition
Gilliams: FDNY Ladder 116

I could start when I first met Kenny, when I got on the job. I didn't know him; I didn't know anybody.

I didn't have an ambition to become a fireman. I guess that is a good way to start out the relationship that I had with Kenny, because I felt that Kenny had a lot more of an ambition to be a firefighter. To me the money is why I did it. In '79 my brother's friends lived in the Bronx and to them it was considered a macho thing to pass the Fire Department physical and become a firefighter. Financially, I was living on my own and had to make a living. I didn't have a mom or dad to support me.

After one weekend with these Italian guys, who were all talking about becoming firefighters, one guy sent me the application. I was twenty years old working at the Health and Hospital Corporation in the Bronx and making $13,000 a year; the FDNY was starting at $17,000-$18,000. I thought, "Wow man! That's great, let me take that test!" I had no ambition whatsoever and as a matter of fact, I was afraid of going into the Fire Department.

I got called for the Academy and I was with these kids that I really wanted to be like. My friend Don, the Deacon, had a connection and I told him that I wanted to go to 289 in Queens, because I lived in Queens and I wanted to be in an engine company. I didn't want to go into a truck company, because I was afraid. I was literally afraid, because I learned in the Academy that when you work in an engine company you go in with the line, you have the water, you put the fire out. When you are in a truck company, you go in and do a search and if you don't know what you are doing, you can get killed. Plain and simple. You have to know what you're doing.

I was in a class which consisted of 50 kids. Usually, there was maybe 200 kids in a class. My class was a special class because they needed manpower. So, I told my hook that I wanted to go to an engine company and out of the 50 kids that were in the Academy, 49 went to engine companies and one went to a truck company… and that was me. When they were doing the analyzing and testing, they thought that I would be perfect for a truck company. I ended up getting assigned to Ladder 116.

I got on the Fire Department, started doing my job, and realized that these people that I was working with were phenomenal. They were phenomenal. They had such great senses of humor, but when it came down to doing what they had to do, they became total professionals. I am talking major league. It was all about business, "Let's get it done. We've got a job to do."

There are two parts of the firehouse: there is the firehouse and then the socialize part of the firehouse. It's part of being accepted into the family. You aren't accepted into the family right away. You have to earn that, then they accept you.

Kenny told me about Suspenders in Manhattan when I was a probie. He said, "Ask for Tom, tell him I sent you." I went in and it was a fireman's bar, real fireman's bar. They had a picture of this guy Fitzpatrick who had died doing a rope rescue. His picture was on the wall and I said to Tom, "Who is that guy? Why is his picture on the wall?" He explained to me and I started understanding that there is something special here. There is something special.

I started to get to know Kenny more from the Skulls. I would go out with him to Suspenders in Astoria and hang out once in a while. It was always nice to go into a place where I knew somebody and if you knew Kenny, you knew everybody. You knew everybody, because Kenny knew everybody and everybody loved Kenny. Everybody loved Kenny. That's what I wanted. It's like being on a baseball team or basketball team and the star is Michael Jordon or LeBron James. That's what Kenny was like. You want to be with the right person, you go with Kenny.

So I started to attach to Kenny, because the way I grew up, you had to have an alliance with somebody. Then he started breaking my chops and I didn't like it. I thought I was the butt of each joke he had and I said to myself, "Am I his patsy? Am I his side-kick?" Indirectly, I wanted it and I didn't want it. I wanted to be friends with Kenny, but I didn't want to be made fun of, but he would do that. He'd make fun of me. I accepted that. I accepted that because it was part of the course to be accepted into the family, because Kenny was Kenny and everybody wanted to be with Kenny. Like on St. Patrick's Day, everybody hung out with Kenny. So, I went with it.

Then one time I was hanging out with Kenny and he didn't have his cronies with him. It was just Kenny and me and he was a different Kenny. He wasn't that Kenny that wanted to break my chops. He was a compassionate guy, very tender, something that he didn't like to show. He invited me to dinner at his mother's house. I'll never forget it. We were in Suspenders and he said, "My mom wants me to come to dinner. Why don't you come over and have dinner?" I said, "Kenny, I really don't want to go over to dinner at your parents' house." He said, "No, no, no. You have to come. Come with me."

I had met his parents before at a Christmas party. His father came in and his mother was … she was like a postcard of what you would want as a mother. An Irish mother. She carried herself with manners and she dressed herself like a queen. His father carried himself like a prince. I remember asking him at that Christmas party, "Kenny, what does your father do?" He said, "He cleans floors." I said, "He cleans floors? He looks immaculate! He looks like an executive in that suit." He had a suit on, tie, white shirt. That was one of the reasons that I was afraid to go to their house and have dinner. I thought it was going to be a prim and proper dinner, but when I got there it was just in the kitchen, me, Kenny, mom, and dad. We ate dinner and we left.

We used to have these big meals in the firehouse and I used to complain about the cost of the meal. They were like $15 a man meals. Kenny always insisted that we go to Alex's, this butcher on Thirty-Sixth Street and we had to get Argentine beef steaks. Then, we had to go to Parisi's and get Italian bread. Then, we had to go to the vegetable stand and get fresh vegetables. Everything had to be elaborate; dinner was a phenomenal thing for him. One night when I was still new on the job, we got a run in the middle of the meal. I grabbed my potato, stuck it in my pocket, and ate it in the truck on the way to the run. I had paid my $15 and didn't want to ruin my meal.

Another night, when I was working with Kenny, the bell went off. I ran out, jumped into my boots, and Kenny had filled them with mashed potatoes. I had to wear them like that. We ended up going to the projects; I got off the rig with all my gear on, going up the stairs, and my feet were going up and down in the potatoes. Kenny asked, "How does it feel Tommy? Do you like it? How about eating those mashed potatoes!" I said, "That's stupid, man." I felt like an idiot. He would do that. He would make me feel like an idiot sometimes.

Another time, I walked into the back room and guys were placing bets. I sat down and asked, "What's going on here?" Kenny turned around and said, "John is betting Patty that he can pull you up the pole hole with one hand with the life rope on." I was looking at John and this guy was like fifty-something years old. I asked, "He's going to pull me with one hand up the pole hole with the life rope on? Are you kidding me? I want in on this bet!" So I threw $10 down on the table and they told me, "Go get the roof rope." I got the rope, Kenny lowered it down and I tied myself up. Eight or nine guys were all placing bets in the kitchen and the pool was up to a hundred-something dollars. I said, "You're going to lose John. You can't pull me up the pole hole. Are you crazy?"

They pulled me up the pole hole, got me halfway and stopped. Then the flour came down and the buckets of water came down and more flour came down, so I looked like the Pillsbury Doughboy. Now I am getting angry. I'm angry at Kenny because he was the one that instigated it. They lowered me down and what happened? We got a run. So I had to put my gear on. I had to put my helmet on. I had to get on the rig and back to the projects we went. All the people there were looking at me like… I don't know if you have ever seen anybody with flour all over them… they were laughing.

Kenny loved to make people laugh. He loved to make people laugh, but there was that other part of him, that part of being a fireman. He was the one who I felt wanted that job when he was a little boy. That's how much he loved the job. He was a fireman's fireman. Those people who were kids that wanted to be firefighters went into it because they had something in their life that told them, maybe it was a higher power, I don't know, but I learned that they were special people. People who will give their life for somebody else. I started to learn that in the Fire Department, because as we went to fires we would find out the men from the boys.

There are people who are willing to give their lives and there are people who aren't. Those want to see the morrow and it doesn't matter if somebody dies. There are people that will go that extra yard and I learned that about Kenny. Most of the people that are on that job, just as some men are called into the priesthood, these people are called to become firefighters. So, I learned to love the job. I learned there was a meaning to what I was doing and not a paycheck. Kenny kind of brought me there.

As an individual, as my mother died, I kind of gave up on life. I was in a group home and when I turned eighteen they showed me the door. One night a couple years later when I was coming out of work at Health and Hospitals, I thought, "I don't give a f*#> anymore." I was so lonely. I don't know if you have ever felt real loneliness, but I was lonely. I felt like there was nobody in the world but me and I didn't like it. I didn't like it. Then in an instant that all changed. That was the first time I felt God. It felt phenomenal. I didn't feel lonely. It was like somebody came down and said, "It'll be all right."

I saw it as the beginning of life, but when I got to the firehouse, that is when meaning started coming to my life. Kenny was one of those people that showed me that by saving someone else's life, I am saving my own, because there is no better thing in life than saving somebody that you don't know. It's like you saved part of God, because you saved a soul. You didn't save a person, you saved a soul. If you look at it that way, you don't take it personally, or you try not to.

The first time I did CPR on somebody at five o'clock in the morning they died on me and I cried. I went back to the firehouse and one of the guys said to me, "If you can't handle this, you need to quit. This is not the right job for you." I had no options of quitting, because I had to pay my rent, so I kept on. But as I kept on and I got to know the guys, I started to love it more. And more. And more. And more, like a drug. If I knew I was working with someone good, and by now

I was working with Kenny and I knew I could depend on Kenny, I knew I could go in further, and I wanted to get further, I wanted to get right on the seat. I want to be able to find the fire. I want to be able to get the call into the chief and let him know where the fire was. Then if we pulled somebody out, and we worked on him, and brought him back, that was a high. That was a high.

Going back to Kenny, as I describe that high, there is also the high of winning a basketball game, like the Queens Championships: we sink the winning goal, and turn around and hug each other. Or another day, we were playing basketball in the city championship in Brooklyn, went to the big party afterwards, then Kenny, Warren, Big Dave, Joe, and I worked that night. We ended up getting a call to the projects for a fire in the top floor. We had gotten the 10-75 on the way to the projects, so we knew we had a job. We got off the rig, threw our Scott air packs on, grabbed our tools, and as we ran towards the building, a guy was pulling a couch out of the building. I was thinking, "Why the freak is this guy pulling the couch out?" We look up and there is a guy on the sixth floor window sill and he jumped out the window and landed on the couch. He was mangled up in the couch. I was upset and Kenny said, "Listen, we're not God. We can't do everything. We can do the best we can and that is all we can do."

I could tell you a story where we saved six people at Goldwater Hospital and the mayor, David Dinkins, flew in on the helicopter onto Roosevelt Island. We were dirty as hell. He came over and congratulated us. It was phenomenal. We succeeded in what our objective was in saving those people. But there are times where it isn't in our hands, it is in God's hands. That's basically what Kenny said to me, "You have to take the good with the bad. Sometimes we can achieve our goals, but sometimes we can't. As long as we can walk away from it and say that we gave it our all, that's all we can do. We can't give any more." That can be applied to any job; you work hard to do something and it doesn't usually turn out the way you want it to, but if you can say, "I gave it my all," if you can live with that, then you will have peace with yourself.

It was a shame when Kenny was diagnosed with the cancer. That was a really bad time for Kenny. Really bad time, because he loved the job so much. He loved it, but he was so brave, he accepted it. But things were starting to fall apart for him, not as an individual, but as a professional, as a firefighter. He wanted to be back out in the field so badly. There's nothing like getting on that big red truck, saving a life, coming back, sitting down at the table, discussing what we did, how we achieved it.

Then things got bad when he went back to 116 and the lieutenant asked him to empty his locker. That is when he really became detached from 116. He felt that he was slapped in the face; that he wasn't wanted anymore. I know how that feels because I went through it at the end of my career. I cried; I looked at my locker and said, "It's the end of an era, part of my life."

When they tell you to empty that locker, there is a lot of luggage in that locker. I am talking about experiences that a lot of people don't understand and they would never understand unless they experience that experience together. I was chosen to do this job, not because I wanted to do it, but because it was what God wanted me to do. This was my journey in life and this was being taken away from me and I didn't want that to happen. That's the way Kenny felt. He didn't want that to happen, but he had no choice. It was being taken away from him, probably the biggest gift in his life beside getting married and having children. At least that's the way I felt. I guess maybe I also felt jealous that they were giving that locker to another young man who was starting what we did. It goes on and it goes on and it goes on.

I always prayed for him; I prayed for him a lot. I pray a lot because I believe in it. I believe in it and I believe the biggest gift that God has given all of us is the freedom of what happens to us. If God had control of what happens to us, we wouldn't learn. We wouldn't learn from pain, from happiness, which Kenny taught me. Kenny taught me pain and he taught me happiness.

That pain was when he broke my chops, I didn't like it. Like I said, when I was going into the projects, do you know how much pain I felt? I felt like an imbecile, because I looked like the Pillsbury Doughboy and I am driving on a truck where I am supposed to be rescuing people. He's laughing and I wanted to strangle him. I literally wanted to strangle him! But I couldn't, because I knew he was laughing because he "got" me. He got me. He didn't do it because he wanted me to hurt; he did it because he thought it was funny.

When you suffer you learn that the little things in life are so much more important. I mean the little things like waking up and seeing somebody you love walk across the hallway and go into the next room. Little things like that, you would never learn were important, unless you suffered. When we suffer, sometimes we get mean and upset, "Why me? Why me?" In my life I had my brother who was a year older than I jump out a window. I had my mother jump out a window. I had my brother shot with a double barrel shotgun, murdered. I had my best friend murdered within four years and that's when I really learned that there is a God.

I think of Kenny when I am on my sailboat. I play that song by Coldplay, *O*. It always makes me cry. I listen to it, and I think about Kenny, and I think about when my daughter left me to go to college. I was listening to Coldplay and I was getting up to Massachusetts and that song came on. You know what was the great thing about it? It wasn't sad. I was feeling love and when we feel love, we can't ask for anything more. Love is not pain. It is only pain if you accept it as pain and I was feeling love, because somebody I love so much was leaving. I had no control over it. Things in life that we don't have control over we have to accept. That's the way it is.

31
Fun

Claire: *Lynda's Queens Friend*

I met Kenny the same day his wife met him. I am the friend in that fateful story. And that's always how I remember him. In my eyes, I never saw the physical changes, even as time went on. To me, Kenny was always the same person. Maybe in the last couple of years, that began to change and I came to realize, as he got close to death, facially how much he had changed. But, I really never recognized or thought about it along the way. He was handsome; he was charming; he was funny. That's what I remember most from that first meeting and all those things, to me, he always remained.

What I remember even more clearly, was the night when he came to the apartment to pick Lynda up for their first date. My parents and I lived in the co-op apartment next door; we shared a kitchen wall. I remember my mother and me trying to look through the peek hole watching him come down the hall, to see what he looked like in daylight!

In one word, Kenny was fun. Everything about Kenny was fun. He was funny. The things he did were funny. And he had a really, really good sense of humor. I think that is why he and my father got along so well and I think that is why he and I got along so well. When I think of Kenny, I think of my father; when I think of my father, I often think of Kenny. They had a lot of similar traits, but the strongest one was their great senses of humor. I think that is why Kenny survived as many years as he did. It is a very under-spoken character trait that people don't think is as important as it is. I think he even found some humor in his illness, although that got very hard to do. He kept his humanity and his humor and he trudged along.

I think that my father, Harry, in some ways was a positive influence on Kenny. He saw my father and saw a guy who really didn't care what the world threw at him, didn't care that he was seventy-five years old and lost a limb, because to my father, life was more important. He wanted to be around; he wanted to be around for his wife; and he wanted to be around for his kids. He would make any sacrifice, big or small, to do that. Kenny was the very same way.

When we think about it, Lynda took an almost life-long bachelor and turned him into a family man. The biggest family man; I'll tie him with Harry. I always think that was my father's purpose and I think that was Kenny's purpose too.

One of my favorite early stories is when Lynda and Kenny would put these kochka things with the rest of our knick-knacks on the living room shelves. It started when they found a couple things in the incinerator room that people from our floor were throwing away. They secretly added them to a shelf and waited to see if we noticed. I think they may have even bought a thing or two at a bargain store and merged them into our collection. Months went by and we dusted them regularly. Sometimes my parents and I would argue, "Where the hell did that come from?" Mom would say, "I got it as a gift at a shower." Or "I got them as a gift at an end-of-the-year party." One day, finally, I realized, "What the hell are those two little Dutch salt and pepper shakers?!" Lynda and Kenny were visiting and could not contain themselves anymore, they were laughing so hard. We still laugh about it today.

When I think of my father, I remember Kenny standing at my father's casket. I remember it was just him and me in the front and Kenny just shook his head and I know he was truly sad. But to that point, for my father, it was okay because he had suffered enough and it was time for me to let go, so he could find peace someplace else. It would be ironic that the only other person that I ever felt that way about was Kenny. I can say that I have prayed for Kenny a lot. Toward that end, what I always prayed for was God's mercy, whatever God perceived that mercy to be. The only other person that I prayed for mercy like that was for my own father. I remember this well, but those aren't the things that I carry with me.

We would have private moments when other people would not be around and he would open up to me. One day, he just matter-of-factly said, "I really just wish I could eat a slice of pizza." It wasn't even frustration, it was just plain sad. That was the food that he missed the most. I knew how much he meant that and I could almost taste the pizza for him, because we ate some good pizza together. When there were things that we prayed for, in the middle years, it would be that he would, at some point, be able to eat solid food again. Then, we came to the realization that was not going to happen. We stopped thinking about wanting that for him and just prayed that he would not have difficulty swallowing and not have any more procedures or choking incidents.

I remember when he stopped coming to my annual Christmas soiree. I remember him trying and Lynda coming with soups, but it just became too hard for him to eat outside of the home. I remember the frustration, yet whenever I see a flank steak, I think of Kenny too. He always made me feel very special that he would grill a flank steak for me, because I liked how he did it on the grill. He would grill it himself and smell it, even though he couldn't eat it. I almost felt cruel watching him doing that, but I knew that he wanted to do that for me and I know that was his way of providing me comfort with food. Food is a great comfort. He especially did that after the deaths of my father and mother.

The day we took the tour of Yankee Stadium may be my favorite day of my entire life. I loved that day and I get emotional when I think of it. Kenny, Lynda, the boys, Lynda's mother Eileen, Linda, Victor, Jo, my parents, and I had an amazing private tour of the old Yankee Stadium. It was a beautiful day and we have beautiful photos as mementos. We had a rough start and my parents were both in wheel chairs, but we had a great day. One that none of us will ever forget.

Lots of baseball stories. When I think baseball, I think of Kenny. I remember one afternoon, in Linda and Victor's yard, Kenny was kind of at a plateau. He was doing okay, but our Yankees weren't. The Yankees lost to the Angels in the playoffs and it was very disappointing, because it ended the season earlier than we would have liked. Post-season baseball with the Yankees gave Kenny something to look forward to everyday and inched him a little closer to spring when it would start again. Winters were very hard for Kenny. They were hard for a very long time. They were very hard on him physically and mentally and sports were a big part of being able to trudge through that crippling season.

I miss Kenny very much when it comes to talking baseball; I miss my father very much for the same reason, because there just aren't people who have the interest that I do and there aren't people that can have a decent conversation about baseball. The second to last time that I saw Kenny, when he was in New York Presbyterian, it was the day after Old Timer's Day. I went on a Sunday morning. We had what would be our final baseball conversation. Of course, it was one-way, because by then Kenny was only able to communicate by writing or just with his

72

looks. And I did get the over-the-eyeglass look that day, which was also a quintessential Kenny. We were talking about the old timers and, "They don't make ball players like that anymore." We were trying to keep it from being melancholy, but it felt melancholy. It would turn out to be Yogi Bera's last Old Timer's Day, because he was too sick to go to the next one, and he died soon after.

We didn't see that much of Kenny in the last couple years of his life because of his suffering. But I remember going to Tim's opening ball game in 2013, right after Kenny had gotten the trach and got out of rehab. He came to the Little League game and talk about a champion, that was a great moment. It was a fearless moment for Kenny. That took tremendous courage to do. It was a pretty cold day for an opening day of a ball game. He came out and you could see how the community was so happy to see him and how great it was for him to be on the sideline to watch some of that game. I remember that very vividly.

I had a difficult time understanding my dear friend after the trach. It was frustrating for him and then it became frustrating and very sad for me. So then I tried not to make conversation, because I didn't want to embarrass myself or him by not being able to understand what he said.

There was one afternoon after he had the trach, Lynda was out running errands, and it was just Kenny and me in the kitchen. My father was probably dead six years already. Kenny and I didn't have to say too many things; I understood, he understood. At that point, after the trach, I thought he was the bravest man I had ever known and I thought my father was pretty spectacular in a very ordinary way. They were ordinary men who had ordinary lives and did ordinary jobs, but they were spectacularly brave.

That day in his kitchen, I told him that he was the bravest man I had ever known and how great his love was for his wife and children that he would endure the suffering that he had. We had our little quiet moment, but he understood and I understood. I've always believed that was his driving factor. He thought that he could still contribute to their lives and he did that in many, many ways and to many, many people.

***

Kenny is a testament to how resilient the human spirit is, because he never gave up, he just kept on going. That resilience of the human spirit—that is my inspiration.

Monica, Astoria Friend, Stove's Wife

32
Impressive
Dr. Fishman: *Local ENT Doctor*

In the beginning of my career, I was doing a lot of head and neck cancer surgery. We would see patients, like Kenny, where we thought we got the whole tumor out, the margins were clear, and then the cancer would come back. We'd see the effect on the family and everybody else. Some people were obviously very depressed and took it very hard and other people had very positive attitudes. The attitude affects everybody, the surgeons, family, everybody, because we want to do what we can for them.

It is impressive for someone who has had this problem for such a long time to maintain such a positive attitude, such good spirits. It is hard; I don't know if I could do it. I don't know if there are any studies on it, but I certainly think that attitude has a lot to do with outcome. I have a brother in California whose wife was never a smoker, but was diagnosed with adenoid cystic carcinoma of the lung. It was diagnosed kind of late. He's a physician, but it just wasn't picked up for some reason. She had a very negative attitude from the very beginning and she didn't last very long. She tried the chemo and the radiation and they would fly her to the best people in the country, yet it was pretty much a downhill course.

Probably, because of Kenny's positive outlook, cracking little jokes every now and then, is why he survived so long. I still think there is something to that. Even though we do what we can do in medicine, we still don't really know as much as everybody thinks we know. We really don't know what is going to happen.

I had one patient years ago, she had a tumor in her neck, in her voice box area, and down into her chest. I had to send her to a thoracic surgeon, who biopsied it and it came back squamous cell carcinoma, which is the same diagnosis that Kenny had on the tongue. She needed to have a laryngectomy done, a radical neck dissection, and more surgery to remove things lower in the chest that can't be reached by ENT surgeons. And she did nothing… She decided that she was just going to leave it in other hands, higher powers; and she is still alive. It went away. We have no idea why. That has to be ten years ago or more.

What is also impressive is the commitment that Lynda had to Kenny. I've known patients in the past that have come down with something like this and then wound up being pushed off to nursing homes, marriages break up, and it is very tragic for everybody. It was difficult to handle, but he was fortunate to have a family to take care of him.

It is sad that these things happen, but it is amazing that Kenny had the support and the attitude that he had. Every time he came in here, he was always smiling and cracking a joke, even though I could tell that he was in pain and feeling miserable. Then I'd go home and look at myself and say, "Boy…" and feel thankful for every day.

I think life is about choice. You choose to make the best of a bad situation or you choose to be miserable. There are plenty of people that choose to be miserable. Kenny chose to be happy. I think it was conscious choice.

Norine, Nurse, Head and Neck Floor, MSK Cancer Center

33

Opus

Jim: FDNY Lieutenant, Ladder 116

I met Kenny in 1990. I was a covering lieutenant and that was the first time I was assigned to work at Ladder 116. At the time, 116 had a very bad discipline reputation; a lot of people didn't want to work there. But I worked there that one night and it was an exceptional night. We had about twenty-five runs and three fires. Kenny was working and Kenny was a chops-breaker too. He was overt and outgoing and welcoming, all in the same way. We had this banter going back and forth, because he went to Power, and I went to Power. So, when I was leaving in the morning, he said, "Ah, we'll never see you again." And I said, "Oh, no. This is only round one!" So I got into my car, went over to the battalion, and put my request in to work there permanently. Kenny was the compelling force of that. That was enough for me to satisfy any inquisitions that I had about the company.

Ends up there were no discipline problems. This was a happy place; there was Bobby and Kenny and a lot of extroverted individuals that were vocal and some people might have felt threatened by that, but I had done twenty years in the South Bronx. I had seen discipline problems; it wasn't that. Kenny galvanized my want to be there and that was it.

Kenny had that switch. When we went to a fire or an emergency, he was able to transpose himself into the consummate firefighter. His precision and attention to details made him the standard that other firefighters would aspire to. As a boss, I was inside the building all the time, but I needed guys who were outside, or on the roof, and he would always be my guy out there. He would do things that I wouldn't think to do. He was a great, great set of eyes for me and that is really what the outside guys are doing. They are relaying information so we can manage the fire. He was able to do that very well.

He also had a certain magnetism about him. Kenny had charm and charisma and took the younger guys under his wing. They all went to him. Like I said, there was more to him than his personality and his humor.

When I met Kenny, he was in a transitionary stage of his life. It seemed like he was putting away his toys. He was very much in love with Lynda. Very, very upbeat about his upcoming marriage. He was anxious to start a family, white picket fence, two cars, thirty-year mortgage, all of the things that we all wind up doing. He looked forward to embracing all of those challenges.

I am sure that Kenny, somewhere along the way, felt shortchanged. Who wouldn't? Everything he wanted to do was taken away from him. One thing I would like to tell Kenny's sons about their father: I wish I had three hours with Kenny to take him to the movies. I'd take him to see Mr. Holland's Opus.

In the movie, Glenn Holland, an aspiring composer and a young husband, takes a "temporary" job as teacher to pay the bills. He believes that he will eventually write a transcendent piece of music in his free time, but the demands of teaching and life whittle the decades away. His paper remains blank, but he makes an enormous impact on the people he touched. At the end, the governor says to Mr. Holland, "We are the notes." That was Kenny. Everybody he touched are the notes that make up his opus.

Another one of my quotes for Kenny is: "*Finis coronat opus—The end crowns the work.*" Once again, I wasn't there with him through the suffering, but I can visualize and imagine what it was. He did so many things with his life, gracefully, with dignity and honor.

So, I take literal exception to Lynda referring to "Kenny's small corner of the world." Exponentially, through him, people became better. Better firemen, maybe better husbands, better neighbors, better friends. It wasn't a small world for Kenny, just as cancer spreads, he was a good cancer that spread positive and good things.

Naval Admiral William H. McRaven was the commencement speaker for the University of Texas in May 2014. He said that the average American will meet ten thousand people in their lifetime. If every one of the 8000 graduates changed the lives of just ten people and if each one of those people changed the lives of another ten, and so forth, in five generations, in 125 years, UT's Class of 2014 would have changed the lives of 800 million people—over twice the population of the United States. In one more generation, they could change the entire world, 8 billion people. I drew an analogy to talking about Kenny and what the admiral was trying to inspire in UT's graduating college students.

I think Kenny's suffering was Christ-like. It was an overt sign to anyone that he came in contact with. It didn't have to be a family member or brother or sister. Just to observe the dignity and how he conducted himself. And not complain. That's a hard thing to do, not to complain.

When we look at Kenny's life on an intellectual level, we rationalize many wonderful things that he accomplished with his friendship and humor. But when we look at it in a spiritual sense, we realize that those things that he did from an intellectual perspective were small potatoes. What he did spiritually was far more uplifting, far more powerful, and meaningful than any human act that he could have done.

***

I found Kenny to be resigned and I noticed that his suffering was not made obvious by what he said and did. God had blessed him with the gift to suffer in public in silence. I would guess that many souls were saved by these acts of quiet suffering.

Deacon John, St. Lawrence O'Toole

34
Kindred
Steve M: *FDNY Ladder 116*

My wife is related to Kenny; her grandmother and Kenny's mom were first cousins. I had never met Kenny, but when I was going through the Academy, Karen's grandmother would say, "Maybe you'll get into Kenny's house." When I received my assignment, it was in Engine 261 which shared the same firehouse with Kenny's Ladder Company 116.

My first tour was a Saturday nine by six tour, so I got there nice and early and Kenny greeted me at the door. He showed me around the firehouse and gave me my first locker. I realized then that Kenny was a practical joker. He always did it in a great way; it wasn't nasty. There were people that broke chops in the firehouse in a nasty way, but Kenny always did it silently and for a good reason. I learned from it. It was good. I always had that in the back of my mind. It was never to belittle, always to joke.

I was assigned to the engine, but not even a year later, I transferred to the truck and Kenny and I really, really became close. He taught me a lot of things as a firefighter and he took me under his wing. I was lucky enough to be in his groups, so I worked a lot with Kenny. I also stole a lot of his material! And I used it quite often in my twenty-seven years on the job. I still use it. Sometimes I would work in a different group and I would use some of Kenny's pranks and they would say, "Oh, you stole that from Holler!" I always looked upon it as a good thing.

What else can I tell you about Kenny? My memories are abundant. I still talk about him every day. Every time I see any of the Skulls and I just went out to dinner in August or September this past year with Danny and Dante and Kevin. We sat down and fifteen, twenty minutes into the conversation, we started with, "Remember when…?" Then I will say, "Remember when Kenny did this?" or "Here is a funny story…" Here are a couple examples:

We had a fellow named John in the firehouse that was an old single guy, rather cantankerous and set in his ways. He would come in at night and immediately after the tour started, he would go into the kitchen, fill up a glass of water, and put it in the refrigerator. Two hours later he would come out and drink it. When Kenny worked, about an hour into it, he would dump the water out and put warm water in there. Then when John would drink it, he would spit it out, and go crazy trying to pinpoint who did it. He worked with Kenny a lot longer than I did and still I don't think he ever knew it was Kenny. That is how good Kenny was at it. A lot would get blamed on me or someone else and we would just go along with it.

Another story about Kenny and John: John was big on watching TV in the kitchen. There was a couch right next to the refrigerator. He would put his show on with the flicker and put the flicker on the table. Kenny would sneak out to the yard with another flicker, go right up to the window, and change the channel. John would get up, get his flicker, change the channel back, put it down, and sit down. This went on two or three times until John got up and said, "These flickers never work!" and threw it across the room. Me and Kenny would be in the alley cracking up! Those are stories that I always share with everybody.

I also remember this… It was New Year's Eve '92/'93 and I was working with Lieutenant Jim, Mac, Kenny, Drew, and Charlie. We had one of those typical Ladder 116 nights where we did twenty, twenty-five runs. I went on vacation right after that tour and got a phone call from Charlie at home. He said, "Did you hear about Kenny? He has cancer."

Charlie telling me that Kenny had mouth cancer hit me like a Mack truck. In our job, we can be working with somebody one day and the next day they are out. Our job is so unique. It is not like an office worker: Joe will be out for a while, because he broke his back or he has asthma or he has a heart condition. Joe's career isn't over. He will be back in the office eventually. But in our line of work, we can be here and then gone and Kenny is a perfect example of it. I worked with him and a week later he wasn't there anymore. I never worked with him again.

But I would go visit him at SOC and put pine cones in his bed. And little sticks. So when he got into bed at night, he'd say, "What the hell is this?"

I prayed for Kenny and went to see him in the hospital. He still kept his sense of humor and that is what I keep in my memory of him. I called him many times, but when Kenny had difficulty talking, I knew that I didn't want to call him anymore. I began texting him instead, because I knew that it would be easier for him. Even though my heart bled when I saw him: he couldn't eat properly, couldn't chew, used a spray bottle to keep his mouth wet, and I hated to see a great guy go through that, I learned that he was so positive even when he was suffering.

I am an optimist, not a pessimist. I thought since Kenny had fought this disease for so long, "This guy is going to beat it." Obviously, there are people that have cancer and are able to live with it and maybe die with it, not from it, but that is very rare. We more commonly hear of people that have cancer and a year, two years later, after trying to fight it, they pass. For twenty years, Kenny fought it, and I thought, in the back of my mind, "Kenny is okay." Little did I know, he wasn't okay. He really didn't let on to people how bad he was.

I still think of Kenny often. My relative, my brother, my friend was my kindred spirit. I like talking about Kenny and I like sharing his stories. I like telling them to guys that never met him, that have gone through 116 or any firehouse. It doesn't matter what firehouse we are in; we all relate to the same stories, just the names change. The same characters are around in every firehouse.

I'll be driving and I'll hear a song. Kenny was famous for whenever it said, "You," in a song, he would change to "Drew," for John Drew. The lyrics, "What I like about you…" he would change to, "What I like about Drew…" So I find myself still singing those. Ask Karen. I keep the positive and the great memories of Kenny and that is how I get by without him. The cancer definitely didn't define him and that being said, he carried that disease for twenty years, so in my eyes, he beat it. It didn't get him. He never quit and he lived such a positive life. We know he died in the end, but it didn't get him. It didn't win.

***

Kenny inspires me to be a fighter. He fought this disease for years and he just didn't stop. He would do anything just to live another day. That is always a good thing. If he can do it, anyone can do it.

Jack, Astoria Steve's Son

35

Lessons

Lorraine: Astoria Friend, Shorty's Wife

My first meeting with Kenny was separate from Shorty and Steve and all of them. I met Kenny first because I worked at the Oak Tree Inn in the Hamptons. Kenny got a job as a day bartender there and because of Kenny working there, Shorty and Steve and all of those Astoria guys came in.

The lightbulb went on and I realized how serious Kenny's disease was in 2003, when we went to his fiftieth birthday party. Steve must have told us on the way home that Kenny had problems again. He was having a big surgery the following week. It seemed like he was doing good, then it got so bad. We didn't know then that he would never eat solid food again.

A while later, they came to our house one night for dinner. I made a big dinner, pork and potatoes, and he sat at the table. That was the first time that I really realized that he couldn't eat normal food. I had known that he had a hard time, but I didn't realize that he couldn't eat any solids.

I felt it; in my heart I felt it, because I saw how hard it was for him to eat. In Lake George, we would go out to dinner; a few times he went out to dinner with us. I was so grateful that he was able to come for the companionship, but then it was so hard that he could only have ice cream. His spirit, he was really such a good example for his children, for all of our children. He impacted all of our children, teaching them that we deal with what we are handed and we try to make the best of it. I am grateful for that, because our kids really learned a lot from Kenny in that respect.

During the 2012 Lake George trip, Kenny was really struggling to eat and he was in the room a lot. They didn't realize it then, but his esophagus was closing up and he couldn't get enough nourishment by mouth, so he became malnourished. Right after that he got the stomach tube. Karen was speaking to Lynda at that time assuring her that he would feel so much better, but that was a very sad time for all of us.

They came to our house the February before he died. The boys came in carrying cartons of stuff. I asked Lynda, "What did you bring? What did you make?" She said, "No, this is everything that Kenny needs." I was so grateful that we had a place for him and his suction machine for his trach, but he spent almost the whole day in that room. Karen was up there with him, because he was having a lot of problems clearing his trach. I give them all so much credit that they came and it was a really good thing for the boys, because I think they needed it. Lynda was able to have a glass of wine and have some food and conversation and give herself a little bit of a break. When they left, Shorty and I were so upset. I said, "He's not coming back here." He said, "I know." It was horrible.

I think of Kenny all the time. A lot, a lot. I am sure that Shorty or Steve mentioned that baby picture of him in the Hamptons. So whenever somebody says something like, "What about the baby?" in a funny way or if we see an adult's baby picture in a movie, Shorty and I will always laugh. It just happened recently.

I think Kenny did a lot of good for many people. Uncle Teddy has bladder cancer right now and he is going through chemo and radiation. He is really not complaining; he is being amazing. Uncle Teddy wasn't around Kenny that much, but he remembers Kenny very well. He liked him very much; they talked about fishing. Teddy always said to me, "He's amazing how he handles his illness." So, maybe Kenny is helping Teddy now. I really do think that as hard as it was, Kenny taught a lot of people a lot of lessons without even realizing it.

***

When you are looking at the family that is going through the horrible time, your heart breaks for them. It does. And now that I just said that, I think it opens our eyes too. Even those people out there that you think are having it so good, we have no idea.

Kathleen, Brewster Friend

36
Determination
Shorty: *Astoria Friend*

The first time I met Kenny I was probably fifteen or sixteen years old. I used to hang out with a group of kids my age and we would go to the Zoo basketball games. One of the things that always used to make me laugh was when Kenny wore the number 747. Whenever a foul would be called on him, the refs would have to say, "7-40-7," and then they would always come up with smiles on their faces, as if to say, "How did he get this number 747?" I don't know for sure, but the legend is that Kenny got the number because he was so fast, like a 747 jet.

When I was around eighteen years old, I started going to McGivney's. One of the things that impressed me most about Kenny from the athletic standpoint, was he used to be able to stand next to the bar, and without really doing anything, just bending his knees down, jump up and land on the bar, which is about four feet off the ground! He had tremendous athletic ability.

As I got a little older, we started getting houses out in the Hamptons. Kenny was the reason that I ended up meeting Lorraine. In the Hamptons' houses, Kenny kept everybody laughing. He would always bring his baby picture with him. No matter where he went, he had his framed 8x10 baby picture.

At one house in particular, we had a player piano and he had the baby picture on the piano. Whenever anybody came over to the house for the first time, Kenny would go right to the piano and make like he was playing. He could basically fool anybody into believing anything that he ever said and did. He was one of those guys that could carry a story without smiling or laughing. It led to a lot of laughs, a lot of good times.

We would go up to Boston every year fishing, and Kenny would bring his baby picture. No matter who was his roommate, he had the baby picture on the stand next to his bed. Kenny loved to fish. Most guys just went to hang out, have a couple drinks, go to a Celtic game, a Red Sox game, but Kenny was there to be a serious fisherman. He would always be competitive. He would find the places in Quincy Bay that he would call "Holler's Hideaway." Every year it was a different hideaway and he would come back with the most fish.

There were a lot of funny Kenny stories. A couple of my favorite stories weren't with the Astoria gang, they are Fire Department stories, where Kenny took an unfortunate situation, helped people, and then added his own signature wit.

Kenny was living in a basement apartment in a three-family home on Thirty-Sixth Street in Astoria. It was a very hot humid day, late July, around lunchtime, and one of the tenants on the third floor, a medical student, tried to commit suicide. He lit camphor candles throughout his apartment, the kind of candles exterminators use to kill roaches, and had some accelerants in the house that would have caused the house to go up in flames. Kenny was home, smelled smoke, called 911, then ran upstairs and somehow forced his way into the apartment. He found the guy unconscious, tried to revive him and was unsuccessful, but he was able to prevent the house from going on fire. He got a commendation for that work.

Because it was an attempted suicide and arson, the Fire Marshalls came a couple hours later and Kenny showed them around. They couldn't stay in the apartment long, because it smelled and they needed fresh air, but it was sweltering hot, so Kenny invited them downstairs to his apartment with air conditioning. Kenny had forgotten that he still had his Christmas tree and all his Christmas decorations up. The Fire Marshalls looked at him crazy; these guys didn't know Kenny, but they continued on with their paperwork, asking him, "So what happened upstairs?" Kenny explained, "Well, I was listening to *White Christmas* for the ten thousandth time and the guy upstairs decided to kill himself." They realized he was kidding, of course, and they just filled out the report and went on their way. It was just a normal day for Kenny; Christmas was every day.

Another story was on the front page of the New York Post newspaper. At one particular fire, there were a couple of kittens involved. Kenny went in and found a kitten unconscious and gave the kitten mouth-to-mouth in order to revive it. He referred to it later as mouth-to-me-ow! That was one of his proudest moments at the time.

Later on, when Kenny and Lynda got married and Kenny became ill, we didn't really know what the extent of his illness was going to be, but throughout his battle year in and year out, he was so determined. He was a fighter. Everything he ever did, he always wanted to be the best and I think that he looked at whatever he was facing and said, "I can beat it. I have beaten other things, and I can always win." I think that competitive attitude of his carried him through his whole life. Right to the end, I don't think he ever, ever really wanted to give up. The things that he was going through the last several years of his life, I don't know how he did it. I look at it and say, "Could I ever do that?" He had a lot of support with his family and friends, but it still required the determination that he had in himself to push to the fullest.

A big group of us started going to Lake George about thirty years ago and for the last twelve years the Holler family has joined us. One of the most amazing things that I found with Kenny, when he wasn't able to eat, was that he still wanted to cook his chicken legs every year. He didn't want help; he would basically cook a hundred chicken legs with his signature barbeque sauce for everybody else, then just walk away. That is how unselfish he was and how he loved to see other people have fun. If they enjoyed something, it didn't matter if it was a hardship for him. He looked out for others first.

Then with the fishing, we would see the happy faces on our little boys. They would go out on the boat or on the dock and Kenny knew his stuff, so he would teach the kids what to do so they wouldn't get hurt and so they would be able to catch fish. The kids that really didn't care about fishing still liked to do it, because Kenny was there.

We only vacation together in Lake George seven days a year, but we are there 24/7 those weeks and it is an opportunity to see how people react to different situations and how they interact with everybody else. I could see that although Kenny realized that he was battling certain things, he was always planning how he could make life better for his kids and his wife. He realized as time went on who he wanted to associate with and who he wanted his family to associate with. He was very protective in a lot of ways. It wasn't that he wanted to shield them, but he wanted his kids to see the values in certain things.

We would have conversations up in Lake George where Kenny would say, "I see you with your kids. You do this, you do that…" He was older than me, but two of my kids are older than his. He would ask, "Why would you do this type of thing?" or "I admire you for handling your kids that way." I really appreciated that, because I looked up to Kenny. Hearing him tell me, "I like the way you do that and how your kids have come along and grown," meant a lot to me.

When we would go to the race track, towards the end, when he couldn't speak, it was frustrating. Frustrating not only for him, but for us too, trying to understand what he was trying to say. He would go to the window to try to bet and there would be somebody that didn't know him, didn't know what he was up against, trying to understand what he was trying to say. We would tell him, "Kenny, we'll take care of your bets." We tried to be more compassionate because of the love we had for Kenny.

Even in the hospital, I would ask, "Kenny, what are you trying to say?" He would write it down, but it was getting difficult, because he was writing all over the place. After a while he would get frustrated. The worst thing to do was to get him frustrated. We would almost predict what he was trying to do and try to get one step ahead of him, but his mind, even at this point, was still three steps faster than everybody else's. He was playing his moves, like in basketball game. He was so sharp and so quick; something would trigger him.

One of the last nights that I was up at the hospital with him, we were watching a Yankee game and they were playing the Red Sox. All of a sudden Pete R's name came up, because Pete R is a Boston Red Sox fan. So, Kenny's mind went: Boston, Pete R, fishing trips… He would be looking at things and taking that one step down the line; he was so good at curving the conversation in the direction that he wanted it to go. Keeping up with him was difficult, but that goes back to his days with all of the pranks that he used to pull. That was him. He was never satisfied with, "I have one thing down." He was already looking at step two, three, and four. It was amazing how he was so motivated to keep people laughing and interested in what he was doing all the way to the end.

Six months before Kenny died, we had a gathering at our house with Steve, Karen, and their kids. We went into the day hoping that Kenny, Lynda, and the boys would be able to come. When Kenny came in, we were all so happy, but then seeing what he had to go through, the amount of equipment that the boys unloaded from the car, and what he had to have here was shocking. I hadn't seen him in a period of time and usually when I would see him, it would be for a couple hours here and there, and he would be able to shield a lot from us. Coming here, being in the car for a couple hours each way, and then staying for several hours, it was a shock on how much equipment and need that he really did have.

He was on the feeding tube and one of the things that really got to me was, although the house was warm, he couldn't get warm. When he started to eat, the chill just went through him and we gave him sweatshirts and blankets to try to keep him warm. It was another thing that made me think, "How much can he put up with?"

It made me think not only about what Kenny was going through, but about Lynda and the boys. I thought, "Wait. We did this for a few hours, how do they do this every day of the week, every minute of the day, not knowing what is going to happen?" That is where you see family, closeness, and love for each other that are just beyond comprehension to a lot of people. When they left, it wasn't the fun day that we had wanted to have. In the past, every day out with Kenny was a fun day; we realized those days were limited, if any.

It started to sink in that no matter how much fighting and battling he has done over the years, he is fighting a losing battle and at some point he is going to lose. It was just a matter of when it was going to be. We had wanted to have good, fond memories of that day and unfortunately it wasn't what we wanted, but I think it showed, not only myself but my kids and everybody else, what it is like to really love somebody and take care of them. I think that really helped everybody realize that life is short, we have to take advantage of what we can, and when people need help, we have to be there for them. They can't do it on their own. Family and friends are what help us get through these things and we not only need to support others, but the time will come when we will need help and support ourselves.

Whenever I am sick or hear of someone else being sick, I think, "Is this going to lead to something? Is this going to be a prolonged battle?" I think of Kenny and say, "How would he handle it?" Like the question, "What would Jesus do?" I ask, "What would Kenny do?" He set the bar high on a lot of things.

***

Lynda referred to Kenny as a regular guy, I don't know that I think of him as ordinary; I think of him as extraordinary. Whether that is because of how he conducted himself, or how he had to persevere and cope with what he had to, or a combination of both, he certainly did it with grace and dignity in a way that in my opinion sets an example. In my family we often talk about leading by example; that is easier said than done. I think that Kenny did that and I do not think that is particularly ordinary.

Greg, Brewster Friend

37
Letters from Strangers

Card sent to Kenny, November 16, 1984
Sandra: *NY Post Reader*

You are truly wonderful! My husband and I have two cats who we love with all our hearts. Having been an animal lover all my life, I actually cried with joy when I read the story of you in yesterday's New York Post and the heroic and humane act on your part. I can only imagine how dangerous your job is and worrying about the saving of human lives as well as of your colleagues coming out of a fire alive and well, but to take the time, love and patience to save a poor animal's life is indeed beyond any compassion I can imagine. Again, thank you for your caring.

Letter sent to the FDNY Commissioner, Joseph E. Spinato, November 20, 1984
Yolanda: *NY Post Reader*

This is to express the appreciation we always had for the Fire Department, and the self-less service rendered by our firefighters to this community.

Our appreciation was greatly enhanced after we read the article in the New York Post about that wonderful firefighter, Mr. Kenneth Holler, who did such a charitable act on behalf of that little animal and its grieving owner. This man not only deserves our heartfelt gratitude, but we believe a citation from you for pointing up the meaning and substance of real humanity toward all living things, man and beast alike. (November 15, 1984)

We thank all of you, for we consider you heroes, every one.

***

I don't know if Lynda even realizes how many people knew her husband. He was just such a presence.

Jackie, Brewster Baseball Friend

38
Humbling
Richie: *FDNY Ladder 116*

"One of Many," was Kenny's mantra. "One of Many" is a term that means we rise and fall together. We are all one, the brotherhood. We all go into the fire, we all come out together.

I remember when I first got on the job, I was into sports and they asked me to play. The softball season was over, so I played basketball with them. We were playing this team from Ladder 163 in our battalion. Me and this guy, Harry O from 163, were underneath the hoop and we were battling and elbowing in the first half and it was getting pretty heated. The second half started and we were going at it again. Harry O turned to me and asked, "You know how to box?" I said, "Ya!" and I put up my hands and said, "Come on, let's go!" Kenny came out of nowhere and almost tackled me; put his arms around me and said, "Ricco! What are you doing? We are all firemen. You can't beat these guys up! What are you crazy?" And Harry said, "Kenny! Who is this guy?" It is a story that I always remembered and I told my sons that story too.

Personality, just great. Great energy. Constant prankster. Kenny could never sit. I could be in the back room with a couple guys and everyone was relaxed. Kenny would sit there for a couple minutes and he was gone; he was in the kitchen, doing something. Always fidgety.

There was always something happening in the firehouse. The biggest thing I remember with Kenny was the flour fights. A little flour gets thrown at somebody, then a little more, then the whole freaking kitchen. Then we had to clean it up; how stupid were we?

When I would walk into the firehouse, the board is by the housewatch. There were ten guys that I was going to be working with that night, nine guys, plus two officers. I would look at the board and as soon as I saw Kenny's name on it, I thought, "Okay, I'm good." Not only that I am going to have a good time, but also a good meal, because Kenny loved to eat. Kenny loved to eat, especially steak. He used to go to Alex's and get steaks all the time. Big freaking steaks. Kenny hated cheap people, so if he knew that we had a cheap guy in the group working that night, he would make the meal cost double. He would go out and get a freaking prime rib, then ask him, "In or out?" Going back to where I started in the beginning, "One of Many." We all rise and fall together.

Loved his parents. Loved his mother. I always felt that Mrs. Holler would pray for us. I just felt that sense that she was always there for us. We would go by their house to see her and she would say, "Oh, boys be careful. God bless you." Kenny had that instilled in him from his mother and that was a good thing, because it carried on into his being, so to speak, his kindness. Now I look at his sons and Lynda; they carry it on.

Never met anyone who didn't like Kenny. Kenny pulled pranks on some people, but everyone loved him. You can just see in the turnout of people that came to his funeral and are contributing to this book. It has to be the constant thread that Lynda hears.

A fireman. Very proud to be a fireman. He thought it was one of the best things a person could do in the world. He just loved the job that much. Good at a fire, never panicked. Calming. Calming not only in the outside world with all the civilians, but inside a fire situation. People would be screaming, and there was Kenny, just looking around, evaluating what needed to get done. He got the job done and never panicked. Kenny was always a good balance for me, because I am high strung and throughout my life I always connected with people like that. It just works. It is a yin and a yang.

Talk about being a proud Skull? He taught me that. He put us on the map. He was the trailblazer for us; we were a good company, but he had a lot of connections with Suspenders, with Pete, and all the firemen. When people asked him, "Where are you from?" He would say, "116. We are a busy truck." The question: "Where are you from?" And our response "116!" gave us prominence throughout the Fire Department. He set the tone for us. Anyone that I ever met who asked, "Where are you from?" When I said, "116," they said, "Kenny Holler!" It was a great experience knowing him.

A kind person. He taught me kindness. When I first came on the job in '84, I had a lot of rough edges. I was a kid from the street, a broken home. He saw that and took me in, "Relax; these people are your friends." He started me on the road to seeing things a little differently. He showed me the Fire Department for what it was. Now, I'll wear you down with love. I just keep coming at you, but he started me on that road. I could have met some jerk that took me another way. For that, I am forever grateful.

After Kenny got ill he got kind of distant from all of us. I trapped him one time and I asked, "How come you don't come by anymore? I want to know. Did we do anything? Are you okay?" Kenny said, "It kills me, because I can't go out on a run. I can't be a fireman anymore. It is all I wanted to do. It is who I am; it is who I was."

Cancer is cancer. Seeing the crosses on his neck, no saliva, radiation, I recognized that it was serious right from the beginning. He was scared. He'd never tell you, but it affected me. It made me humble. I'm complaining about money and this guy can't even chew a steak. He can't enjoy a beer. He can't taste anything. Twenty years, I don't know how he did it. I don't know how Lynda did it. Lynda deserves a gold star. Look, raising two boys, Kenny sick, it was a lot. The boys seeing their father sick; I am grateful.

Just be grateful man, be humble. It's not about the money; it's about life. Kenny embraced life. He lived every day. No holds barred, he lived. Kenny's like me. He comes from humble beginnings. He grew up in Astoria; he lived in an apartment. His brother was a cop; he became a fireman. He did the best he could; his mother did the best she could. I guess that is what we are all doing, the best we can.

Kenny's suffering teaches us to be humble. We think we have problems, because we are not driving a new car or have a big house or our kid can't go to that school. Think about Kenny Holler. Think about what he went through. It is humbling. He was in my life for a reason. He helped me become a man, he really did. Warren, Gilliams, Kevin, really nice guys too. Good people. We're intertwined; we're always going to be there for each other. We'll see each other on the other side; in the meantime, we'll look out for each other's children and grandchildren.

**

No one is bitching about the little things in their life that they can't accomplish or do at this point. We need to keep a picture of Kenny Holler on our refrigerators.

Chris, St. Lawrence O'Toole Friend

LISTENING

You know when you meet someone and you just start talking and one thing leads to another? He was that type of person. You could keep talking to him all day long, even though you didn't know him, and you would want to tell him everything.[9]

Kenny's unique quality was that he would find what he had in common with me and just focus on me when he was with me. He would always give the impression, and it was genuine, that he really enjoyed my company. He did that with everyone. I cherish that memory of him.[10]

I spent a lot of time talking to Kenny. Kenny always listened. Whether it was talking about the weather or the field or second base, he always made us feel like what we had to say was worth listening to.[11]

I was afraid that I didn't know Ken well enough to say anything, but the funny thing is, with Ken, you knew him when you first met him, because he instantly would make you feel comfortable. I could talk to him about things and it wasn't just a silly conversation; it always had a little meaning to it, and always was something that would brighten my day, or make me feel good or make me feel meaningful.[12]

I lost my brother on 9/11. He worked in the Trade Center. In Yonkers everybody knew; everybody knew me, there was a lot of attention around it, but when I moved up here nobody knew and I enjoyed keeping it sort of quiet. I didn't really want to get it out there, but I did tell Ken, because for whatever reason he came across as the kind of person that I felt I could talk to about anything.[13]

---

9 Anne Marie, Neighbor

10 Linda, Lynda's Friend

11 Lisa, Brewster Baseball Friend

12 Janice, Brewster Friend

13 Paul, Brewster Baseball Friend

39
Remarkable
Christa: Brewster Friend

I met Lynda when Will and Colin were about a year old. Sometime later, we had a play-date at their house and I saw the article about the fireman who had given mouth-to-mouth to a cat and I remember thinking that I had seen that story on the news. Then Lynda said that was Kenny. I thought, "Wow! That is remarkable. What a small world."

Then I remember the morning of 9/11. We were so shocked and stunned by the whole thing. We decided to try to carry on a normal day and continue with our play date which was planned at the Holler house. What a beautiful day it was; the sun was shining, the weather was perfect, and we couldn't believe that sixty miles south of us such a terrible thing was happening.

Kenny came out on the porch and said, "Lynda, I think I should go down and help out. Maybe I can help out with the phones." They were unsure what to do. Everything was so uncertain in the city, and they didn't know if he would even be able to go over the bridges to get there.

He didn't go that day. But Lynda told me that was the day he hung his fireman coat on the garage. He pulled it out of the box that he hadn't touched since he emptied his firehouse locker. He hung it in memory of the firefighters that he knew were dying that day. The rest of us had hope that most would get out. He and Lynda had heated discussions about it. She was thinking about all their families and struggled with the idea that they would go into such a dangerous fire knowing they might not come out, but he knew the truth before it was reported. He knew they would be going in to save total strangers, putting their own lives on the line, and demanding that their own families accept the sacrifice too.

That was a tough day, but the years went on and we have so many fun memories with the Hollers. Fireworks at the park on the Fourth of July. The Halloween parties. Those were fun. Kenny was Frankenstein one year with the green face. He would go around making sure that everybody was having fun. I'll never forget the tissue paper mummies and all the friends running around outside. The cupcakes. Those parties went on for many years. Those are memories for the children that will last a lifetime. I was the tattoo gal. It is funny all those children that I put the tattoos on, as they get older, I say, "I know you from somewhere!" And it is from those parties.

And Thanksgiving at my mother's house. One year I happened to ask the Hollers to join us and they didn't have plans. It was really a nice day. Kenny couldn't chew solid food by that time, but he made due with mashed potatoes, gravy, and cranberry sauce. Lynda may have brought him soup too. But I will never forget when Kenny took the first bite of pumpkin cheese-cake and his reaction. It was a new flavor for him, something different for him to eat. It is my favorite too. My mother made whipped cream to put on the coffee and I asked him, "Would you like some whipped cream on your coffee?" He seemed very hesitant, but said, "Ok." I think he was being polite, but he drank it and I'll never forget he had whipped cream on his lip. Then he said, "I'll take another dollop!" So I gave him a big dollop and I think he had another cup of coffee too. He really liked that. They came for two years. It was fun.

As time went on, our children went separate ways and we didn't see each other very much. I didn't know that Kenny had gotten so sick until I saw him up at the high school at Will and Colin's baseball game. He said to me, "I am back." And I said, "I didn't know where you were." Then I could tell that he had been very sick.

I prayed for Kenny at that point and I still pray for him and for all the friends that we have lost. Seeing their suffering makes me realize just how wonderful life is and how vulnerable we are. Many have passed quickly, but I think Kenny was remarkable that he was able to survive all that he did for that amount of time. It could not have been easy.

***

I remember how upset he was about 9/11. I remember him telling me that on September 11th he took his uniform to the dry cleaners because he knew he was going to need it. It broke his heart, it really did.

Maureen, Halloran Fund Friend

40
Words
Grace: *Colin's Friend, Age 18*

I find myself thinking about Kenny most often in my Anthropology class, which is kind of interesting, because you wouldn't really peg that as somewhere I would think of him. We have been learning about how linguistics has such a big impact on evolution and how language is not only changed by the people who speak it, but also how much people are affected by the language they speak. My teacher has told us that the way we speak is a reflection of how we see the world, which got me thinking about what happens when speech is changed or even taken away in some cases, like with Kenny.

Words are our most efficient means of communication, but there are also other ways to communicate, which is how I thought about Kenny with his notebook. His notebook is representative of how he took this challenge and was able to use another method to do what he would do in his daily routine anyway. That motivation definitely inspires me.

When I picture Kenny, I picture him in four places and in each of these places there is a certain way of speaking. I find that interesting, because he was able to participate equally, even above some other people, and his words were effective. The first place is in church where everyone is singing and chanting and praying. Everyone does it together and he blended in.

The second place that I picture him is at the Dennis P. McHugh Annual 5K Run and Family Fair working behind the grill. He would call out my order and that sound of his voice has stayed with me.

At their annual Halloween party, he always used to say, "Happy Hollerween!" I always thought that was funny, but again, it was just another word that stuck with me and represented Kenny and who he was in his goofiness.

The fourth place I always think of Kenny is on the baseball field and in the dugout. When you think of a baseball field or a baseball game, automatically the sounds come to you: people cheering and clapping, coaches yelling, the kids. There are so many different little sayings that come with baseball. He was still able to communicate his love for the game with these words, and his actions.

Kenny lost his ability to use words, but he was still able to communicate and show his love and his spirit. In a way, Kenny had a language all his own, a language that affected everyone around him, a language that reflected how Kenny saw the world.

***

It was in his voice. When we came upstairs in the morning at his house, it wasn't just "Good morning Liz." It was "How're ya doing Liz?!" Not really sing-songy, but kind of cool, suave, upbeat, and very cheerful. Uncle Kenny didn't just say things, it was the way he spoke.

Liz, Lynda's Niece

41
Script
Marie: Lynda's College Friend

How did I hear about Kenny? I heard about him from Lynda, of course! I am still very excited about the idea of when she first met him; she called me and said, "I met this guy!" She gave me his name and said, "Talk to Vince and see if he knows him." So I called him immediately and he didn't even pause or take time to think about it.

The way firemen are typically, they know everybody. You know that. Anywhere they go, they know people and it always amazed me. We could be in North Carolina and they would run into somebody. I think that is a great part of the job.

But back to Kenny, without a hesitation, the response was so positive. Vince said, "What a great guy. What a nice guy. She should definitely go for him!" And she did.

I remember their wedding. It was beautiful. Lynda's dress was gorgeous. Kenny was always so handsome, OMG. So handsome.

Time goes on, the babies, seeing the kids. It was always easy whenever we were together, because the guys got along well. The funny thing was, whenever we got together their discussions were about what was on sale at the grocery stores! I found that to be one of the big benefits of being married to a fireman. They really took an active part in the household and raising our children; you can't get better than that.

Thanksgiving weekend 2000, two of our college girlfriends visited from Ohio and Pennsylvania with their families. We all got talking about our families going on vacation together in the Outer Banks the following summer. Lynda and Vince were the planners. I remember pulling up in front of our rental house and Vince saying, "A pink house? We rented a pink house!" Out of the thirteen kids in our group, there were only three girls, so that was kind of funny!

A lot of it was hanging out, sitting and chatting on the back deck. The guys would read their newspapers, and they were sharing a pair of glasses. It wasn't even their real glasses, they were little cheater glasses. That's when we girls realized that our husbands were middle aged! It was just so nice to regroup for the last time, so to speak. A month later, September 11th hit and Vince was killed at the Trade Center.

With his food issues, his speech issues, it always amazed me. Lynda would call, "Marie, come over, Kenny is going to make a pot of sauce." He loved to grill his sausage for it. For a man who couldn't eat it, I always felt like that is the worst torture. Food is socialization. And drinking, he had to give that up as well. I don't know how he did it. We would come and he would have a smile on his face. He would be grilling and stirring his sauce. We'd be hanging out; he just liked to do for others.

I saw Kenny in Putnam Hospital during his admission there after the 911 call and before he was transferred to Sloan for the last time. Lynda was very involved on the phone with Sloan's medical staff. Kenny was lying in bed and was still so funny. He wrote me a note, something like, "I am driving her crazy; Lynda is going to jump off a bridge." Then he added something about it being fortunate that there aren't any high bridges in Putnam County.

I think I pray more because of Kenny. I definitely prayed for him when he was sick and I pray for him and to him now. It is crazy. We start thinking about everybody we have lost, and we're not that old yet. My list is long; it is amazing how long it is: the people that have passed and the people that are struggling now. I know a lot of strugglers.

I am going to contradict myself a little bit. I hate that saying, "God only gives you what you can handle." I don't know how many times, people asked me, and they probably asked Lynda, "How do you do it?" Well, we just do. So, even though I hate that saying, we have kind of lived that. You handle what you get.

Lynda describes it as superhuman powers. It was more than a person can do, what she was doing, so she knew that she wasn't just doing it by herself. She had superhuman powers and God was sending her people to help her when she needed them. People would just show up at her door with something that she needed or call and ask, "Can I drive you?" on a day that she needed to be driven. So those things would happen that gave her that superhuman power, gave Kenny the superhuman power, to do what needed to be done. We need to be open to and aware of those powers.

I had superhuman powers at times too, doing things when they needed to be done, but the superhuman powers and the special things that came to Lynda were definitely different than for me. We needed different things. Lynda's went on so long and that is a whole different game plan. Both of us, we are not done yet, but we have been very successful at drawing upon the powers that are available to us.

Kenny was one of the best. I have to say, Lynda and I lucked out. We really did and even though the time was much shorter than either of us would have liked, we would do it again, because we got good guys that cared, who were kind. Lynda and I got talking about it and she told me about something that happened to her after Kenny died and how it helped her perspective:

A few months after Kenny died she was in the bathroom, looked in the mirror, and this thought came to her, "I just didn't know how long he was going to live. That's all." She started to ponder it and realized that when we marry someone we have this unrealistic expectation that we are going to live to be eighty-five, sit holding hands in a rocking chair, and die together in our sleep. We don't voice those expectations, but it is what we have in our minds. It is what we want. It is that scenario that we think should happen, especially when we find the right person. But it doesn't work that way, very few people's lives follow the script, so people actually approach life with unrealistic expectations and then are disappointed when it doesn't turn out the way they planned it. People become bitter, angry at God, depressed, etc.

It didn't used to be that way. A hundred years ago, people didn't have the same expectations and they expected to suffer. They expected to have difficulties. If they had ten children, they might lose four or six of those children before they reached adulthood. So they lived their lives not expecting everything to be perfect, where in this day and age we kind of expect everything to go the way we want it to go and when it doesn't, we are mad, we are disappointed, we are resentful… Of course, we are going to be sad, but do you know what I mean? Lynda and I are disappointed, of course, because Vince and Kenny aren't here anymore, but we understand that we just hadn't been shown the final script.

When the underpinnings of your house get pulled out, and you are fighting the fight of your life for everybody, for everything you love, how do you hold up everything? You can't. Lynda went through it with such grace, not ease I know, but grace. It's amazing.

Ellen, Brewster Friend

***

Humanity has permanent need of supernatural power and strength. When we are tired and tempted to give up, instead of blaming fate and circumstances, we should ask ourselves whether we are living sufficiently close to God, whether we have called on him earnestly enough.

Father Alfred Delp, German Jesuit Priest

42
Heart
Anne: *Brewster Friend*

I first met Kenny and Lynda in 2000, when Grace and Colin were three years old and in preschool at St. Lawrence O'Toole School. At that time, he was doing scheduling for FDNY's Special Operation Command (SOC). One day I arrived at St. Lawrence and he was so excited; he had found out that he had gotten approval to retire and that June he did. Three months later, September 11th happened, which is where, although we hung out and did a lot the year before, my relationship with Kenny took a whole different turn, a much deeper turn.

I clearly remember walking into St. Lawrence with the three kids the following week when school resumed. I turned the corner and Kenny was standing in the doorway of the Pre-K4 classroom. He watched me walk down the hall and he asked, "Did you know anyone?" and I said, "Yes, my cousin. Did you?" He responded, "Yes, my friend Vinny." Meanwhile, he didn't say all the hundreds of people that he had known and been acquaintances; he just singled out Vinny.

It's hard to describe, but from that moment on, that event took our relationship to a whole new level. We would try to find out information to pass along to the other. Anytime I saw him after that, for years, it was all about September 11th for him. Any spare moment we would get, within seconds, we were in deep conversations about life, about death, about fears, hopes, about everything. I didn't have a relationship with anyone else like that, obviously other than my husband Tim, but no friends did I ever discuss that level of death with.

For Kenny, it was so real, because he had come into contact and worked with so many of the fallen firefighters. Also, by having so recently worked doing the manpower staffing for SOC, he had not only known many of the men killed that day, but also their wives. He had spoken to many of them on the phone, joking with them and encouraging them to convince their husbands to come in for overtime, so they could buy a new pair of shoes or something silly like that. Now he felt a lot of guilt and a lot of compassion, not only for those families, but for the man that had his job on September 10th. In conversation after conversation, he would refer back to the fact that he didn't work that day. I think part of him felt like he should have been there; that maybe he could have saved people. What he wasn't realizing was that he saved people in his own way, through his personality, and he was such a support to so many people in that time period.

So it was crazy. Anytime we saw each other we would back away from whoever was around and we'd get into these deep conversations. He'd tell me about every funeral he went to. He'd tell me about every family, every story he heard. It just weighed so heavily on him. I remember a particular time, we went to the soccer field and Kenny had gotten there first. It was probably a month to six weeks after September 11th. I looked at him and he just looked tired, he looked worn; he had been to funeral after funeral at that point. I said to him, "Are you okay?" Without talking we backed away, sat on a rock, and he said, "I don't know where this disease, the cancer, is taking me. I've no idea what road I'm on, how hard it's going to get, what I'm going to do, but Anne, I will take it any day over losing my life on September 11th."

I have always remembered that, because he had no idea what was in store for him; how hard it would get. He just felt such pain, not necessarily for the people that lost their lives, it was the people that were left behind. That's what really got to him and I think he was thinking of Lynda, Colin, and Tim and realizing, through these experiences, how hard it would be for them. I think for years to come, he was able to prepare them and all his friends for that day, whereas he felt on September 11th, nobody was prepared. Slowly we would meet at the sidelines of a ballgame and we got out of that constant talking about death or life, but I always knew that if either one of us had to talk, we would go to the other. That was nice.

I miss Kenny; I miss him a lot. There are constant reminders all over the place. A lot of people would have just stayed home with family, but he didn't do that. He was volunteering; he was asking, "How can I help you?" He gave so much of his time, which brings me back to September 11th. In one of our conversations, all the memorial fundraisers for different people who lost their lives popped up. He was telling me about the golf outing that they were going to do for Vinny and I had said, "We're going to do a race for my cousin." Without even a hesitation, he said, "Count me in," and sure enough, he was there.

It was a matter of getting to Piermont by seven in the morning which was not easy; although he was an early riser, he was leaving Lynda and the boys behind for a day packed with all their baseball games and stuff. He left them behind to volunteer for somebody he hadn't ever met and of all things, he worked at the barbecue. That always struck me, because he couldn't eat and yet that's where he was happiest, at the grill.

So, our first year was so crazy, was so busy. The race went off and then we had the fair. By only ten o'clock in the morning we were exhausted. I was standing with my mom and Kenny came over and asked, "Can I get you guys something to eat?" I remember saying to him, "Ahh Kenny, just anything is fine. We're starving, that would be great," and so he disappeared. My mom and I got busy at doing something and he tracked us down and in his hands were two wrapped sausage and pepper sandwiches. He said, "I loaded them up for you." We ate them and they were the best, the best sandwiches, perfectly put together with love. So every year after that, we didn't even ask, Kenny would hunt us down and at some point, no matter how crazy the day was, he would give us our sausage sandwiches. Throughout the year, my mother would talk about it, "Kenny's sandwich was so good!"

The last couple years before he died, Kenny couldn't make it to the event because of his health. Then the event after he died, my mother turned to me and said, "I don't think I have the heart to eat a sausage sandwich." I said, "Mom, I know exactly how you feel, I don't either. I'll go get something else. I'll get burgers." So I walked up and I was thinking about Kenny the whole time, because I thought, "Gosh, I'd love a sausage sandwich!" As I walked up to the barbeque, there was a sign: "No Hamburgers or Cheeseburgers." They had run out! I laughed and thought, "This is such a sign!" So I ordered two sausage and peppers, returned to my mom, and she laughed too. We toasted with our sausage and peppers to thank Kenny.

Kenny was part of the Dennis P. McHugh Foundation which has raised over $350,000 over the last eleven years. With his help so much good has come out of it: the Piermont Public Library; we built a playground; we built homes for heroes; we help people in the community. It took everybody's help to do it and he understood what the results could be when one person steps forward to help. How one person can totally make a difference, an impact, and he was determined to show that good things can come out of bad things.

One time, towards the end, I drove Lynda down to see Kenny at the hospital. I was so happy to do it for Lynda. I remember we got to the lobby of Sloan and she said that Kenny may not be up for visitors.

A couple hours later she came down and said, "Kenny would like to see you." We went up to his room and I was happy, because I missed my friend. We started telling stories and catching up on what people were doing in town, what he was missing. Lynda and I were talking and he was using his whiteboard trying to catch up with the conversation. I remember looking at him and knowing that he was frustrated because he loved to tell a good story and he loved the corny jokes, but the whiteboard wasn't fast enough for him.

At one point, he put the whiteboard down and shooed it off with his hand, frustrated. The room went quiet for the three of us. Then Lynda climbed into bed with him and they looked at each other without any words and there was so much communication between the two of them. I remember at that point thinking, "Oh my gosh, I totally feel like I just invaded your space." I felt awkward and then I watched them and I thought, "I'm here for a reason."

I get goosebumps to this day thinking about it and I think about it almost every day. That I witnessed such an unbelievable love story; that they had been through so much. Lynda could have asked anyone to go down with her that day; she could've gone alone.

In our everyday lives we are in such a rush. We're coming from one field, we have one kid in one car, one kid in the other car, and although we see each other every single day practically, we don't see the love and the intimacy between couples. That was such a rare moment and it was so raw, because they weren't talking, they communicated everything through their looks and it was as if I wasn't even in the room. It is one my favorite memories, because it's so vivid in my mind; something I will never forget, witnessing that between Kenny and Lynda.

***

I remember when I saw Lynda cry at the wake…. I knew she was devastated, but she was always so strong. It was a reminder of the love story too. She was taking care of so many things, the kids, Kenny, but there was also that other part, that other piece of the two of them. We forget that sometimes.

Denise, Brewster Friend

43
Unique
Jimmy: *Astoria Friend*

Everybody is trying to figure out a word for Kenny and I would say Kenny was "Unique," because Kenny was not like any other person I knew.

I worked on an ambulance for thirty-two years. On 9/11 I was down there. I was in my ambulance when the towers came down and I spent the day shuttling people to the hospital. Back and forth I went, helping as many people as I could. It was terrible, so much loss, so many painful memories. Kenny was the one that always would get me to the side and no matter how sick he was, he would have time to ask me how I was. He became a little more serious with life as his illness went on, but he always had time. He would call me to the side and ask me, "Are you doing ok? How are you feeling? If you have any problems, call me up." We had a bond there.

Every time we were with a group, I would always ask, "Is Kenny coming?" The group without Kenny was like a four-wheel car with one wheel missing. He brought out the best in a lot of people; he would make people smile. There's no better joy in the world than to make people smile. He knew that and he could do that. He was unique.

***

Most everybody saw that movie, It's a Wonderful Life. *If Kenny was sitting here right now, and you said, "Ken, what impact do you think you made on society from the time that you realized there was people on earth?" Do you know what he would say? He would say, "I didn't make much of an impact." Even through his end was painful, he had a wonderful life with everybody around him; he made their existence better.*

Bill, Brewster Elks Lodge

44
Welcome

I met Kenny when we moved up to Brewster from Long Island in 2005. He was probably, if not definitely, the first person that Sal and I met. I remember how we met him, where we met. It was on the field at JFK. Kenny walked over and introduced himself to me and we started talking. I told him how we had just moved up here and how we didn't have any friends yet, just the neighbors we had met. I remember thinking, after speaking to him, whatever little conversation that we had, "If most of the people up here are like him, we will be so comfortable here."

Annamarie, Brewster Friend

***

The first time I met Kenny we were new here. He was one of the first people that I met, like number one or number two.

I think the boys were playing soccer. He was standing by one of those rocks and I was by that post that has the chain on it. We were both just standing there, watching. He made a comment about the kids and we both started laughing and we just started talking from there. I don't even think at that point we had even introduced ourselves. Then it became every Saturday with the practice, every Sunday with the soccer; it became a regular thing that we would see each other all the time. It was always, Kenny being Kenny. Always a hello. Always in a good mood.

Sal, Brewster Friend

***

My family and I moved from the Bronx to Brewster in 2010. One of the first things we did with our kids, our youngest kids Aiden and Eve, was to sign them up for Little League baseball and Little League softball. As I think about and reflect upon my experiences, I remember that the first person I interacted with was Kenny. It was at Markel Park. Kenny was there helping out and that was how I perceived Kenny, always helping out. We met at the concession area between the girls' softball and the boys' baseball fields. I remember the introduction, "I am Kenny." "I am Robert." Da da da ... and that was kind of it initially. I am a person that believes in vibrations, vibes, and gut reactions; I knew immediately that Kenny was a good guy.

Robert, Brewster Baseball Friend

Whenever I saw him I would always see that big huge smile and he would always give everybody a big hug. It could have been a year ago, five years ago, or ten years ago, he always treated you the same. He would always welcome you with open arms. And he had that little smirk to him, that little smile that he gave which was very nice.

Mike M, FDNY Engine 261/Ladder 116, SOC

***

Kenny was the most easygoing guy that I ever met. I never really saw him mad. And Kenny knew everybody. We would work with guys from other houses and everybody felt at ease that they were working with Kenny, because Kenny made people feel at home.

Mike P, FDNY Ladder 116

***

There are people that even though you don't know them that well, you kind of get a feeling for who they are. You meet them and talk to them for five minutes and you feel like you have known them for a very long time. I got that feeling from just the little bit of Kenny interaction I had: that he liked everyone, wanted to include everyone, wanted to make them feel part of the group, and it was genuine.

Maria, Brewster Friend

45
Firefighter Kenny

Swearing-in to FDNY by Commissioner Augustus Beekman
April 5, 1979 - Kenny front row aisle

Action photos taken by Kenny's father
at a fire in his Astoria neighborhood

Kenny with his parents on his Fire Academy
Graduation Day

Mouth to Meow

Mike M's catering staff - Kenny second from left

Firehouse fishing trip - Kenny on right

Mike, Kenny, and Gilliams with Ladder 116's truck

Firehouse ski team - Kenny back row center

Firehouse Halloween Party - Kenny as the Tin Man

Photo printed in the Rocky Mountain News of
Kenny holding his hat at Tommy Kuveikis'
Memorial Service

46
Buddy
McCormick: Astoria Friend

As one of the Astoria crew, you know all about us growing up together, but then Kenny and I separated for many, many years. Getting married at twenty-five, me and Pat moved out of Astoria and left that whole bar scene. Then we had the babies. So the group sort of splintered a bit, between the guys that got married at a younger age, and the guys that got married older. Which makes sense in a way, right?

I always remember, and I knew it was special at the time, not just now looking back at it: the 9/11 anniversaries that I spent with Kenny. Being able to spend hours, picking up where we left off, with that big gap in our lives. Those were very, very special times for me. To look forward every year to 9/11 is kind of creepy to think about, but once a year I would get to see Kenny there. For some reason, when I think of the past with Kenny, that's what comes into my mind. How enjoyable that was. Very special, very special.

We would talk: family talk, work talk, sickness talk, just general guy-stuff. We would just sit down and freakin' talk. Him being in uniform gave us access to certain areas. So right on Church Street, right across from the site, there were park benches and that's where we would sit. We would stay until maybe the second set of bells, then we would get up and walk. One time we even signed a beam; there is a beam in One World Trade Center with mine and Kenny's signatures on it.

Church Street was pretty empty because of security concerns, but one year a girl was walking past and she was crying. We stopped and asked, "What's the matter?" She just got diagnosed with cancer. I said, "I have cancer; Kenny has cancer; you're talking to the right people right now." So we did our best to help her along, not to be so upset and everything. She thanked us and she moved away.

Another time we were walking down one of those streets and we saw Mike Lupica, the sports writer. Lupica gives the impression that he is really not a big fan of the Yankees. I forget exactly what transpired between the three of us, but Kenny started right away with what Kenny was famous for: good natured busting chops. Mike Lupica came back with something, I came back with something, and we all ended up in hysterics! All three of us, in the middle of downtown Manhattan on 9/11, laughing our butts off. As we were leaving I said, "Maybe we can make the paper!" We never did. We were in hysterics, all three of us, just people passing. Strangers passing. And Kenny made that happen with the stuff that came out of his mouth. It just works. We've seen it a thousand times.

I hid my cancer for a long time. My voice changed. I guess I thought of every excuse in the world to not go to a doctor. Months passed and then six or seven years ago I was at a birthday party in Pennsylvania with Pat's family and I started to hear comments about the sound of my voice. That was the first time I really realized that something was wrong here. Being a heavy smoker, I didn't need Sherlock Holmes to figure out what might be going on. Then I said, "I've got to stop the BS; I've got to go see a doctor and get this taken care of." It was on one of my vocal chords. One thing led to another, I ended up in some great hands along the way, and I'm fine. I'm considered cured.

You belong to a club you don't want to join; you are one family with the other people you meet in treatment. I was there every day and to see what other people were going through, my stuff didn't even compare. That I didn't like the taste of chicken? That I sounded like a frog? My side effects didn't even count. Piece of cake.

Kenny definitely had my back, that's for sure. Just like I had his back—that was unspoken. We would talk about cancer, but it never would be a woe-is-me kind of thing. It was just part of a "how's it going?" When we are going through certain sicknesses, the last thing we want is for someone to feel sorry for us. Dealing with Kenny, that was a no-brainer. We didn't feel sorry for each other. We just were, "Hey, we have to roll up our sleeves and go to work." That's the best way I can explain it.

The bond that was created a million years ago remained intact. Forget about miles… and time… nothing ever changed. My friend is my friend.

My mother was extremely religious. She was a big pray-er. Anytime anybody was sick, I would tell Mom and she would put him on the list. She had a book with all these names and everybody had a saint attached to them. Every once in a while she would give me a call and we would go over the list of the names. I remember towards the end when she called me about Kenny, I said, "Mom, he's still doing bad." She said, "You know what, I'm putting his family in."

She died in June 2012 of cancer too, small cell lung cancer. Maybe we were blessed in a way that it was undiagnosed for such a long period of time. Her doctors missed it. She lasted a month, six weeks, but she could have had it for years. She was eighty-six. It worked out the way it should work out.

Kenny had been battling his cancer for many, many, many years and I knew it wasn't an easy thing to do. I remember August 2012 in Lake George and him struggling to drink coffee. I thought, "This is going to be a really tough road."

Over the twenty years, when Kenny went in for surgeries and he had all these procedures being done, he never wanted visitors. Obviously, we did not agree with that statement, but we respected it. The day I was told that I could go see him in the hospital at New York Presbyterian, I knew right then and there, "This is bad, really bad. This is not normal." That's when I knew, I really felt, that the road was going to end.

Shortly after, I knew there were some mental problems, because Kenny started to text me a lot of gibberish. One day, Steve called to tell me that Kenny was acting paranoid and Lynda needed one of us to go stay with him. I said, "No problem, I'll get down there." I got there and I remember being very, very concerned, because I was looking at all the monitors and even though I am not a friggin' doctor, I could see heart rate and I could see blood pressure. I could see how freakin' agitated he was. Restless. I was sitting there, he couldn't communicate, forget about writing anything down. I could see him tugging on his oxygen. I'd say, "Kenny, you can't be doing this. Put it back, put it back."

I forget what time during the night, not a sound came out of his mouth, but he was screaming, screaming! Not a sound. I said, "Kenny, I don't give a shit what you're saying. I don't give a shit what you think. I ain't leaving." I had no idea what he was thinking. Was he enraged at me? Was he enraged because of the craziness of the medication? I had no idea. He was enraged though and he tried to rip everything out. All kinds of crazy stuff. And that's exactly what I told him. "You're not pulling anything out. I ain't freakin' leaving. I'm here all night long, so calm the hell down."

Then the monitors must have alerted the staff and they came in. He did calm down; he was laying there and there were two doctors and a nurse. They were talking all sorts of stuff to him, trying to get an answer somehow, and I'll never forget: he was looking at the doctors, he was listening to them, and at the moment he seemed quite calm. After all that, I wasn't calm; I didn't see how he could be calm!

All of a sudden, he just took his sock off, in front of the doctor, reached out and just dropped it... Almost like giving him the finger... That's the impression I got, like he was angrily saying: "I've had it!"

The doctors looked at each other... They didn't know what in the hell was going on. Then they gave him medication, he calmed down, and the rest of the night was uneventful. The nurse came to me asking, "Can you stay the night?" I said, "Absolutely! That's what I am here for." They couldn't get an advocate there until the next morning.

It is a night I will never forget. I think the advocate came to relieve me, but there was definitely a rotation with me and the guys. I went back again. Me and Steve relieved each other and Pete R spent the next night there. I remember giving him a heads-up that things could get friggin' stupid. Completely, completely out of character for Kenny. It had to be the drugs or some temporary malfunction in his brain. Fortunately, after a few days, the craziness passed and Kenny settled down again.

Our retirement club is getting bigger and bigger and sometimes I think, "Man, man, we're missing a couple people here." That's when he comes into my brain. Not in a sad way, just that we miss him. The looks, you know that freakin' smirk. Little stuff like that, that little thing in his eye. That's what comes to mind. Not the corny stuff he did. I'm sure there are a thousand stories. I can't recall any of them at the moment, but it was that freakin' look, the devilish, harmless look, that I remember... and I miss.

***

Forces beyond your control can take away everything you possess except one thing, your freedom to choose how you will respond to the situation.

Viktor Frankl, Austrian Neurologist, Psychiatrist, Holocaust Survivor

47

Peace

Pat: *Astoria Friend, McCormick's Wife*

We went on vacation with Kenny in 1978. We were in a bar in Fort Lauderdale and behind the bar they had a swimming pool with mermaids swimming around. All of a sudden, Kenny was gone. Where was he? He was swimming with the mermaids in that pool behind the bar! That was so typical of a Kenny move.

That's the kind of stuff I remember with Kenny, just laughing a lot. We didn't get to see that very often in the latter years, I guess, especially Lynda. He got sick so early into their marriage. Every time something new would happen, I would think, "Dear God! Now how is he going to survive this?"

I think of that a lot. His kids. What they had to go through. Just having their dad sick for so long, not having the Kenny we had. They never knew that Kenny. The fun Kenny like we see in pictures from those young years. There is a picture of Kenny and Tommy in the boat—it is one of the most beautiful pictures. They both look like movie stars. I always used to say that Kenny was the best looking and they would all get mad. Yes, he was extremely good looking, Kenny, but never cocky about it. I don't think we realized it, because he was not one to be conceited at all. There was not a conceited bone in his body. He was just one of the guys.

Kenny had faith. I think when you are put to the test like that, is when you've either got faith or you don't. Sometimes I wish I could have more of a faith like that, because everybody with it seems so peaceful. I hope his faith gave him peace too. It is fantastic that Lynda and the boys feel peace since Kenny died. You see people years later that are still struggling. Their life was so… complicated. Now it's not and Kenny's at peace. They miss him, but he's at peace which is probably the most important thing for them. For me too.

We were down in Virginia at my brother's house in Richmond, when we got the word, and my first reaction was relief. More than a feeling of "Oh my God, Kenny…" it was, "He's at peace. Thank God."

***

At the funeral home, the thing that had the biggest impact on me was the pictures. I got to see the Kenny that I didn't meet. I thought, "Look at this guy! This is Kenny? OMG! Wow dude! This guy must have been amazing!" I saw all the people around him and I could tell they were at parties and picnics and just having a nice time. I thought, "Wow! I never met that guy." But I guess in a way I did, right? Because it doesn't matter what we are going through physically, our soul/spirit will always come out.

Robert, Brewster Baseball Friend

48
Respect
Will: *Colin's Friend, Age 18*

I have known Kenny my whole life. I don't know how old I was at the time, but he was the one that taught me how to properly shake hands. When he first shook my hand, I thought, "Geeze, that really hurt!" After that, every time I would meet him I would always give him a firm handshake. He respected me that much to give me a firm handshake and I would give him the same amount of respect by giving him a firm handshake back. That has carried into how I shake hands with other people. I credit Kenny in helping me know how to properly greet and present myself to people.

There is so much to say about Kenny, I don't know where to begin… It's a lot harder to talk about him than I thought it would be.

I love the fact that he considered me one of Colin's good friends. During Little League, I would see him around the baseball fields and he would always take the time out of his day to come and talk to me. I respected that so much; I didn't really have a lot of friends back then, so the fact that he came up to talk to me, I couldn't thank him enough.

The Halloween parties were an absolute blast! I always looked forward to them and would ask, "When is Colin and Tim's Halloween party coming up?" Then I'd finally get the invitation and say, "Yes!!"

Kenny and Lynda both cared a lot to set up this party for their kids and teach them how to be grateful for what they have. Instead of presents, they'd ask for food donations for the food pantry. The fact that they instilled that so young, I respect that so much. The fact that they would teach them, "Hey, you have so much. Why not give so much to someone else who has so little." That is a great thing.

Kenny made sure to talk to everyone; he was always helping out with the activities. He was taking pictures, making sure everyone was laughing or smiling. He was always in the background making goofy faces. He was a special part of why those parties were so much fun.

I remember my mom telling me about four or five years ago that Kenny had been sick earlier and it went away. I had known him my whole life, but when you are a kid, you don't really notice those things; you notice the character and the person. I noticed that he was so healthy with life, enjoying the little things, enjoying people. I did notice his raspy voice, but that's pretty much it. Other than that, as a kid, I just saw his energy and kindness, not the negative things.

Then, when I was fifteen, she informed me that the cancer had come back. I just felt all this sorrow for him, because how can that happen to someone so good? It's unfair. He doesn't deserve that. Why him? Why someone that everyone respects and has done so many good things in life? I was just in shock for days. I felt like he was a second father, because I was always at their house. I was devastated. Absolutely devastated.

I saw Kenny out once or twice with the trach. I would always go to talk to him and make sure to make eye contact with him and not take a single glance at his trach. Again, he showed me so much respect, that I felt the most respectful and honorable thing to do was to look him in the eyes. I felt that anything else would be disrespectful and rude and he did not deserve any disrespect whatsoever.

When it got really bad and he was in the hospital, Mom would tell me what was happening. Whenever I would hear that news, before bed I would pray for him. I still pray for him now. Whenever I think about baseball or school, he will always come back to me and I pray for him, absolutely. It's the least I can do.

I carry myself differently, because Kenny taught me not only to respect other people, but to respect myself. He gave me a lot of confidence when I was a kid, a lot of good advice. I feel that it is only right that his advice and his willingness to give it, wasn't in vain. I owe it to him to carry myself as a better person, as a better man.

When I first arrived at his wake, I was just in awe by the amount of people that showed up. I thought, "This man had an impact on this many people's lives!" Not just an impact, but how great the impact was that they would all come and show their respect.

He had two firefighters standing honor guard by his casket the whole time. I could see his life in that one scene. He was so respected by his coworkers and so respected by everyone else that came.

When I die, I would want to have made that much of an impact, if not greater, because that's how we should live, making that great of an impact on other people's lives.

When we first showed up at the funeral home, I felt like I was underdressed. So I thought, "I can't do this to Kenny, man. I respect him too much." I forced my parents to drive me back, so I could change into proper clothes: nice dress shirt, tie, dress pants, shoes. I said, "I am not showing up to Kenny's wake looking like this, I have to show him the respect I gave him in life, even after he has passed. He still deserves that respect.

***

A distinct memory is one time at the end of church our families were talking and I went to say hello to Mr. Holler. I shook his hand and I remember that he had one of the strongest handshakes I had ever felt. He just crushed my hand! I remember at that time thinking, and looking back on it now thinking, how strong Mr. Holler was. Not in a physical sense. Even though that handshake showed physical strength, I realized how strong he was to go through all of the obstacles that he had to go through.

Kyle, Colin's Friend, Age 18

49
Really-Nice-Man

Fran: *Brewster Baseball Friend*

We were never introduced until Mark and Colin were in 9th grade, but I first saw Kenny at a baseball game; it was in the summertime. Mark played for Patterson Little League, Colin played for Brewster, but we would pass each other coming and going.

As I was going in, Kenny said, "Good luck."

And I said, "How did they do?" Real quick.

Then the second time I saw him it happened again and I remembered, "He is the really nice man that asked me that before." I thought, "Was it just a fluke?" But I knew it wasn't a fluke at that point.

I asked Mark, "Who is that?" He goes to school with Brewster kids, so I figured Mark would know, but he didn't.

I said to my husband Scott, "See that really nice man over there? You have to find out who he is." But he didn't know him either.

I asked my friend Susan, "Do you know who that really nice man is?" She said, "No, not a clue." So she started calling him "that really nice man."

So periodically I would say to Scott, "I saw that really nice man," and he knew exactly who I was talking about.

I would ask Mark, "Did you ever find out who that really nice man's son is?" And he still said, "No."

This went on for years.

Then I met Lynda at Danbury Baseball and I still didn't know who her husband was. She could have said his name and I wouldn't have had a clue who that was.

Finally, one day Mark and Colin were playing their first Brewster High School game and I saw him there. I went over to Maria and asked, "Who is that really nice man?"

She answered, "That is Lynda Holler's husband, but why are you calling him that really nice man?"

That is when I went up to Lynda and said, "I have been calling your husband 'that really nice man' for years!"

I saw him out with the trach and the bandages on his fingers and he would still make a point of saying "Hi." That's just the way he was. When I found out he was sick he was in my prayers all the time. I kept him in my prayers because he was so special to a lot of people. I didn't know him like a lot of people, but he touched me because of the way he was.

I don't think you could meet anyone that would say, "I am not a big fan of Kenny Holler." Or if you did, you probably wouldn't be a big fan of that person!

Denise, Brewster Friend

***

I never heard anybody ever say anything close to negative about Kenny and in certain company if they did they would lose some teeth.

Kevin, Brewster Baseball Friend

50
Grace

Sharon: *Brewster Neighbor*

I don't really know when I first met Kenny. I tried to think back if there was some sort of an event we were at; I really don't remember. I think maybe it just started out as neighbors, seeing each other, waving. He would be driving by; I was probably walking. It started out as waving, then maybe eventually it turned to a greeting: a simple greeting, you know, "Hello. How are you?" Then eventually he would stop and we would chat a little bit. I don't remember a time that I was walking that he wouldn't pass by one way or the other. He was taking the boys out to practice or he would be going over to work on the field or something like that. And I looked forward to it, because when he wasn't driving by, I noticed that I didn't see him.

The thing that sticks in my mind most is when he left, when he drove off after a chat, I would think to myself, "What a truly nice man." Of course, I realized there was a health issue. I didn't know what that health issue was in the beginning, how it started or anything like that, but it didn't define him. He was just who he was.

Then, I remember at one point, when he was going through a difficult time, he passed by and we would chat about it. He would say that he was going to do what he had to do, and that it would be okay. Then he had to have some procedure done and he was waiting for test results. That was the first time that I sensed maybe some sadness in him, that maybe it was recurring, because he had always seemed so upbeat and always seemed so positive. Then I said, "You know Ken, you just have to keep fighting." He said, "Oh, absolutely! Absolutely! That's all I can do. We'll just wait, we'll see."

At one point, he couldn't speak, so it was just sort of a wave. That was probably the last time I saw him. Then I took notice of the fact that I'd be walking and I wouldn't see him drive by. Then I would notice that Lynda would be driving with the boys or Colin would be driving Tim. That's when I started to notice that maybe things weren't going so well.

The biggest thing I could say about Kenny is the grace with which he handled everything that was happening to him. I guess that would be my word, "Grace." It was clearly not good and he had been through so much already, but he just did his thing. You could tell how much he loved his boys, how much he enjoyed being part of their lives, and the activities, especially the baseball. I would hope that if I were going through something like that, I would handle it the same way. Wanting to fight it, but doing it with such grace.

***

There are people in our lives that for whatever reason touch us so we don't forget them.

Jack, FDNY Chief Special Operations Command

What gives somebody the will when he or she is feeling crappy, when he or she is looking like what people may consider crappy, to take the attitude of, "This is what I have always done. This is what I will continue to do." Where does that come from? It is easy to be selfish and close ourselves out when we are down and out, whether it be health or finances or things not going right in life. What I have mostly seen is people shutting themselves out. What I am trying to say is that I never saw Kenny like that. I am not saying that Kenny didn't go through that. I am assuming as a human being he had to go through that as part of the process, but that's not the guy I ever saw on the field. That's not the guy that I saw when we went to the pizzeria or the ice cream spot after the game. I knew he was struggling just to talk sometimes, but he said what he had to say. I felt bad to ask him to repeat something, but when he did, it was with the attitude of, "Here it is, you'll get it."

Robert, Brewster Baseball Friend

51
Outstanding
Glenn: *Brewster Neighbor*

When I think about Kenny, I go back to when I first met him, when Colin and Eric were in third grade. Now they are first year of college, so that is ten years.

I consider Kenny as one of three people that I have known that really "got" life. What I mean by that is they knew what was important and they knew not to get bogged down with work and all kinds of problems that really are insignificant in the grand scheme of things.

When he was in remission he was always still kind of concerned that it was going to come back. He didn't know how much time he had left on the planet. There was always a concern in his mind, yet he was always willing to talk about it and it kept everyone grounded.

I remember one day we were sitting out by our pool at the end of that third grade year. We had to write a letter to our kids that would be sealed in their time capsules and opened when they graduated high school. Kenny was in great shape and didn't have any active issues at that time. He said, "You know, it took me three days to write that letter. I had to push back on it a couple times. Glenn, I may not be here when that letter is delivered."

That always weighed on me. I remember telling him, "Ken, you know, I might not be here either. Who the heck knows?" But obviously he had more of a concern than me, because I didn't ever have cancer or any chronic illness. I never forgot that conversation with him and how emotional that was to think that we might not be here when our kids graduate from high school.

Of course he was an avid Yankee and Giants fan like I am. When the Yankees won the World Series and when the Giants won the Super Bowl, he took my son down to the parades with his family. His buddy, Pete, owned a restaurant named Suspenders along the parade route. He was always willing to do stuff for people; to have fun and take advantage of life.

When the friggin' cancer came back, how concerned we were! We were praying for the guy every night: "Whatever it's going to be, let it be. If he isn't going to get better, don't let him suffer. If he is going to get better, let's get him better."

I remember one of the last things he said to me before his voice went. I remember exactly where we were on our road. I stopped the car, he stopped his car. He said, "I can't believe this came back." I said, "Ya, I'm feeling for you man." He said, "Glenn, I'll be all right."

Kenny was a tough guy. He didn't back down from his illness; he tried to really battle it out as best he could. He took it till there was nothing left to give at the end and that's a good way to live. Flat out, just don't stop until it's over.

When he died, I got the call at work. Over the last couple days, we had known it was coming, but when I got the call, I realized how ironic it was that the three guys that I think "got" life the most were no longer with us, at least on this planet. I remember saying to my buddy John, "All the good guys are gone." He's an Irish guy too and I told him about the wake and we were cracking up. He said, "A good old Irish wake. Those are the best."

I love the guy. I miss Kenny and I wish he was here to see some of the stuff that has been going on with the kids, when they graduated from high school, went off to college, and now me shifting careers. He would have really enjoyed it. Whenever I see his kids, I see him in them. Colin clowning around and Timmy shooting hoops.

I think he is up there looking over us. When something falls into place that I think he would really care about, I think that he has had his hands in it, as crazy as that may sound. I'm hoping to get a new job and I really hope he has his hands in that! He would be happy if that happened for me. When I pray at night, I always pray to Kenny saying, "Hey, if you can pull a string up there for me and help me out with a new job," (or whatever the battle I am facing). "Do it!" but I'll add, "If you have to pull a string and not help your kids or something, don't do it. Take care of the kids first!" I don't know how it works up there, if there is a quota system.

And I tell him that I'll do the best I can with his kids down here. I'm always thinking about them and will always be here to give them advice. I keep the conversation going back and forth. I want to say that I think of him daily, certainly multiple times a week, if it isn't daily. That's saying a lot with all of the people that I have known. I can't even say that about relatives that have passed away.

***

When he was in remission, every single time I saw him, he would say his time frame of how long he was in remission, like: "It's almost a year!"

Maria, Brewster Baseball Friend

***

We all know that Glenn has been miserable in his job for so long, to the point that he got annoying. He complained for years, but Kenny is the only person in our life who was really not bothered by Glenn saying it again and again; he really cared and understood. Glenn always felt that Kenny really "got it." Even if Glenn had said it ten trillion times, Kenny acted like he was hearing it the first time. It is a rare person that can make you feel that they really care and value what you are going through.

JoAnn, Brewster Neighbor, Glenn's Wife

52
Humble
Jean: _St. Lawrence O'Toole Friend_

The first time I remember seeing Kenny was at the 9:30 Mass at St. Lawrence. I noticed a gentleman sitting at the very end of our pew who had bandages on his face and I thought, "Wow, he is really very courageous to come to church." We feel very vulnerable when we have something noticeable about us. We feel like people are watching us. I thought, "He must have faith to come to church through all that." Then Father Doughty came over and spoke briefly to him, so I thought, "That's wonderful that Father knows him and knows of his challenges and was smiling and welcoming to him." I felt good about that.

Then I suppose, I began to notice his family, the boys especially as they started to be altar servers. But the first time that I really communicated with Kenny was probably when we were doing the new church presentations with Father McKeon. Lynda and Kenny came into the auditorium where a bunch of us were fielding questions and explaining things. I noticed Lynda, particularly, because she was bright and upbeat and interested and happy. Kenny was happy to be by her—as simple as that. He didn't say much. He had a few questions, but he listened. That was my first encounter with him.

Once Kenny was too drained from the treatments and could no longer go to church, the only times that I saw him was when I went to their home. I was so appreciative that Kenny and Lynda allowed me into their home when he was really suffering and they all were really struggling. That was an amazing gift. I felt very privileged. I know how it is to not feel well. We have limits to how much we can expose ourselves. So that was a very precious time.

It did create a funny situation for me, however. You see, I am hard of hearing. I have to watch people when they talk. And Kenny's speech was so muddled by that time that I'd be looking at him wondering, "What is he saying?" I knew he was talking to me very earnestly, but I'd look at Lynda from time to time as if to say, "Translate, please!"

From the time I knew him, Kenny was always sick. If he wasn't actually in therapy, he was struggling with the consequences of the last illness and learning how to live with the latest deprivation. So I never knew him as an athlete or a vibrant person, still I am just in awe that he was so present when he was present and so willing to be part of things as best he could. He didn't have to be a great contributor. He didn't have to be a sporty, healthy, robust guy. He was happy to be present. It showed his great love for life and his appreciation for others. That was beautiful.

When we think about Kenny as a gift from God and we think of this process of reflecting on him, it is something like Lectio Divina (praying by meditating on Scripture—the Word of God), in that we are looking to see, to discover, all that is there. And being created by God and being faithful to God, there is so much to discover. We are all part of the Body of Christ, so the more we look and study Kenny, the more we learn about ourselves and about God.

The thing about faith is, we should have faith all the time, in good times and in bad, in sickness and in health, constantly have it in our lives. Some people give up on God when things get tough, others don't even think to pray to Him unless they need help. Other people preach it, but don't live it.

Camille, Astoria Friend

53
Brave
Michele: Brewster Friend

It is great that Lynda is doing this because I think it will carry on that tradition of reaching out and impacting other lives. Kenny impacted a lot of lives; this book will impact a lot of lives. It will multiply.

Our boys ran both cross country and track and played soccer together. Kenny and Lynda were fixtures among the parents, just like us. We'd see them on fields and pass the time at games, but it was when our family was impacted by illness that we really came to know Kenny and Lynda.

Greg's stepmom contracted ALS and it had gotten to the point where they were talking about, "Should we do a feeding tube? Should we do a trach? Should we do a breathing machine?" This was the decision time. I recalled having a conversation with Kenny on the field at a track meet; he had just gotten the trach, but he took everything in stride, so it didn't stop him from attending any sports events. When I was talking about it with Greg and his family, I said, "Well, we were on the field. He was participating. He was active. He was out and seemed to have a good quality of life. Let's talk to him about it."

Kenny and Lynda agreed, so we arranged a conference call when Greg's parents were at our house. Phyllis, at that point, had completely lost speech, so she was working with a keypad and app that would read what she typed. There were times when it was hard for us to understand Ken with the speaker phone and Lynda would repeat what he had said, but basically it was a very candid conversation. I was impressed with the openness and his ability to take the conversation in stride.

I didn't know that he was on the feeding tube at the time, but as a result of that conversation, we decided that we were going to go with the feeding tube and stay as non-invasive as possible in terms of breathing for as long as we could. That bought Phyllis months of a quality of life that she might not have had. That was huge.

It's funny; we know a lot of people in the community, but that conversation gave us an intimacy with Kenny and Lynda that we didn't have before and we wouldn't have had otherwise. We were so grateful. We were so grateful, because we didn't have access to that kind of information. If we are only talking to doctors, we are not getting the perspective of those that are living through it and dealing with it. When our paths crossed like that, it had a huge impact on the decisions that we made as a family and ultimately Phyllis' quality of life.

One thing stands out in my mind from the Memorial Service for Kenny when they dedicated the tree. Mike said in his speech, "Kenny was a firefighter and he knew the difference between a life and death situation and a Little League baseball game." I thought, "Absolutely, absolutely!"

That is something that is so important, so one word I would choose for Kenny is "Perspective." Being able to cope with what we are dealt and keeping it in perspective. He seemed to just take everything in stride. Some days were hard; some days not so hard, but when he could go to games, he would go to games and be present. Being able to pass that perspective on was an important part of the example he set. You could see him. He didn't have to say anything. He was there, he dealt with it.

But ultimately I want to choose the word "Brave." I'll take that, because not only was he brave with all of the other aspects: firefighters are brave, parents are brave, but I think the most brave is being a very capable person, that was always taking care of other people, becoming helpless, having to be taken care of, and not feeling that sense of control. That takes a lot of bravery. To talk about it and cope with it and deal with it and take it in stride and demonstrate to his kids that that is what bravery is really about: when we don't feel like walking up a flight of stairs, but we do it. When we aren't hungry, but we know we have to take in sustenance and we do it.

If I had to choose a word for Lynda: "Grace." That is the word, because she to me is the embodiment of grace. When I see her in situations, like that memorial service… the Holy Spirit was in her and she was orchestrating and channeling a powerful presence, helping everybody to move forward and to plant a tree, to start something positive. We never know what it is all about and what the purpose is and why the paths cross, but I feel very, very fortunate that our families have crossed paths.

***

Just because someone is battling a disease, do we automatically label them as courageous? I don't think that always applies. It is our natural instinct to stay alive, so people are going to do that naturally. Not necessarily in a courageous way, more in a life-preserving type of way. When you have a desire to go on despite your suffering and you want to be there for others, that becomes courageous. Without courage we might just give up if it gets too hard.

Christine, Massage Therapist

54
Invictus

Max: *Tim's Teammate, Age 15*

The one word that I think would best describe Mr. Holler as a human being is "Invictus." It is Latin for indomitable, indestructible. He seemed to be the sort of person that could take any situation, keep a level head on him, and keep going.

When someone carries themselves the way that Mr. Holler did, it definitely changes the people around him for the better. He had a trach and other things to be able to breathe and talk and eat and do things that we take for granted, yet he never stopped smiling. Never.

Mr. Holler seemed to have this magical ability to brighten up a day no matter what he was going through. If we were having a bad day and we bumped into him, we could take our minds off what we were dealing with and stop worrying so much. Even after his passing, he still seems to be doing that. I almost hear his voice...

That's why it doesn't seem like the disease won. I feel that he took more power away from the disease, than the disease took from him. He had a very strong will and that was evident; look him in the eyes and you could see a fire constantly burning. He'd always find something to be positive about. He didn't let it control him. Like my mom said earlier, "He had cancer, cancer did not have him." What he was struggling with, it did not own him. He took it by the reins until the very end and that is why he was unbreakable.

That is why "Invictus" is my chosen word to describe him. You could see the iron fibers in his will. He was a man that was truly impressive. I live to be like him. That would be an honor.

***

Many athletes at cross country meets are upset because they have to run a race; running cross country is exhausting and painful. The courses are long and challenging; every course is different; it is a fall sport and the weather is usually uncomfortable—either too hot or too cold. I too was upset before my races. I think back now and consider how my fellow healthy athletes and I were upset that we had to run a race, but Kenny was going through some very tough stuff, far worse than running a cross country course, yet he was always happy and pushing through his challenges.

Chris, Colin's Friend, Age 18

55
Memorial Day Community BBQ

Let's talk about the park.

Kenny was always the most enthusiastic. Always. He would call, "What can I do? What can I bring? I'll get the worms." He always volunteered to bring the charcoal, get the grill started, get down there early to set up, grab the tables, BBQ, do all the work. He made it so much fun for everybody and I don't know if everybody really appreciated or knew how much work he did to get it together. My kids still talk about it.

Denise, Brewster Friend

***

Another example of Kenny's selflessness is Memorial Day. I don't remember the year. There must have been 10-15 families that gathered for a picnic, food, fishing, talk, tall tales, etc. Kenny was flipping burgers and roasting hot dogs and yet not one of them were meant to cross his lips. It was hot and I wandered over to ask if I could help. This was his response, "Ellen, if you don't mind taking over for a few minutes, so I can have an Ensure, this grilling is sure making me hungry." Right then and there it hit me that this man was amazing. An amazing friend to all he met.

Ellen, Brewster Friend

***

A big memory I have is of Kenny and me standing at the barbeque, food was being cooked, yada, yada. Ken and I were talking, he was getting one of his shakes to drink, and for the first time I said something to him about not being able to eat.

I said, "Do you mind me asking? Is it hard for you to be here, because I can't wait to sink my teeth into a cheeseburger." He said, "Susan, you have no idea. Day to day I can handle it because I don't have to put myself in a position to focus on food, but these big gatherings are difficult for me. I would love to be digging in to all the great things that are here to eat, but I can't." Then he added, "But it's okay." He still didn't pity himself. He didn't approach it as though somebody should feel sorry for him. It was just who he was and it was very natural.

Susan, Brewster Neighbor

Joy is different than happiness. Happiness is a feeling from and in the body. Joy is more. Joy is from and in the soul. I am sure that Kenny wasn't always very happy about his circumstances in life, but I believe he was always joyful, as strange as that seems. I think of Kenny cooking the food that he couldn't eat at that barbecue. I think he wasn't happy that he couldn't eat it, but it brought him joy to cook for the others. I think he realized that he was leaving a mark on the world no matter what, through his love for family and friends. I think he realized that he was going to be with his God sooner than most of the people around him. I think he found joy in all of that stuff. Outwardly happy most times, inwardly joyful all the time: this is the way I want to remember Kenny Holler.

Charlotte, Brewster Friend

***

It was such a powerful thing when Kenny would hang the flag at our community BBQs on Memorial Day weekend. It was so great to know someone who was so patriotic and so faithful to God. I don't think you can be one and not the other. It always made me think about his dedication to our country and his service to our country as a firefighter. I get the same feeling anytime I pull into their driveway and see the flag and fireman's coat. Kenny was so proud to be part of this country; he so loved the country and loved people.

Denise, Brewster Friend

56
Genuine

Tommy: *Golf Partner, FDNY Fireman*

I never worked with Kenny in the firehouse and I didn't know him when he was still an active fireman. I met him through Mac. I got invited to play golf with Mac, Mike, and Kenny. I am sure everybody knows that Kenny had quite a special place in his heart for fellow firemen, and the cast of characters that we can be at times, so right off the bat we got along well and became friends through playing golf.

The thing that I remember most about being on the golf course with Kenny was it was never about golf. He would just hit the ball and forget about it and we would talk, all over the place on different tangents—talking about everything except golf. He would always, always, always stop, take in the beauty around him and be thankful for every day.

He told me that before he was married to Lynda, firemen were regular houseguests at his apartment. Kenny was always the guy taking everybody in, at different points in their lives, in different situations, getting them back on their feet.

He told me one time, a guy called him up early in the morning, "Kenny, Kenny, can I come over? I have to talk to you." So Kenny said, "Sure, sure, come over." The guy said, "Do you have any beers in the house?" Kenny answered, "I might have one or two in the frig." So the guy said, "Don't worry, I'll pick up a twelve-pack." The guy shows up at the apartment; Kenny is fixing him breakfast of course, and the guy puts the twelve-pack on the table and starts popping open beers. After the hellos, Kenny asks, "What is the problem?" The guy said, "Kenny, Kenny," and he opens up another beer, "I think I have a drinking problem!" Kenny and I laughed about that. Having beer for breakfast, I guess he did have an issue there!

Kenny would take the shirt off his back for others. He never spoke about it. You only heard about all the things that Kenny did from other people.

One of the firemen at Kenny's funeral told me a story. He said that he went into Suspenders and Kenny was bartending; he had never met Kenny before. He was watching the game and Kenny was going to give him another drink. He said, "No, no, I have to go. I don't have any more money." Kenny reached right in his pocket and gave him forty bucks, without even knowing the guy. The guy said, "You've gotta be kidding me, you don't even know who I am. How can you trust me to give me money?" Kenny said, "You're a fireman. That's good enough for me."

That's the way he felt from his heart. I'm sure there's a million stories out there that Lynda isn't aware of, nor am I, but that's the way he lived his life.

I helped Lynda and Kenny once or twice by driving them back and forth to the doctor. He never complained about how he felt. If he was uncomfortable, he kept it to himself. He was good at keeping that veil, just to enjoy the day and he didn't want to ruin anyone else's day.

I only saw Kenny get angry one time. He was upset about someone that was a chronic complainer. He was always complaining about little things that everybody has in their daily life: bills or shopping or this or that. Kenny just felt he wasn't living his life, enjoying his life.

The biggest honor for myself, was to be considered a friend by Kenny. I live right down the road, so I am always driving by the house and I always bless myself on the way by as I see his fireman's jacket out there. God bless you brother.

***

I view people who complain differently because of Kenny. When people complain about miniscule things, I think of him and what he went through and think, "There is a guy that didn't complain." I wish other people would be like him.

Dan, Physician's Assistant, Neighbor

57
Optimistic
Lisa: Tommy's Wife

As a dental hygienist, I think I am more keenly aware of how painful and uncomfortable everyday life was for Kenny. Oral is one of the most painful types of cancer. Radiation burns the salivary glands, sometimes permanently, causing a lack of saliva flow and sores. Saliva helps heal our mouth, so when it is missing, it takes longer for sores and surgeries to heal. Sometimes the saliva gets very thick and patients have to spit or swab it out with gauze or paper towels. They may drool uncontrollably. This is all very anti-social behavior, making patients feel very uncomfortable around other people.

I would tell Tom, because this was my area of expertise, that Kenny's cancer is a billion times more painful than he even thought it was. Just imagine the pain when you have a small sore in your mouth and multiply that times one hundred. Consider how it affects your speech and your swallowing. Kenny was so amazing, in that even with all the pain and suffering that he was going through, he was always so sweet and so kind, not angry, not bitter.

When I think about Kenny, I think about how my husband's whole persona changed after spending time with him. Tom, you might be surprised to know, tends to see the glass half-empty and can be very pessimistic. We are childhood sweethearts and we have fought about this forever, because although I had a very difficult childhood, I was a half-full person. So, I always tried to look at the positive, but he didn't. The only time that I ever noticed his personality change was after he spent the day with Kenny. He would say, "Oh Lisa, you wouldn't believe Kenny. He is in so much pain and he will say, 'What a blue sky! What a beautiful day! Oh, I love the smell of spring! Isn't this great!'"

In contrast, they knew other men that tended to be very negative also. Tommy would come home and say to me, "How is it that these other guys complain from the moment they arrive to the moment they leave? 'Oh, this is too much money! This is too much this! This is too much that!'" Kenny was so optimistic and appreciated life and everyone in his life more than most people do.

So, in that way, it reminds me of my own father. When he had cancer he said that the happiest days of his life were the days that followed his diagnosis. For that same reason: food tasted better, the sky looked bluer, everything was just clearer, crisper, and wonderful. What I think Tom learned, and then translated to me from Kenny, was to focus on all those wonderful, good things. Towards the end I am sure it was very hard, extremely hard for Kenny, but he was always able to stay positive and focus on the good—the good of everybody.

I saw him at a football game and he was so frail. He was cold and I said, "Kenny, you should go home. It's too cold." He said, "I know, I might have to." He never complained and after living with someone who tends to complain a lot, it was refreshing. It really was.

Kenny definitely impacted Tom. He is aware of it now, but I don't know if he is as aware of it as I am. Tom is much more optimistic now; he's more positive. He'll stop himself when he gets cranky and starts to say something negative and the only person that I can say was responsible for that is Kenny.

Kenny suffered more than any person I have ever seen before my eyes.

Claire, Lynda's Queens Friend

58
Honor
Tara: Palliative Care Home Care Nurse

I met Ken in 2012 when he was pretty much at the end stages of his illness. I had just transitioned into palliative care and it is a different world from hospice where I had worked before. So when I came in to their home, my thought was, "This is a very sick man," and speaking honestly, I didn't think he was going to be around very long. He was actually the turning point that made me see that just because a person might have all these things going on and look a certain way, it doesn't mean it is going to follow that path. Ken's desire and his fight were truly amazing.

When I think about the hours that I spent with him, half of it was clinical, but the other half I just enjoyed being in his presence and talking with him—in his own way of talking. Once he had the trach, it was very hard for him to get his words out, his thoughts across, but I got him. I enjoyed finding time to hear about who he was, not just the illness. His love for his kids, his determination to still go to their ball games... How he was a fireman, a dad, a coach, involved in the church... It was really nice. Like I said, that was a turning point for me.

Kenny had the trach and recurring wounds surrounding it. And the suctioning, the constant suctioning from the build-up of secretions consumed him. I think that played a lot into depression for him. Not the fact that he had the trach; I don't think that bothered him one bit, because he would tie the scarf around it and want to get up and go. It was unfortunately the need to be attached to the home, because of all the equipment he required to maintain the trach and keep it clean. If he was up eighteen hours a day, I think his care consumed about fifteen or sixteen of those hours, without exaggeration. He had very little free time, but he still managed to maintain a positive spirit until the end.

Aside from the trach, he had the peg, a tube connected directly to his stomach for feeding. That's how he got his nutrition. So, if he wasn't suctioning or using the nebulizer, he was feeding himself through the tube. How independent he was! Fiercely independent and you don't see that very much. That said a lot about his spirit and his character. He got little infections in the skin around his peg and he had to have it changed once or twice. Every now and again his mood would be down when I was there, but very few times I saw him down and feeling sorry for himself.

Not sleeping... he couldn't sleep because of the secretions. He would get a half hour to an hour of sleep before he would wake up.

The big devices... his home was transformed into a hospital, between the poles, the pumps, the tubes, and that ungodly humidification device. They couldn't tolerate the sound of that thing; it was like having a generator in the living room. It made it impossible for Lynda and the boys to hang out with Ken, so they MacGyvered a better device. That's what you do in the home. You take what you have and you make it work.

And his nails... Ohhh, his nails! His fingernails, his toenails, so many of them removed, needing to be cared for and bandaged, and the polish… We used to do manicure and pedicure time at the end of our visits! The polish was to prevent fungal growth, but it seemed like just another burden to Lynda and Ken. I remember the first time I wanted to do it he said, "No," but by that time we had a good rapport, so we just made a joke out of it. I enjoyed seeing him laugh. That's one of the best parts of my job, helping distract my patients from what is going on and helping them focus on living and enjoying their time.

He was in and out of the hospital a lot throughout the time I knew him. After one of the later admissions, I noticed that his mood was down a little bit. The interactions with his sons, I saw they were distancing. After Ken died, Lynda told me that she realized that they had started mourning him while he was still alive, although they didn't realize it at the time. They were losing parts of him little by little. Lynda and the boys were going through that process and it is one hundred percent normal. It made that transition easier for them.

I prayed for Ken and I also prayed with him. I knew from the start that they were very strong with their faith. I am a firm believer in faith myself and I believe that the power of prayer is very strong. There is some kind of peace that people find in prayer. When people are seriously ill and haven't gone to church for many years or when they reflect on their lives, there is always a time when people ask for forgiveness, for repentance, for peace.

We offer chaplain services under palliative care. I often make calls to people's parishes for them. I won't bring it up when I first meet someone. I look around and I try to get a bond established before I speak to people about that. It's touchy for some people, but it is an important part of my job. That's how I feel and if I can make the transition easier for my patients and my families, then I have done my job.

Ken pops into my mind frequently. If I drive past their road, I'll remember the fireman's coat and the American flag that I saw when I pulled in their driveway. If I meet a young man or a young woman who has a trach or has trouble with secretions, I will flash back. Sometimes I will use Ken as an inspiration without using names.

Every case that I go on is an honor, and I was truly blessed and grateful that Ken, Lynda, and the boys let me serve them for as long as they did. I don't remember every case, it is just impossible, but there are certain cases that I just form a bond with and it is almost instantaneous. Ken will be in my heart forever, as well as Lynda and the kids. Always.

***

The fact that not once did I see him slow down or stop, it almost seems like he was just taking whatever diseases he was struggling with and telling them, "Listen here! I will go when I am good and ready! Until then, you sit yourself down."

Max, Tim's Teammate, Age 15

59
Talking

Marty: *Lake George Friend*

I met Kenny about twelve years ago. I was introduced to him by Lorraine, Shorty, and Steve. He seemed to be a very, very nice person. He would always say, "Marty, can I help you? Can I get something for you?"

There are some people that when you meet them you know that you want to see them again. Then there are people that you meet, that you think, "Oh, I hope I don't see that person again!" Kenny was the kind of guy you wanted to see, because he was full of spirit. He was happy. He was happy with the job he had. He was happy coming up here to Lake George with all of us together and sharing like we always do. That's what sticks out in my mind. I didn't know him for a long time, but in the time that I did, he had an impact on me.

I used to tell Kenny that I go to the dock where I live in Port Washington and I see veterans there. I welcome them and buy them coffee. One day, we were up here playing the horses and he said, "Marty, Dock Master is running today." So we all put a few dollars on this horse for a long shot and the freakin' horse won! We all made money! He was all excited. We were all excited. Dock Master! I still remember that day that he gave us the tip. I don't remember everything, but that is one of the things.

Last year I was doing a painting for everybody, so they would have a nice scenic view of Lake George after we leave. When I finished it, I thought it came out really nice. I dedicated the painting to Kenny.

This is life. I couldn't change anything, but I was Kenny's friend up here in Lake George.

***

I don't know why I continue to think about Kenny other than the fact that I believe we are all connected. We still are. He was a connecting principal for some reason. It's strange because although he was a special man to me, he was also just Kenny, just a regular guy.

Carol, Auto Repair Shop Office Manager

60
Tapestry
Cheryl: *Lynda's Cousin*

I think what hit me the most is every time I saw Kenny, the first words out of his mouth were, "How are you doing? How are your parents doing?" He was always so much more concerned that my parents were in poor health. His health came up further down the conversation and even when I tried to bring it up he would always go back to, "Did your dad go to that doctor? He was going to that doctor, right?"

Part of it might have been avoiding talking about himself, but I never got that impression. I got the impression that he truly remembered what I said last time, that Dad was going to get this test or going to that doctor, and he truly wanted to know what was going on. He was just very concerned, empathetic. And the fact was, he was going through what in my mind was much worse than what they were going through.

The kids prayed for Kenny. Jillian is sensitive to other people's feelings and when we came back from Kenny's funeral, she decided that she wanted to pray for him. She prayed that he was happy there and that he was okay.

With my husband Joe being sick, I think of Kenny more now, more of a guardian angel kind of role. There are symbols that I see that cause me to think of him.

Right after Jillian's eye surgery earlier this year, she insisted that she wanted to go for a walk. I said, "Jillian, You can't walk, you can't see." My sister Chris was visiting. So, we put Jillian in the stroller and I said, "We'll push you." We went down the road and we were talking about Kenny, because the St. Lawrence O'Toole CYO had decided to establish a scholarship in his name. I was telling Chris about it and I remember seeing in the distance a mylar balloon coming our way. I didn't think much of it; we were caught up in the conversation. The next thing we knew this mylar balloon was coming directly for us. And it continued to come directly for us and it went right to Jillian. It was a heart balloon. I thought it had to be from Kenny. It went right to her and we couldn't have avoided it if we tried.

I had an admiration for Kenny that he could just continue to plug away, continue to do it, and that his faith didn't waiver, because mine would.

One time when we were going through the infertility and miscarriages and stuff, I was crying at work. One of the chaplains came by and he said, "You don't have to tell me what is wrong. I don't want to know, but do you want me to pray?" I said, "Of course you can pray. I'll tell you what's wrong." And I told him.

I couldn't understand it then, it is all in retrospect that we get it, but he told me that life is like a tapestry. On one side, we see all these knots and strands, this horrible jumble of stuff. It doesn't look like anything. It is when we turn it over and are able to view it from the other side that it makes total sense. My tapestry makes sense to me now. I guess it's not at this point, and it's probably not in this life, that the whole tapestry of Kenny will be revealed.

We started the CYO college scholarship in Kenny's honor, to carry on what he is all about. The money isn't going to pay for all of college, but we hope the fact that they won the award can spark something in our young people. Hopefully the kids we select each year can keep that spark going, keep them interested in doing things to help others. That was the purpose in it.

Tim, Brewster Coaching Friend

61
Fighting-Irish
Karen: Nurse, Head and Neck Floor, MSKCC

I first met Kenny when I was on nursing orientation in August 2013; I was brand new. I remember going into his room. He was always reading his newspaper and listening to his little transistor radio in the morning. We would chit chat. We were managing his pain at that point. I would ask him, "What can we do? How is the pain?" If my beeper would go off, he would say, "Karen, don't worry about me. Give me the pain medicine, then go take care of that patient. They need you more than I do."

I was there for Kenny's first Code Red bleeding incident. All of a sudden, out of nowhere, he started bleeding. We all ran in, everyone had a position: someone was suctioning, someone was manning the IV fluids, and once the head and neck doctors came in, we were able to stop the bleed in the room. Kenny was so calm. He knew us all so well and he knew we would be able to take care of it. He wasn't scared, because we weren't scared. He was just like, "Ok, we fixed that." I wasn't there for the second one, the last Code Red, where he had to go across the street.

We were getting to know each other and one day he said that I looked upset, that he could tell that something was wrong. I told him, "My mom is sick too and I am trying to take care of her." I explained that she was diagnosed with brain cancer and she was really bad. He said, "Oh, I'm so sorry. I am going to say prayers for her."

I was running around; I was still on orientation so my head was spinning, because I was trying to learn and my preceptor was on top of me making sure that I was doing the right things. Kenny went downstairs and when he came back up he said, "I just said a prayer for your mom downstairs in the chapel." That touched my heart; I cried. He was sick in the hospital and needed us to be taking care of him, yet he was thinking about me, thinking about my situation, thinking about my mother, and he went downstairs to say a prayer.

He didn't have that long of a stay that time. He left, but soon after he dropped off a package. He gave me a St. Peregrine statue, the patron saint of cancer, and he wrote a note saying: "Thinking of you. This is for your mom. Wishing you well and hopefully she is doing well too."

A few months later, he was back and asked, "How is your mom? What is going on?" The cancer was coming back for him and he was getting worse. When my mother died I told Kenny and we cried together. He told me that I was doing such a good thing being a nurse here, that my mother was living through me, as I take care of everyone else.

It was hard, but I look at it that way too. I meet so many different family members and I can help in a way that I wasn't able to help my mom. I can feel what the family members are going through. If my mom hadn't had cancer, I wouldn't have had that perspective. It's interesting, because it helps me; it helps me grieve, because I am able to help others that are grieving and are where I was.

When I see someone do an act of goodness that just comes out of nowhere, that is when

I think of Kenny. And if I see a patient that is really upset or having a bad day, because of Kenny, I go down to the fifteenth floor, where we can get a little cheer-up balloon or write a sign. If I can give them a more positive experience and show that we are their cheerleaders, I'll do it. I'll write, "You Rock!" posters and things like that. That is something that Kenny would have done.

I pray for my patients too. I have gone down to the chapel and said prayers. If I can tell that patients are religious and they pray, I will tell them, "I am going to say a prayer for you tonight before I go to bed. You're going to be in my prayers." They'll always say, "Thank you;" then when I come in the next day they will always ask, "Did you say a prayer for me last night?" I will say, "I did! You thought I would forget, but I didn't! I said my prayers for you."

I feel that the whole time Kenny's disease progressed, he still was helping. We want our patients to feel like we felt. I feel like the spirit of him is still here. He shines through all of us in the way that he touched us, and then we spread it to everyone else.

***

I believe in the wisdom of God and when we cling to the things that cause our suffering here, we perpetuate our own suffering. If we can let those things go, we can find God's freedom.

Cyndi, Accountant

62
Devotion
Lynda

It was probably about five months before Kenny died; he was an inpatient at Sloan. A Code Red was called because he began bleeding from his voice box area. If it had been an artery, it could have been fatal. Unchecked, he could have bled to death. Immediately, his room was filled with doctors, nurses, the medical team needed to save his life. They pulled his bed away from the wall and surrounded him on all sides, doing what they were trained to do.

I wasn't there. I was told about it later by the doctors and by Kenny. He explained that in the frantic happenings all around him, he just stayed focused. Focused on the foot of his bed where Mary stood with the rest of the team. He kept his eyes on our Blessed Mother and prayed to her, asking for her intercession to her Son. Asking her to ask Jesus to save him. He could have asked Jesus directly, but it was Mary that came to him, that comforted him, like his own mother Mary would have done if she could. He knew that our Mother of Compassion loved him as her own son and it was her divine presence with Sloan's best that saved him that day, that bought him more time, that granted him life.

***

I wondered, "How do people, when they are faced with a no-hope situation, how do they go on?" Lynda told me that they always had hope, even if they didn't know what they were hoping for. They didn't know where life was leading them, but they still stayed hopeful. By having faith they had hope. My sister also is very religious and she tells me the same thing. She says that you have to have faith to realize the hope.

Linda, Astoria Friend

63
Healer

Tim: *Kenny's Cousin, FDNY Lieutenant*

About Kenny, we could write novels, all of us. The thing that struck me the most after I talked to Lynn was that she asked me to come up with one word that would describe Kenny. I thought about it for days and I wasn't sure. First I thought of "brave" for he was certainly brave. All the good words, all good things, but then one word just stuck in my head and I couldn't get it out. And it was, as ironic as it seems, the word "Healer." The reason that I consider Kenny a healer is that everybody needs some form of healing: physical, mental, emotional, spiritual; everyone in this world has something going on, all the time. Whenever you saw Kenny, were in his presence, and then he left, you felt better. You were smiling inside and out.

Somehow, no matter how bad things were, something could blow up at work and he'd say, "Hey, we'll get this done. Four hours from now we'll be back here and everything will be fine."

It was just so enjoyable to see someone with such challenges go on and lead a normal life. He never said, "Poor me," never made excuses, never needed a break—he just participated, no matter what the situation was. He participated as if he had nothing wrong with him. And boy, he had all of the potential excuses that he would need, if he ever wanted to use them, but he never would.

He was a great family man and obviously, one of the funniest people anyone had ever met. I guess those were fundamentals that he learned early from his dad.

One Saturday, when we were kids, we were waiting at our house in Rosedale, Queens for Uncle Rod, Aunt Mamie, Gerard, and Kenny to come. Kenny being close in age, I just couldn't wait to see him. They all showed up and Uncle Rod came through the door and said, "Sorry, Kenny couldn't come, he was busy, but I brought this other guy." The other guy was a mannequin's head that Rod got from a window display at work and put over one of his coats. Kenny was hidden underneath, walking around, like he was the mannequin. I was thinking, "Who is this guy?!" I was only a little kid. I will never forget, like it was yesterday, how much we laughed when Kenny came out from underneath!

Kenny was just easy in life. He didn't look for any problems. They say that the difference between the words "untied" and "united" are where you place the "i;" and he was definitely a *uniter*. He brought people together. His fun in life, that I saw, was making other people happy. Most people go through life and they want their piece of the pie. He always made sure that other people got their piece. When we would go to visit them, he couldn't even eat, and he would say, "I've got this cake from this great bakery, just wait until you taste it." He wasn't even eating, but you could see that he was *tasting* it with you. Or he would be *eating* a meal with you or *drinking* a beer with you. Some of the things that he really enjoyed he wasn't able to do anymore, but he still enjoyed them, by watching you enjoy them.

I think of him all of the time, for simple reasons. Kenny gave me a vise. I took it and of course, I shined it, painted it red, and it is on my workbench, so every day I see it. A friend, Jack Kelly, gave me a door stop and I think of him every day. I have realized how important it is to have these simple little reminders in our lives.

Something Kenny would say is, "You have to go out and make it happen. Life isn't going to come to you. You have to go create great memories." That made him just simply enjoyable to be around. That's the best way to put it. When we were at work and we saw his car pull up, everybody would start grinning. Everyone. I don't know how he was able to pull it off. He would collect frogs in coolers and bring them back to Astoria to put in the pool table pockets and stuff like that. He always had something funny going on.

He was a man's man. I had never worked with him in the Fire Department before he came to Special Operation Command (SOC) on light duty after his first surgeries and radiation treatments were completed. As the headquarters for all of the FDNY rescue and special units, days were completely unpredictable and the pressure could be overwhelming. I never realized how competent he was at paperwork, because he wasn't really a college student. I knew he could do the firematics part of it, but when it came to doing his desk job and all of the things that were associated with that place: paperwork, phones, staffing, juggling at least three things at the same time, he was a pro. I was proud of him. He had a little trouble speaking, but he still was able to do it and hold down the job. He loved coming to work. He had all of the excuses in the world to stay home, but he loved to come to work.

One day at SOC, there was a bad collapse in Brooklyn and Kenny was on the desk. So he had to call home to get Chief Raymond Downey to come in; it was really important. His wife, Rosalie, answered. Kenny was trying to tell Rosie that Ray has to get in there first hand and Rosie kept asking, "Kenny, how are your two kids?" And you could hear Ray in the background, "Rosie, give me the phone!" And she'd be saying, "Wait, I need to find out how Kenny's boys are doing." Ray would get on the phone and say, "Where do I have to go Kenny?" Downey would come in the next day and shake his head and say, "Rosie is tough when she talks to you Kenny, she loves talking to you and I can't get the phone away from her." Ray thought the world of him too and Ray of course, had a very high standard.

One time we took Marie's kids to Madison Square Garden for a game and we lost one of them. Kenny said, "Wow, what are we going to tell Marie?" Those were his first words. I said, "What are *we* going to tell Marie!" I can't remember which kid it was, he had just walked away from us for a little bit. My heart almost stopped, but we had a couple of good laughs—after we found him! After that, I never let go of his hand the whole time we were there at the Garden.

It always worked out when you were with Kenny. No matter what you did, things always worked out.

No matter where I went, people would say, "How is Kenny? What's he doing? How is he doing? We miss him. We miss him." I guess that was the most common thing that I heard, was people saying that they missed him, because he was their therapist. People would go to work and he would come and put a banana in their pocket or something like that and right away they would say, "You know, you are right. These crazy phones, it doesn't matter. It is more important to be happy and calm."

Does he inspire me? Well, anyone that can smile against all of the odds is an inspiration. I think of the simple things that used to make him so happy, like just standing at the side of the grill, flipping burgers, for us. He'd say, "I got this one perfect for you! Go get a cold beer and you're going to love it. I'll make it medium in the middle." It was like he was our personal chef.

He was at our service no matter what we were doing. Like I said numerous times, he enjoyed a good time, but he made sure that no one was left out of the good time. No matter where we were. Even if it was a kid standing off in the distance, he would go over there and tickle them or something.

We had a Christening at my house and we had, maybe a hundred people. All of a sudden I looked and everyone was on our deck. I said to myself, "Oh my God, the deck is going to collapse!" I said, "What are you all doing up here?" They said that my young daughter Kristin was telling everybody that we said to get off the grass. Kenny had told her to tell everyone that. So, after I wrung his neck, everybody returned to the lawn and the deck didn't fall off the house. Then the next day, I got in my car and the windshield wipers were on, the radio was blasting, and he got me back. He didn't leave without getting the last laugh.

Even when Kenny was very sick, he didn't carry himself as a sick man and to some degree, I guess I didn't consider him sick. I didn't think of him that way. He just performed: this is my job; this is my life; this is my role as a husband, a father, a neighbor, a friend, a cousin, an employee of the Fire Department.

I remember when I went to see him at Sloan one day. He couldn't speak and he had a white board. When I walked in—I think of this every single day of my life—he took the white board and wrote, "Tim I love you!" with a big exclamation point. I almost started crying, really. The next time that I came in, he wrote, "Tim you are the best!" To hear that from him meant a lot, because he had such high standards. We were close and will always be close. What I try to tell people is to hold fast, because one day we will all be called home. I am sure he will have the barbeque going when we meet again.

He'll be smiling. The first thing people thought of when they thought of Kenny was his smile. Even though he had so many surgeries and his face had changed, he'd still smile. His eyes and his smile were still beautiful. And that is how I will always remember him—as a smiler.

Like I began, the single word that best describes Kenny is "healer". Wherever he went, people felt healed to some degree. And of course, he was brave and courageous and above all, through it all, he followed Christ. He never gave up on Christ, he never gave up on his faith. When he had all the reasons in the world to say "oh poor me", he never did. He will be sainted and hopefully he will work on getting us there to meet him.

I remember his mother, Aunt Mamie, saying to me, that when Kenny was a little past his mid-thirties, he had told her that if God was to take him tomorrow, he had lived. He had no regrets and had gotten so much out of his life, and was so content, that he would not feel cheated if it was cut short. Little did he know that shortly after that he would meet Lynda and have these beautiful kids, have a wonderful family and would make sure that he lived another whole wonderful life as a family man. He did that to the nth degree. Well done Ken.

There is that one line in the movie It's a Wonderful Life, *"To my brother George, the richest man in town." I always had this thing with my kids. The kids would ask, "Daddy, are we rich?" And I would answer, "I am the richest man I know. I have you two." Kenny has more love coming at him; he really is a rich, rich man. It's not about money. It is about family and love and friends. That is what I think he is, on top of everything else. He is a rich, rich man and we are all better for knowing him.*

John, St. Lawrence O'Toole Friend

COACHING

The legendary running back for the Chicago Bears, an individual by the name of Gayle Sayers wrote an autobiography called, I am Third. *According to Sayers, God is first, the family is second, and he was third. Had Kenny Holler written that book, he would have agreed with Sayers with regard to God and family, but third would have been his friends and his community, especially the Brewster Little League.*

Kenny was a quiet leader both in the dugout and in the community. Kenny worked tirelessly until his body gave out to make sure that each and every one of the kids in Brewster Little League played on the best possible field. He wanted to make sure that Brewster had a home field advantage at all times. His knowledge of sports, and particularly the game of baseball, helped Bryan Brooks and a young team of ten, eleven, and twelve year olds put at least three of the championship banners up here before you.

It was Kenny's leadership off the field and in the face of adversity that is an inspiration to every kid that ever had the opportunity to play for him and every coach that had the opportunity to share the dugout with him.

In short, Kenny Holler's love of family and community will forever shine as examples of how we should all treat each other. For those of us that coached with Kenny, who played for Kenny, or simply shared a laugh along the sidelines with Kenny, we are the better people for it.

Joe: Brewster Baseball Friend, Excerpt from Tree Dedication Speech

On April 18, Opening Day of the 2015 baseball season, friends from Brewster Little League planted a Crimson King Maple tree in Markel Park in Kenny's memory

***

I see that tree and it makes me think of Kenny every time I drive by. The field itself too, but I see the tree. The Town hasn't killed it, the landscaper hasn't chewed the bottom of it up; it looks good. It does look good.

Bryan, Brewster Baseball Friend

64
Supportive
Rosanne: *Brewster Friend*

The very first time I was aware of Kenny was when my oldest son, Nathan, was going to try baseball for the first time. Because he is my oldest, my heart was on my sleeve when I put him into the Instructional division. He hadn't done tee-ball and didn't know how to play baseball; he was a lefty and he wasn't very coordinated.

I dropped him off at practice and when I came back, Kenny, who I didn't know, was down on one knee pitching to Nathan, over and over, and over… My first thought was mortification because that's my kid and he is not hitting the ball. Yet when I took a step back from that, I loved how Kenny, said, "Oh! You almost had that one!" Afterwards, Nathan hit one and it was a great hit; he nailed it, and it was satisfying for me to see a coach who could be quietly encouraging and not get frustrated.

He must have been out there for a very long time pitching to all of those kids and yet he saw something that he was helping to correct—and Nathan was listening. If it had been somebody who was abrasive or coming at it from a competitive way, it would have shut Nathan down. Instead he became the go-to pitcher for Nathan. Kenny came in in a couple of games and pitched to him. I think he knew Nathan's sweet spot or something or it just helped Nathan to succeed when Kenny pitched to him.

Truthfully when I saw Kenny with all of those pitches that first day, I kind of wanted him to just stop. I wanted him to stop and say, "Ok, that was good, nice try, now go play in the field." He never did that. It was a good thing for me to see also. I have patience with other people's children, but at the time was I an overly patient athletic mother to my son? No, not really. Yet here was somebody that didn't know my son at all, who either saw something in him, or within himself just wanted to reach all of the children on that team and make them feel like they could do something. And he was right. That meant a lot to me.

I think of Kenny now and my memories are connected to the way that I view my children. I still see the image of Kenny pitching over and over again and not giving up on my son. It is a powerful metaphor in terms of valuing something and knowing there is progress being made. It is not just in sports; it is remembering to give them the chance that they deserve, or maybe more than they deserve. I love that that is my take-away from it because it is very tangible. To kind of take a step back and instead of being critical or frustrated, to see it as a process, that growing up takes time.

Kenny was always a good example of how you should work with kids. He spoke to them in words they could understand; they knew they could trust what he told them; and he would demonstrate time and time again how to play the game. He was a person that could clearly get down on their level and relate to the kids to make them perform. He was a very strong motivator in a lot of ways.

Larry, Brewster Friend

65
Safe

Jane: Brewster Baseball Friend

My first impression was that Kenny had had a struggle with something, but it disappeared immediately, because I would make a connection with his eyes. I didn't see anything else except his really happy, friendly demeanor. Always so positive. Not to sound cliché or anything, but if I was having a bad day, and at that time I was going through the divorce and there were a lot of bad days, when I went to the baseball field it all went away.

With Anthony and his competitiveness, he was his own worst enemy. He didn't want to let the team down, he didn't want to strike out; he didn't want to get out at all. Even if he had a hard at-bat, I just wanted him to get to first base. Just to get to first, because I knew that Kenny was always waiting for him and I knew that his morale and his self-esteem would be safe if he got to first, no matter what he did. Although I really was happy those times that I saw Kenny waving him on, "Go to second, go to second, go to second!"

Kenny was all about the kids. It wasn't just his kids; it was all the kids. They were all his kids. This came at a very important time in Anthony's life. I told you it was during the divorce. Anthony and his father had their battles. There were a couple of years where Anthony didn't see his father. It was really important to have that male time and that male role model with somebody that was positive, showing how a dad can be. I knew that he was safe with Kenny, well taken care of on every level.

I never knew until today how long Kenny had been sick and the extent of his struggles. How did he keep it together all the time? My mom has had cancer twice, every time she goes to the doctor, she holds her breath because she is waiting for another diagnosis. Lynda told me that every time Kenny went to the doctor he held his breath too, but twenty-one years is a long time to battle, a lot of uncertainty.

We were in Canada when Kenny passed away; we didn't even know he had gotten that bad or that it was back.

How often do I think of him? I think of him all the time, especially during baseball season. He is one of the people that I think about that makes me feel positive. There are a couple of people in my life and he is one of them where I get a warmth when I think of him.

***

Kenny had a way with his eyes of wanting us to be okay with his suffering. He didn't want us to feel bad for him. He didn't want it to be about that.

Rachel, Brewster Friend

Kenny was like the Wizard of Oz. Both in Majors and in travel ball, he made magic happen! He did. He made a lot of wishes come true for those boys.

Bryan, Brewster Baseball Friend

66
Rangers

Tom: *Brewster Baseball Friend*

I really got to know Kenny the first time when Rory and Timmy played on the same soccer team. Rory was in fourth grade and Timmy in fifth. Before that I knew of Kenny, like an acquaintance, just saying "Hello," just being around the school and the kids and everything like that, but it was during that soccer season that I really learned who he was, what he did, fireman, Astoria, Rangers, kids.

The thing that struck me before I met him and got to know him, when he was just an acquaintance, was that I could obviously see that he had been through something. I thought, "Wow. He has a really positive attitude. He's got a lot of energy and he is really out there with people. Somebody else who is feeling sorry for themselves could just be introverted, but not him."

He was always positive with the kids. This is going back five or six years, so my younger son Shane was six or seven years old walking around with a football or soccer ball or baseball glove. If I wasn't paying attention for five minutes, Kenny was there having a catch with Shane on the sidelines. Just always engaged with the kids; always engaged with the families, got to know everybody.

Then I got to know him really well when Kenny and Bryan and I coached the eleven and twelve year old Little League Majors team together. It was so much fun; half the time it was just the three of us breaking each other's chops.

Cleaning up the field, he was great about that. That is a big part of coaching that people don't really get. They really don't understand how much time goes into being a groundskeeper. You are a coach, but you are a groundskeeper: getting the field ready, dragging it, raking it up, putting the lines out there, and everything. Part of me would think, "We have a game tonight, great! We get to coach and watch the kids play baseball. What a lot of fun! But, ugh! I have to get to the field an hour early and sweat and drag it and rake it."

But Bryan would say, "No. Kenny's got it."

I would respond, "What do you mean? I feel bad. He's going there every time?"

He said, "I have been trying to help, but he just does it."

I remember how meticulously Kenny would do it. We would get to the field and it was just immaculate. A few times I got there early, when he was finishing up; he would be looking across the field, surveying it. We would be just sitting there chatting and he would get up, walk across the field and grab a pebble, and throw it off. He took care of it like a collector car or something.

The one thing that he and I had in common was our passion for hockey. He was such a big Rangers fan. Not a lot of hockey fans around here. I have known this my whole life, so when I find a hockey fan, I gravitate towards the person. Every time, whether it was in the middle of the season or playoff time or in between seasons: "Who are they going to draft? Who are they going to trade for?" All that kind of stuff. So that was great, just talking to him about hockey. He always asked Rory about it, because he knew Rory played. He'd ask him how his hockey games were; they would talk about the Rangers. Kenny would poke Rory with, "What do you think? Should they start McDonagh? Should they start Girardi?" Giving it a little bit to him to try to elicit an answer out of him.

All of my times with him were the parts of my life that I enjoy the most: being with the kids, watching them play sports, being a coach, being around my friends, and he was a big part of that.

I think of all the times when I am feeling sick, or I hurt, or feel like I am getting old and I am sore because I was throwing the baseball too much, and I think to myself. "I wish I didn't have this. I wish I didn't have a cold. I wish I wasn't tired."

Then I think, "Who the heck am I? I have everything."

So feeling like that, because of getting to know somebody like Kenny, changed my life for the better. I think twice before I ever think about feeling sorry for myself. And I tell my kids too, "Don't ever complain about anything. You've got everything in the world. We have everything in the world when we have our health and we have our family."

Kenny epitomized that probably more than anyone I ever met in my life. And the time that I knew Kenny Holler was a brief window of my life. I am forty-six years old; I probably really got to know him five or six years ago. So I only knew him for four or five years, less than ten percent of my life, but I feel that he has had such an impact on it.

And I feel like in getting to know him, after only a couple weeks, it was as if I had actually known him for my whole life. He was that kind of person.

Lynda is talking to a lot of people. I think it is great that she is doing this. I am sure everyone is telling her the same thing. I am sure that if they have known him for their whole life, or if they only knew him for a day or six months or two years, I am sure they are saying the same thing. That's the kind of impact he made.

I prayed for Kenny. We didn't know them in 1992 or even when the kids were younger. Then, immediately after I knew him, we didn't pray for him because like I said, his personality transcended everything. But when the cancer came back, yes, we started to pray.

We went to the healing prayer service and that impacted me a lot. But after the service, Kenny was back and he was as alive as he had ever been, but I knew that it was serious and unfortunately cancer is very serious, so I would pray every time I would see him. I would see him and we would talk about the Rangers and we would talk about the kids and he would have a catch and I would be happy for that moment, but then I would pray. Rachel and I would talk about it a lot. We would talk to each other; we would talk to the kids in church, reminding them to pray.

Colin has worked as an intern at my engineering company, but I have known Timmy better. As one of the old guys, one of the dads, Timmy is very quiet, very reserved. Rory tells me that he is mostly quiet and reserved, but he is pretty funny, a jokester, breaking everybody's chops all the time. And I think, "Ah yeah, that is just like Kenny." Because Kenny would zing you. I have talked about how nice and polite, but once he got to know you and know who you are, he'd break your chops about stuff.

In both Colin and Timmy, I see very proud, responsible young men who are what a lot of us want our kids to grow up to be. Just like Kenny, all that suffering he was going through, Lynda was suffering, Colin was suffering, Timmy was suffering. In a different way, emotional, not physical, but I never saw signs of that in them. I never heard Timmy complain that his dad was not feeling well so he couldn't do something, come to the game, go to the practice, or have a catch or whatever.

Kenny passed away while Colin was working his summer internship, but nobody knew. I tried not to make it known that I knew Colin, just so that his employment there would be perfectly on his own merit, which it was. Somebody found out that his father passed away and found out that I knew Colin and they contacted me and asked, "By the way, did you know that Colin's father passed away?" In that fashion.

The point I am trying to make is the quiet nature of "Don't let anybody know that you are suffering. Be a bigger person. Be happy for what you have in your life," has clearly passed on to both of them. I have never heard Rory say anything about how Timmy is sad or upset or angry or any of that. I have never seen it. They just go about doing what they are doing and they seem to be happy for what they have and they are just both great young men. I think that is what Kenny passed along to them.

The good that came out of Kenny's suffering is how he lived his life and in a way that was epitomized while he was going through that suffering. I am sure there were really, really hard times for him and Lynda. Just the cumbersome nature of going through all the things that everybody takes for granted in life. You have a sip of tea; you just do it. You take a breath of air. We are speaking all these words and how difficult that was for him. Further, you can talk about his hands and his fingers, the pain that he must have been in.

I guess the good that I take out of it is the lesson that he taught me in my forties, that I believe he taught my kids in their early teens or younger. We learned how to respect life and to cherish all the blessings that we have, our health in particular. If you have your health, and you have your family, every single day is a blessing.

***

Kenny was somebody that I found, as a cancer survivor myself, incredibly remarkable. What he portrayed to other people: the strength that we can have regardless of the suffering, gives other people strength to get through what they have to go through. I believe it is a contagious strength. I know in my life there will be other times that I will call on that strength again. Kenny may be gone, but his spirit is still alive and contagious.

Barbara, Halloran Fund

67
Role-model
Rory, *Tim's Teammate, Tom's Son, Age 14*

Mr. Holler showed me that we don't know how long we are going to live, so we have to try to affect the most people and be nice to everyone. He lived such a short life and he affected so many people and he made so many people change. Mr. Holler was what everyone tries to be like: nice, kind, funny, easy to talk to—what everyone wants to be like when they grow up or be right now. I always try to be nice to everyone and he is a role model.

***

It is funny these days we expect to live to ninety, but it is not how many years, it is what you do with them. One hundred years of nothing is not anywhere near as valuable as fifty years of something worthwhile. You can make those years special, leave your mark, impress people, impress your children. We were lucky to have known him. That is really true.

Janice, Brewster Friend

68
Tried-and-true
Lisa: Brewster Baseball Friend

Hearing the stories that Kenny's friends were telling at the wake gave me a new perspective on somebody that I had already admired and respected. I always saw Kenny as a gentleman and kind and loyal and somebody that I wanted to know, but in hearing those stories, he became somebody that I would have liked to have been friends with and hang out with when he was feeling well.

I first met Kenny when Colin and Joey were in fourth grade, eight years ago. I had seen him before I met him, but I didn't know who he was until somebody told me he was Colin's dad and that he was sick.

I remember that Lynda and I had a conversation and she was so excited because he was going to be able to start eating solid food. I remember being astounded, because I had no idea that he hadn't been on food. Then in what seemed to me like only weeks, they found something more and Kenny had to have another surgery. That finished their hopes of him getting teeth and being able to eat solid food again. I remember feeling so let down and I didn't even know him then. I didn't really know any of them that well. I was just thinking, "Oh my goodness, he has a kid the same age as my kid and what must that be like as a family?" I mean food is such an important thing. It is the first thing we do. If somebody comes to the house, "Can I get you a tea? Can I get you a coffee? Can I get you something to eat? Are you sure you don't want something to eat? You have to have something to eat!"

A few years later, my second son Michael and Timmy started playing together. They've played on the same soccer and basketball teams, but it was through travel summer baseball that we really got to know the Hollers.

Kenny was quiet, partly because he was forced to be because speaking had become so difficult, but he always made an impression. Particularly in the dugout with the boys, it always made a difference when he was there. In his quiet way, he always somehow made it more of a safe haven. He never treated them differently, it didn't matter if they had gotten a home run or they struck out, he made everybody feel valued. That may be one of the qualities that he had that I didn't really think a lot about.

Kenny always seemed to bounce back. I know he had pneumonia a couple times, but then he was back out there raking and coaching and talking. Somehow he always made everything seem like it was going to be okay and I used to be astounded by that. I think the most difficult thing for him as he became sicker, was the idea of not being there for Lynda, Colin, and Timmy.

So Kenny spoke to people. That was one of the ways he dealt with it. He wanted to make sure that everybody knew that was important to him: that his family was going to be taken care of when he couldn't be here to take care of them anymore. I know he spoke to my husband Joe.

I spent a lot of time praying for him and I remember in the last few weeks that I found it hard to pray that he would find peace and comfort, instead of praying for healing. I really wanted the miracle.

I don't think I realized how serious it was until the end. Even when he was in the hospital all those weeks down in the city, I think my denial was really strong. I still felt like he was going to come home. I didn't have a feeling on what that would mean exactly, but going into hospice wasn't part of my plan.

I guess if I had to define a moment, it was when Lynda said to me, "They are waiting on an ambulance, but they don't know if he'll make it in the ambulance from Yale New Haven Hospital to Rosary Hill." She rode in the ambulance with him because she didn't want to risk him dying alone on the ride. He had shown such strength and rallied so many times, but when Lynda said that, I just felt a big sigh. That's when it became real for me, three days before he died. I guess that was the moment. It just didn't seem possible.

***

I don't see value that came out of Kenny's suffering. Lynda may, because she lived it, but it just made me sad. It made me sad for him; it made me sad for Lynda and the boys. He was such a happy guy and to have him knocked at the knees just makes me sad.

Patty, Brewster Friend

69
Hearty

Rory: *Lisa's Daughter, Age 11*

I remember sitting up on top of the hill with Mr. Holler at the baseball field. I was probably six or seven. We'd set up our chairs and just talk. It was a relaxed setting. We'd watch the game and talk about school, about the game, different things like that. We talked about catching because I wanted to be a catcher. We talked about the different techniques Timmy used. We talked about Michael and the different people on the team. It was fun, because he was really easy to talk to, very kind.

I had known he was sick because I could tell by the way he was talking. So even though sometimes it was hard to understand him, I felt like I connected to him. My mom had told me that he was sick and I prayed for him every night while he was sick. I didn't know how bad it was. He didn't really change too much. He acted pretty normal, his normal.

I thought about when I am just regular sick and how it must have been ten times harder for Mr. Holler. He was constantly sick, whereas I get sick every once in a while. I had strep throat recently and I was thinking how it was hard for me to talk, but it must have been even harder for Mr. Holler to talk. That definitely made me think of him. Even eating and drinking were difficult for me. I was sick for three days; Mr. Holler couldn't do those things normally on a day to day basis.

Hearing about Mrs. Holler writing a book is pretty cool because his life is definitely worthy of a book. He is definitely someone you can't forget once you meet him.

***

Out of anyone, Kenny knew how precious life was and he knew how precious his time was. I do believe that he knew there was an end coming, but yet he wasn't afraid to share that with everybody.

Anne, Brewster Friend

70
Perspective
Jen: Brewster Friend

I actually do not remember the first time I met Kenny. I just remember that Liam and Colin became such good friends in third grade, and in the process of that, we all got to know one another. As I reflect back on memories, I see that Kenny has impacted my entire family in a number of ways.

Liam's little sister is much younger than Liam and she used to go to the eight thousand, million baseball games that we all went to. She was always on my hip and talking and distracting me. I clearly remember being at Scolpino Park and during many, many games the only time that I got a break, and could watch the game, was when Erin would go to Kenny. They would sit on the stairs leading down to the field and talk away. She was probably about two, three, four; there were a lot of years that we had baseball.

I would go over to Kenny and say, "I am so sorry. I know you want to watch the game. Let me take her." Kenny would say, "No no, we are having our conversation." Erin didn't even know his name, she would just call him, "Colin's daddy." She would say, "I am talking to Colin's daddy." That struck me as a sign of how even Erin at that age gravitated towards Kenny.

When they held the Healing Prayer Vigil at St. Lawrence for Kenny, my second son, Sean, who is a year older than Tim, had some modified school baseball thing he had to go to that night, so he couldn't come with us. We took two cars and I scooted off early to get Sean and I had eight million of Sean's-aged kids in the car with me, because I was on driving-home duty. They are close in age to Tim and Colin, but they aren't the exact ages or grades. In the car, they all started talking, "We're so bummed we couldn't go to the service." They all knew about it and they all just talked, without me saying a word. I was just driving and listening, because that is when we get the best information from kids, when we just drive and listen.

They all started spontaneously talking about Mr. Holler as they were saying, "Oh my gosh, he is the nicest dad." They were sharing memories of either watching him coach or him coaching their younger or older brother's teams. It struck me that I had just left the service, with all of the kids that were there, and here was a whole other carload of kids that just spontaneously had all of these memories. I remember thinking what a legacy that was, and how his influence had spread to so many in ways that we didn't even realize.

Another impact on me and I get teary-eyed thinking about it, includes both of my parents who were sick and ultimately died. My dad loved Kenny and would talk about him. Even at the end when my dad was pretty sick and had trouble remembering things, he would still ask about Kenny and how he was doing. I remember that he would tell my sister and I that as hard a haul as he was going through, he would think of Kenny and it would put his own suffering and his own feelings that this was not right, or whatever, in perspective. My dad was not a religious man, but what he was talking about, I think without outright saying it, was that it spiritually helped him by thinking of Kenny and putting his life in perspective.

We talked about fairness before. There were times when both of my parents were sick and we were going constantly. I would think, "Enough is enough! I would like a break now. Can I just have two months of no illness so I can get my own life together and watch my own kids and whatever?" Then I would think of what the Hollers were going through, not in a comparison way, but in a perspective way. I'd remember that my dad had lived through his life, my mom had her grandchildren. It would have been nice had they lived longer, but putting it into perspective was a comfort to me in a lot of ways. That as unfair as it might seem at times, life isn't fair; that's not the point of it.

I am a therapist in Carmel and I see people often who come in with traumas or losses or terrible things that have happened to them. Often, they come to me, because those terrible things have led them to make bad decisions, be it drugs or getting in trouble with the court and they get mandated to come to me. Every single day at work I hear, "It's not fair." "It's not right." "It's not my fault I am choosing to live this way. It's all the bad breaks I have gotten." I use Kenny's story, without names or identifying details to help people put their own lives into perspective. I will tell them, "You know there are other people who have hard things that happen to them, much harder than you have had in some ways, but they don't choose to live or make the choices you make." I think he's actually helped quite often.

We have other friends of our family who have a very sick baby. The mother is a hospice nurse with two healthy children, but her third child has heart disease. For my kids, we use both lives as examples of how to put our thinking in check. If you think it isn't fair that something happens, that you didn't make a team, you didn't get this or that, put yourself in other people's shoes. I use that family quite often in my work too. Not that Kenny and this four-year-old on the surface have anything in common at all, but their commonality is how adversity can help others. They aren't just helping people that know them; it's like six degrees of separation to Kevin Bacon, but six degrees of separation from be it Kenny or this baby: they help me in my work, maybe those people say it to someone else, and the effects ripple across the world.

When the boys and Erin were little, we would pray all together at night. We would always say, "God bless all the soldiers and sailors that keep us safe." Then we would pray for individual people that were going through things. We often prayed for my mom and dad at that point, but Liam started to throw in prayers for Kenny. He didn't understand at first what was wrong with Kenny. I didn't say much, I let Colin say what he knew. So Liam would come home with different understandings as time went on.

At first, he would say, "Mr. Holler just got sick." Then he'd come home another time and say, "Did you know that Mr. Holler has been sick as long as Colin has been alive?" He'd take it in, then a couple days later he would come back and say, "But thank God he gets to come and coach and stuff, so he can at least see all Colin's games." Then there would be another sleepover or they'd hang out and he'd come home and say, "Do you know that he is probably not going to get better? Wow. I always thought that he was going to get better, but Colin said that he won't." It was interesting to hear that these boys, that we thought were just playing whatever they played on these sleepovers, used some of the time to have pretty deep conversations.

So at one point, Liam added to the prayers, "God bless Mr. Holler." At first he would say, "God bless Mr. Holler, so that he will get better." Then in the end he changed it to, "God bless Mr. Holler, so that he doesn't suffer." I remember Sean saying, "Why are you saying that? You are supposed to pray so that he gets better." Then Liam said, "But Colin doesn't think that he is going to get better, so we just have to pray that he doesn't suffer and that he does as good as he

152

can do." Which I think is something that he must have heard from Colin, because I don't know how he otherwise would have said or known that. So it is interesting, that Kenny impacted all of our prayer lives too and expanded everybody's thinking.

Liam did not cry at either my mom or my dad's funerals, but he actually cried as we were standing there at Kenny's. When we talked later, he said to me, "I am not crying for me, I am crying for Colin." The conversation led to, not in these exact words, that at least Kenny's not suffering anymore and he is in Heaven now. With all of the other impacts that Kenny had on our family, it is interesting that this dad, coach, and friend may have had the biggest impact of all on our spiritual lives.

***

The example of the faithful often transforms the hearts of listeners more than a teacher's words.

St. Gregory the Great

71
Wisdom

Chris: *Brewster Rec Sports Friend*

I first met Kenny when my son Liam and Colin were little and began playing sports together. We coached rec basketball for our older boys and also some summer baseball for our younger sons Sean and Tim.

It was an honor to coach with someone who played basketball at Power Memorial. I had someone standing next to me, who I looked up to in more than one way. Not just height-wise, but the fact that he was a humble and mature guy.

He and I had a very close philosophy of coaching that we really appreciated the kids that struggled and found success and felt sorry for the kids that were talented, but didn't work as hard. There is nothing sadder in this world than wasted talent. We never expected anyone to make it into Duke or St. John's on a basketball scholarship from our team, but we had the same expectation that if they want to play organized ball, the least they could do is try hard.

Kenny wasn't the kind of guy to just let kids sit on their laurels and the ones who wanted his help got it. A couple times it drove me crazy when the kids wouldn't listen and I would complain to Kenny. He would say, "Don't worry about it. There is nothing we can do about them. Let's concentrate on the kids that are going to listen to us and do as we ask."

He also said, "They have all the answers and we have none."

I would think, "They have all the answers and we have none... and here is a guy that played on one of the most competitive teams in NYC which is probably one of the most competitive basketball markets at the high school level. Not only did Kenny make the team, but he was on the court, getting court time." As we find when kids get older, not every kid in high school gets on the court. Some of them just sit the bench their whole high school career.

In spite of his experience, Kenny's accepted that, "If they don't want to listen to me, I can't do anything about that."

It probably goes back to his faith: "God grant me the serenity to change the things I can, accept the things that I can't, and the wisdom to know the difference." It is as if he had that little saying hard-wired into him; it was who he was.

Sometimes it's not bad to pull back. He had the wisdom to understand when he needed to step in and when he needed to not step in. By not stepping in at every opportunity, he was teaching not just those kids that didn't want his help, but he was demonstrating to the other kids that sometimes there is nothing you can do. Those people are outside of your control. He was going to let them be and make their own mistakes. Allowing them to make mistakes is still an impact. It has impact on shaping lives, shaping mentalities, shaping philosophies.

Kenny wasn't out to set the world on fire. He was just a guy. He thought of himself as just a guy, but very few people in this world have that kind of impact. I wish there were more.

When you talked to Kenny, he would tell you the truth. There was no sugar-coating, no diplomacy to tell you maybe what you want to hear. He just was a very honest, down-to-earth, caring individual, but you knew it was sincere what he was saying.

Dave, Aruba Friend

72
Graceful
MaryAnne: *Rec Basketball Director, Hair Salon Owner*

I met Kenny through basketball, maybe when Colin was in first grade, second grade? When Kenny and Lynda introduced him to Southeast Rec Basketball, I ran the basketball program. The first thing I think of Kenny is his smile. He was always so happy, always so cheerful, just a real genuine man and he had his little one in tow! Colin was always there; I felt that he was an extension of Kenny.

I thought about this one time... I am going to cry... I thought about this one time, and it was years after, I said, "Kenny, please coach! Please coach; you are such a great guy."

He said, "I can't yell."

I said, "That's why I need you!"

We were probably in the age of everybody getting a little crazy with coaching. All I could think of was if Kenny coached, things would be a lot calmer, and they were for all the teams I can remember him being on.

The other thing I thought of was the phone, the phone camera. We didn't use it as much then, but looking back I wish I had. That's what's etched in my mind: all the kids all around Kenny looking up at him or sitting down and all crouched around him. It was as if we were looking at a professional team, intently looking in his eyes, waiting for the words to come out of his mouth. Because he was so calm, they respected him. He gave that respect right back, I could see it. That's etched in my heart forever, as the good things that came out of all the hard work he did. I wish I had photos to remember and to give to Lynda, because that's what everybody saw, just a very gentle, kind, loving man. It showed in everything he did.

To tell you the truth, if I didn't know from other people saying, "Kenny is sick," I wouldn't have known it. Even when he was coaching I never knew of his cancer history, and I think until the end I didn't really understand that he had been sick for so long. Never knew that. Even when he was in the salon getting his hair cut at the worst of times, he never talked about himself. He never said that he wasn't feeling well.

I wrote down some words that describe Kenny: proud, strong, resilient, loving. I thought of graceful because when I realized that I hadn't known how severe or how sick he actually was for such a long period of time, I thought, "How could he go through life not woe-is-me-ing?" I thought he had done it with such grace.

I hope that what we have taken out of Kenny's suffering is that we shouldn't complain. No one would have known he was sick if they didn't know him and most people that knew him didn't know the severity of it. He leaves that legacy of never giving up. We need to go to the last moment.

He definitely made an impact on all the kids that he coached. You don't have to be wild and crazy and get all riled up about things. Just play the game. Stay calm. Kenny was always there for the boys, even when he was sick, and I don't think any of the kids ever realized. That says a lot for that man. I don't think that anyone ever realized that there would come a time when they wouldn't see him.

Kenny's personality inspires me. I never saw him mad or upset—always positive. If I ever feel down, I think about what I have and just keep thinking positive.

Aiden, Tim's Brewster Teammate, Age 15

73
Spirited
Julie: St. Lawrence O'Toole Friend

My earliest recollection of Kenny was when he was coaching Andrew's CYO team.

Then, at one game, Lynda and I were sitting together and she asked me for the recipe for the lentil soup that I made for the CYO snack café. She told me that Kenny didn't eat solid food, so she made him soup. I thought, "Why doesn't he eat?" Literally, it had never occurred to me that there was anything different about him. Now I think about how ridiculous that is, but it was true that it hadn't occurred to me that he had had any surgeries.

After Lynda said it, I started to realize, because my dad had surgery when I was ten. He had oral cancer and part of his tongue was removed. He had the radical neck dissection and he always had the scar. So since I was a kid, he was very anxious about people knowing. He would wear clothing that covered it. He wouldn't speak much; he became very shy, very into himself, so I had the experience that oral surgery kind of makes you a different type of person.

When I think about how Kenny was, it was the absolute opposite, because he was just full of life when he was on the court. In fact, have you noticed how many people seem to drag themselves through the doors when they arrive at a gym for a game? They might moan, "There was so much snow." Or "I got lost." Or "I couldn't park." With Kenny that was never the case. He would come in, have the basketballs, have the kids, and be excited to play. Excited to be there. Being a coach was natural to him, knowing his background, but it isn't something that you get paid to do. He was just passionate about being there on the court with the kids. He would talk to them and he liked them. That was exciting for him. There is something beautiful there. It is really a love of life that impressed me.

Lynda and I became closer friends and I would pray for Kenny. She had told me about the St. Agnes connection and that church was right down the street from where I worked in Midtown Manhattan. There were days, and I am certain of it, that I would tell her that I would pray and I prayed only because I had promised her. I prayed more when I knew something was going on: either they were coming into the city or going to the hospital or just got back from the hospital, or were waiting to hear a test result, whatever. I remember on those days I would think, "I am going to pray for Kenny and I am going to offer my Mass." So I would get my butt out of my desk and go to Mass at lunchtime. That whole relationship increased my prayer life. In my mind, I was praying for Kenny, but I realize that when we pray, God is changing us.

So while going to daily Mass, I remember looking at the picture of St. Agnes. I remembered knowing that she suffered so much; she was being tortured, but she had a holiness about her, an acceptance of it, and the knowledge that she was doing it for the Lord. That gave her joy and peace. When I would be praying for Lynda and for her family, it wasn't that I was praying for healing or for a miracle or a cure in a frantic kind of way. I was adding my prayers to the peace and the joy and the patience that Lynda already had. I felt that. I wasn't just saying the words and thinking about her; I actually had a feeling inside of me that kind of confirmed that I was praying for peace and joy and comfort, rather than healing.

I remember knowing that in that type of prayer, I felt something different. I didn't know what that meant at the time, but I know now that it was a consolation. God sometimes gives us the grace of a consolation to know that he is with us in prayer. I don't always have that and it is not something normal for people to always have, but I remember knowing that I felt differently when I was praying for Kenny and Lynda in those moments.

When I went to their home I felt sadness. It is probably the closest that I have seen suffering. I haven't had a lot of sickness or long suffering illness in my family. There is a scariness about it. Some of the great saints ask to suffer, but it is scary and it hurts. At the same time there is a peace in there for me, knowing that people like Lynda and families that have gone through that stuff can use God's joy and peace and maybe even receive more of it. There is a peace with the Hollers now, a peace that you wouldn't see in a family that is not faithful, even if they are experiencing only the slightest little problem.

There is a teaching moment in there.

Lynda was always strong and there were times that she would just say, "I don't want to talk about that." She had it together; maybe it is a personality thing, maybe it is an Irish thing, but it is like she surrendered it at some point and said, "I am going to leave it with you God." Then she would come back tomorrow and it would still be there, but it was a resolution for her to say, "I am here and I am going to wait on You." That is the realization that God is working in it and it is His time. So knowing Kenny and Lynda is a critical part of my growth in faith.

Their experiences help me to have that kind of hope. Help me feel peaceful in the waiting part. So if a day is really bad, I still feel peace; I know God is holding me. Whatever happens, I know God is there and that life goes on and I will find joy. God will always use it.

***

When Kenny was sick, many times I would go into church, light a candle and pray for him. I mostly went to St. Patrick's, near my office, but there were times that I tried to go to St. Agnes, because that is the church where Kenny made his First Communion and Confirmation. I felt that St. Agnes was special because that was the start of his life, start of being a Christian. It is a cute little quaint church on Forty-Third Street in Manhattan. I would do that, not because I am Catholic, I am not, although I do believe in God. I did it not just to pray for Kenny, but to make me feel better. I hoped that if I prayed for Kenny, somehow he would be healed and I just felt better when I could go into a church, light a candle, think of Kenny, and pray for him.

Sue, Astoria Friend

74
Praying

I remember praying for Kenny when he was sick. Every time I went to bed I leaned against my bed and prayed one or two times. In the middle or the end I would say, "I hope you feel better Kenny. Get well."

After the funeral I started praying mostly every night, I pray for him when I read. When I have extra time at the end I drop my book and then I start praying.

Jillian, Cheryl's Daughter, Lynda's Godchild, Age 9

***

I have become more religious and feel closer to God. I remember before Kenny passed away, I didn't know how to pray, but I would try; I would say stuff in my head. Seeing how it clearly helped Colin's family through hard times to feel close to God, I learned that it can help me too.

Cara, Colin's Girlfriend, Age 18

***

One night when Kenny was really sick, my daughters and I prayed the Divine Mercy Chaplet and we had never done that before together. It was great.

Then one time Kenny must have been pretty sick and I went into the boys' room and said, "Make sure you say a prayer for Mr. Holler."

My oldest son Teddy said to me, "Mom, I pray for him every night." I should know that, I am his mother, but sometimes things like that surprise me. He was 18; how many 18 year olds…? And Thomas had that prayer right by him too and we would talk about him praying also, it just struck me when Teddy said, "I pray every night for him."

Denise, Brewster Friend

I prayed for Kenny when he was sick. He was really sick during my eighth grade year before Confirmation. In our religious education program, they asked us to write a name on a notecard, someone to pray for; I prayed for Kenny.

Brendan, Tim's Friend, Age 15

***

There are certain people that every Sunday when I go to Mass I pray for them and Kenny would always be one of those. You have to try to ask for help for these people.

Victor, Lynda's Friend

***

I prayed for Kenny when he was sick. I talked to myself. I don't go to church and pray. I talk to Mary, because it is always better to go to the mother. A son can't deny his mother if she tells him something. So that is what I did, I talked.

Jack, Brewster Elks, Golf Partner

***

I prayed for Kenny. I always pray for my patients. Very much so. I always did. Praying for my patients helps me too. I see God in people and I definitely know who those people are. Kenny was one of those because he was genuine.

Annette, Dr. Herrera's Nurse

***

Lynda asked whether I prayed to Kenny. I never prayed to any person besides God, Jesus, and Mary, not even Joseph. That's giving me something to think about. I talk to my parents; maybe that is a form of praying, but I don't think I have even said to my parents, "Hey, pray for me." I can use all the help I can get, so that is something I think I am going to start doing proactively. Kenny is not physically here with us, but his presence will always be here. It is an interesting approach and to have a guy like Kenny praying for me can't go wrong! It gives me a chance to step back and say, "Wow, I need to talk to him some more." I will. I absolutely will.

Frank, Brewster Friend

75
Prayers
Linda: Lynda's Friend

We of course prayed for Kenny. Whenever Kenny needed prayers, when some particular crisis or problem was brewing, I would go to people that I worked with and ask them, "Could you pray for my friend?" I had no qualms asking on his behalf. I would lose shyness or hesitation when it came to Kenny. People always respond beautifully when it comes to things like that. It doesn't matter religion or whatever way people think, when you ask for prayers for somebody, they respond. So, Kenny had a way of bringing out good things in people, even if he didn't know them.

Victor and I visited Kenny at New York Presbyterian and we prayed the Divine Mercy Chaplet with Lynda. It was a prayer that brought her comfort and we felt good praying together with her over Kenny.

It is a great grace to see somebody accept help. Kenny, in his illness, accepted whatever help was available to him, whether it was the doctors, the nursing professionals, or his firefighter, Astoria, or Brewster friends. That helps people do the right thing. When you need help, and are willing to be helped, that brings out the best in other people. So through his own needs, Kenny helped other people be as good as they can be.

***

Kenny's name came up when we were in Arthur's restaurant one time. Arthur asked about Kenny. I was with another friend of mine, Gary, who had never met Kenny. I explained to Gary who Kenny was and what a good friend he was. Gary said, "I'm going to say a prayer for him." I said, "Look at this, even somebody that didn't know him is praying for him."

Stove/Bobby, Astoria Friend

162

76
Crocus
Grace: Denise's Daughter, Age 12

Mrs. Holler emailed us a prayer to say for Mr. Holler. Me and my sister have bunk beds and I am on the bottom. I would tuck the prayer in the holder above me so that I would always remember to pray for him. I would pray in the night and in the morning. I remember how sad it was, but I would always pray.

The funeral and the wake were really sad, but also really nice. There were so many people. So many people really, really, really loved him. I didn't know them all, but they were all there and they were all smiling and laughing and telling stuff about him. They really loved him and he made such an impact on their lives.

I went to their house to help with the garden and I really enjoyed helping plant all of the daffodil bulbs and the two trees. I loved seeing his fireman jacket hanging outside on the garage. It always reminds me of how brave he was.

Do you know those flowers, the first flowers to bloom? Crocuses? They bring me such joy and I always think of Mr. Holler. They make me laugh. I love the crocuses. They are so pretty and they grow over by our forsythia, right underneath it. He always just pops in to my mind when I see them, because one day you don't see them that much and the next day they are right there in full bloom. Seeing them always makes me laugh; we are happy that spring has come.

***

Please pray with me today and each day for as long as it takes for continued miracles for Kenny. Now I am praying that he be able to swallow, that his throat tissue return to healthy tissue, that he regain his full voice, and that the cancer be eradicated once and for all. Anything is possible with God. Anything.

The prayer request that Lynda emailed and Grace tucked into her bed.

77
Community
Angela: *St. Lawrence O'Toole Friend*

I complained to God that this "getting to Heaven" thing was
too hard, and lonely…

God revealed to me:
An image of a wide dirt road, in the sunlight,
surrounded by hills and woods.
The road crested over a hill a little bit before me,
and continued on to crest over another
and pass through shady woods to continue on again.
But I was not on this road alone—the road was busy with people.
People around me, people ahead of me—
the people that walked along with me,
the people that gave me a push or a pull,
the priest that pulled me back on when I wandered off,
and gave all of us the nourishment to stay strong for the trip.
There were people up ahead who had made their way long before me
and in the distance, at the farthest rise, the great saints
who've blazed the trail and helped us make sure we follow it.
I think about this image and I know what Christian community is.
It is all of us, helping each other every day, in everything,
to remember that ultimately,
our goal is to be happy in Heaven with our God.

I remember when we found out that Kenny was sick again; Bryan came home crying, just heartbreaking. Heartbreaking. That was the first relapse that we were aware of. Then he was all right for a year and then it just kind of went downhill.

But I always remember thinking that Kenny would be fine, of course he'll be fine. I would think, "He's just going to keep beating it and beating it." It was shocking to realize that he wasn't. "He's not going to beat this? How is this possible?" We just assumed; he was so resilient and he had been through so much, we just assumed he would be fine. All the bad news, I thought, "No, no, no, no, no. That's not right. You have that wrong. You have your information wrong!"

It is really important that by Kenny persevering he taught the boys that life is going to throw us lots of bad stuff, but when things are hard we just do what we have to do to keep going. Kenny's suffering is a lesson that we have to just pick up our heads and carry on. We keep living, stay happy, be kind, and make an impact on everyone around us. I hope that Brendan learned that and he takes that with him through his life, that he thinks of Kenny and remembers that situation. I think Brendan got that. I think all of the boys did. They just loved Kenny and they were all so heartbroken. He made such an impact on them.

That whole summer, especially during the 12U District Championship games in West Nyack with Evan not being able to be in the dugout, because of his wheelchair and finding out that Kenny was sick again, that was just such a motivating summer. Fighting for Evan; winning for Kenny. Evan and Kenny. Going to the sectionals, it was baseball and we were winning and that was great, but there was this back story, this underlying theme that we were not just winning to win, we were also winning for them.

Then two years later when Kenny died, the team had a game the next day. I remember crying when we won that game. Timmy wanted to play and it was just so impressive. He played so well. And the kids, after every inning they all went to Timmy, patting him on the head, whether he did something good or not, they all just went to Timmy. It was so cool.

And the other team was so cool. Bryan had called and told the other coach what was happening. At the end of the game, their coach told his kids that our catcher just lost his dad. You don't realize the impact you make on random kids that are realizing that they just played against a kid whose dad just died. They're thinking, "Look at him. He is here; he played awesome."

The other coach showed Bryan the scorebook and Timmy had three hits that game, but he said, "Every hit Timmy had should have been an out, but my kids made an error! I wonder who is kicking the ball around up there? Timmy definitely had an angel with him today." That was a good day.

I still think of him—I have a vision of Kenny. It is so funny, the other day Lynda was texting me updates on Timmy's varsity playoff games. I always think of Kenny whenever anything good happens in baseball. I got this picture of Kenny sitting on a cloud wearing a hat, eating popcorn, watching the game. He can eat popcorn now! That's how I picture him and I think, "Kenny must be so happy. He must just be beaming." When Lynda texted that they won, that was the first thing that I thought of: "Kenny must be so excited!" And I talk to him during baseball games all the time. When Brendan is up to bat, I'll think, "Come on Kenny, help him out!" He's my baseball guy.

***

Baseball makes me think about Kenny. He's the one that got me into baseball. He told me to keep my eye on the ball when I am catching it. I would look away and try to go catch it, then it would hit me. Now that I keep my eye on the ball, I can actually catch really high ones, ones that are coming at me fast, and ones that bounce on the ground. I think about him telling me those things.

Kellen, Cheryl's Son, Kenny's Godson, Age 10

79
Facet

Kevin: *Brewster Baseball Friend*

I learned a lot from Kenny on the baseball side on how to be a sports parent. One of the things that stuck with me early on is you don't remind a kid about the mistake he made. They know they made a mistake. You don't need an adult reinforcing that mistake. That struck me, because up until that point listening to parents, not so much coaches, but parents, I could see how they would harp on the negative. Kenny was all about the positive.

I started to learn more about Kenny and the more I learned, the more I admired. As the boys were maturing our friendship was maturing and our discussions were maturing. I was learning more about Kenny the man, not so much Kenny the coach, Kenny the father. What I was enjoying with Kenny was a genuine friendship. But he was also helping me learn a little bit more about my faith without it being from somebody who was preaching; it was just naturally evolving.

I learned how I could incorporate my faith and some of Kenny's life learnings into mine. Learning how to treat others and lead by example, not so much demanding, "Look at me, this is what I do or this is what I am." Actions spoke much louder than words with Kenny.

Our circle of friends here in Brewster is much wider due to people like Kenny and Lynda. Kenny opened a lot of doors for me to be welcomed by other people in the community. He helped me a lot as a parent, as a coach to a certain extent, and definitely as a person; he helped me grow.

I don't have any older siblings. I don't have many close friends from my youth around here anymore. They are all gone. All scattered to the wind. As an adult I have had to make new friends. Kenny was one of those friends that opened a lot of doors; he introduced me to people, he included me in conversations. That definitely changed me. It changed my relationship with my son. It changed my relationship with hundreds of people now. It was all because of one man.

Even now I think of Kenny and another facet of his personality or his life clicks together like a puzzle piece and my understanding of him grows. I miss him for the things he could have taught me.

Kenny, Lynda, Colin, and Tim have given so much to our family, and not just our family, our community. Although Kenny and Lynda didn't ask, a time came when folks in the community said, "We have to start doing something." The folks close to them would find out what they needed and the word would get out.

When the call for prayers came out, it made me start reflecting more. It brought Kenny and Lynda and the boys into the forefront of my prayers and what I was praying for made me reflect on what I have learned. There were things that stuck with me from the day that Kenny said them or did them, from our conversations. But it also made me reflect on the things that were never said. That might not have been noticed at the time because they were just part of Kenny. When I stopped and reflected on these things, it made these instances, these life moments, more powerful. They made more of an impression. It was a way of reflecting and realizing the things that Kenny had done and accomplished. The things Lynda has done and how she has handled this type of adversity. I have been amazed on how she and the boys have handled everything.

Even today there are enough people around here that would drop what they are doing to help them. It is a monument to Kenny, but also a monument to Lynda. Most conversations weren't Kenny, it was Kenny and Lynda, Kenny and Lynda and the boys. Team Holler.

***

My first impression of Kenny was when he was coaching Ryan in Minors baseball and how Kenny's gentle personality came across. He was great with the kids. He was understanding, because they were really little at that point. He would try to take them all under his wing, so to speak, and try to develop a relationship with all of them in different capacities.

Alexis, Kevin's Wife

***

If you ask me one thing that stood out about Kenny, it was that he made me feel comfortable around baseball. I never played baseball. I wanted to be part of my son Dominick's life, so when his Brewster Little League team came together, I didn't feel part of the team until I met Kenny. Because he taught me to do the book, I was able to sit in the dugout. I wore a coach's shirt and the kids called me "Coach!" I was able to be part of Dominick's life and that was important to me. I was glad for that.

Dom, Brewster Baseball Friend

80
Positive

Jackie: Brewster Baseball Friend

I am sure you see this in every community; it is always the same people who are volunteering and helping out. So many healthy people will be sitting on the sidelines, not picking up a rake or doing the simplest tasks, but no matter how Kenny seemed to be doing, he would always be in there helping. That always stood out to me.

How Kenny handled his suffering was a great example for the kids. Especially for the kids that had seen him over the years, the teams that his sons were on. They need to see that, because everything in this day and age is immediate gratification: you do something and immediately you get something back. For Kenny, he kept plugging along even though he wasn't necessarily getting something back. He continued to persevere and work hard, and be giving and kind, no matter what he was going through. I think they all saw it.

We can all contribute. We can take away what we learned from watching Kenny, watching him persevere, not complain, being so positive, then bring a little of that into our own lives and spread it. I hope that is part of what people can learn from Kenny's life.

***

One compliment I can say about Kenny is people used to ask to me, "Who is his kid?" He wasn't there just worried about Colin, he was there because he wanted to help coach. I remember a bunch of times when Colin was one of the younger kids, Kenny would say to me, "Take Colin out of the game." He was not there to coach his boys and get them extra playing time, because some people do. Whether baseball or basketball, he was there because he wanted to spend time with Colin, but also he liked kids, was very nice to them, and was a very good coach.

Joe, St. Lawrence O'Toole Friend

81
Husband, Father, Friend, and Coach Kenny

Kenny and Lynda's Wedding, May 1992
Our Lady of Fatima Church

New dad with Colin
November 1997

Some of the Astoria Crew - Friends for more than fifty years
Kenny, McCormick, Steve, Jimmy, Chuck, Hut, Johnny, Gary

Coaching Tim's 9 and under travel team
2009

The Ultimate Yankee Stadium Tour - Spring 2006

Aruba!
Left: Pete and Sue; Right: Lynda's mother Eileen, Joann, and Nancy

Kenny's fire coat hanging on
the garage since 9/11

June 2001

Montauk fishing trip - August 1997
Rich, Kenny, Pete, Captain Tom, Sean

Halloran Fund Golf Outing - September 2008
Kenny, Larry, Mike, and Jack

Tim's First Communion
Kenny's Second First Communion
May 2008

82
Magnetism
Brian: *Tim's Friend, Age 15*

One time we were playing baseball at Tim's house, because Tim had a party. Kenny wanted to join the game and play with us and have fun. First we didn't know what to think of it, but when we started to play it was fun. I connected with him; it was easy for me to talk to him. I felt like he related to us and if we were hanging out, I never thought, "Tim's parent is in the room." He was like another friend of ours. He was like one of us.

Kenny worked through his adversity by sticking to his roots and beliefs and kept pushing on. "Things will be okay. Don't get too high on the highs and don't get too low on the lows. Stay steady and we can push through anything," is what he taught me.

Kenny's life taught me to cherish everything and cherish my family, my neighbors, my community. It brought me a lot closer to a lot of people that I don't think I would have been that close to otherwise. It caused me to go out of my way to do little things for my neighbors. We don't really know who needs it and it makes me want to do more.

Hopefully people will continue on what he started and make an impact on their people in the same way he did on us.

***

Kenny's wake and funeral made me realize not to take life for granted, because we only get one. We need to make the most of it and help others like he did.

Sean, Tim's Teammate, age 16

***

Kenny inspired me. I will be running the Disney Dopey race for charity and cancer is one of the charities. We need to make progress battling this disease.

Jimmy, Lake George Friend

83
Impact
Dennis: *Retired NYPD, Septic Driver*

I knew Kenny Holler for forty-five minutes, just forty-five minutes, which has to be the least amount of time knowing him of anyone contributing to Lynda's project. You have all spent more than forty-five minutes stuck in traffic or in a doctor's office waiting room, or even on hold, while trying to get a live human being to help you on the phone. My forty-five minutes with Kenny, however, was a brief period of time that has left an indelible mark on me.

I am a retired New York City Police Lieutenant and I currently work for a septic service in Brewster. In my time with the NYPD, I always had great interactions with firefighters.

I met Kenny in the spring of 2012 while on a septic service call to his home. I had never met him before, but when I pulled into the driveway, I saw the FDNY turnout gear hanging proudly on the garage and felt that I was pulling into a friend's house. Kenny answered the door and I immediately noticed that he had had radical surgery on his jaw and neck. I introduced myself as a retired NYPD Lieutenant and asked him if he was the owner of the turnout gear. He acknowledged that he was and we shook hands like old friends, which, is a big deal in my line of work because nobody wants to shake a septic truck driver's hand!

Kenny showed me where the septic tank was and we talked briefly. I have witnessed many horrors and injuries and tragedies in my years with the NYPD, so I put my best game face on and asked, "What happened to you?"

Kenny replied "Oral cancer."

"Agh, sorry brother," I offered.

And to my completely unprepared astonishment, Kenny replied "I'm not."

What did he just say? Did I misspeak? He must've misunderstood the sentiment that I was trying to convey.

No, Kenny did say that he wasn't sorry and then he explained why. "Cancer forced me to retire on June 29, 2001. Prior to my retirement I was working at Special Operation Command on Roosevelt Island and on 9/11, I would very likely have been driving Chief Raymond Downey, who was killed in the Trade Center. I would've been killed too."

So being afflicted with oral cancer gave Kenny fourteen more years with his family. I stopped what I was doing, trying to absorb the meaning of what this man just told me. He has cancer, apparently pretty bad, and he finds it something to be thankful for? It was then, at that very moment, that I realized that I was in the presence of a very special person. I needed to learn something here, about life, about faith, I needed to remember this.

So what do you say to someone who has just laid that deep, unfathomable appreciation for life and family on you? Sadly, I had nothing. I was still trying to wrap my head around it. I'm sure I said something like "You keep fighting the good fight," or "Your family is all the inspiration that you need to keep going." I wish I said more to him, I wish I spent more time with him. He had a lot to teach me; I had a lot to learn.

When I was done, we parted with a handshake and a smile, and as I climbed into the truck, I shook my head. Life is so unfair... why this guy? He dedicated his life to the service of his people, a loving husband, great dad... Why? I am reminded of a passage written by an NYPD Chaplain about faith:

"Some of us have a faith that shrinks when it is washed in the waters of tribulation. We forget that trouble and sorrow have a passkey to every home in the land; no one is exempt from suffering. To believe in God does not mean that we, and those who are dear to us, will be spared those burdens that are the universal destiny of the human race."

I would drive by Kenny's house from time to time, see the turnout gear on the garage and say a quick Hail Mary for the positive, inspirational, and faithful family man that resided therein. I prayed that he would triumph over cancer.

Not long before Kenny died, I met Tom, a friend of Kenny's and a fellow firefighter. I asked him how Kenny was doing. I saw the expression on his face change, then he said, "Not good." I hated to hear that; I almost wished I hadn't asked. I asked Tom to give him my best when he saw him. What I should have done is drive that septic truck right over to Kenny's house and gave him my best in person, but I didn't, and Kenny died.

This past spring, I looked at my work schedule for the day, a job on Maplewood, one on Lakeshore, then... Holler. Honestly, I hoped no one would be home when I got there. The man left a mark on me, the man was gone. If anyone was home, could I hide my feelings? I mean, really, who am I? What could I possibly say to his family?

I knocked on the door and Lynda came out. I said, "My name is Dennis. I met Kenny the last time I was here and I am so very sorry for your loss." Lynda was wonderful, one of those people that try to comfort us, that try to make us feel better about their loss! Amazing. We talked about Kenny, the kids, faith, and all the while, this big, tough, truck-driving, retired cop is waging an all-out internal war to fight back tears. I lost, the tears won. We talked about her writing a book and she asked me if I would contribute my interaction with Kenny, those forty-five minutes that changed my perspective on life.

So what did I take away from meeting Kenny? A profound appreciation for life. No matter what our lot is, no matter what circumstances we find ourselves in, deservedly so or not, someone always has it worse. To appreciate love and be thankful for family and friends. To be blessed to meet people like Kenny, who are purposefully put into our paths for a reason, however brief.

Faith, Kenny and his family are true believers. I draw great strength from people like that. Life has put them to the test and that has only strengthened their faith and conviction. Personally, God knows I'm weak; He has only thrown me softballs of hardship in life. I pray that when I am tested, when the fastballs come, and they will come, that I find the strength, faith, conviction, and purpose displayed by the Hollers, all of them.

Forty-five minutes, wow. That turnout gear... I still see it... I hope it hangs there for a very long time. By the end, Kenny couldn't speak, but to many, myself included, he spoke louder and with more meaning than anyone with a voice. Rest in peace my friend.

There are people that you know are special, but I have never experienced it like I did with Kenny. It was as if I had known him for so long when I hadn't, this comfortableness, that we really only get after knowing somebody for a long time.

Rachel, Brewster Friend

84
Kenny

Lynda found this letter to Tommy with some of Kenny's things on Mother's Day night 2016, almost two years after Kenny died. Tomy must have died before Kenny was able to send it.

6/1/12

DEAR TOM,

WE'RE SORRY TO HEAR ABOUT YOUR ILLNESS. HAVING GONE THROUGH 4 BOUTS OF IT, I TELL PEOPLE, IT IS THE MOST POWERFUL WORD IN THE DICTIONARY. WE ALL UNDERSTAND THE WHIRLWIND THAT YOU'RE GOING THROUGH RIGHT NOW, BETWEEN DR.'S- TRAVEL + CRAM COURSE ON CANCER + HOW TO GET BETTER, WHICH IS THE MAIN FOCUS RIGHT NOW. REMEMBER, THEY'RE TRYING TO GET RID OF THAT FOREIGN MATTER (CRAP) IN YOUR BODY. AFTER BEING RADIATED 35X, I ALSO WAS HOSPITALIZED, + LOST 40 LBS. I JUST WANT YOU TO KNOW, THAT THE BODY CAN TAKE A BEATING, BUT IT ALSO CAN COME BACK, JUST AS WELL. (NO PAIN - NO GAIN). BESIDES YOUR PHYSICAL STATUS, ALSO TRY TO KEEP YOUR MIND DISTRACTED. YOU KNOW BETTER THEN ME, BUT MAYBE MUSIC, CROSSWORDS, BOOKS, RADIO TALK OR MAYBE YOUR LOVE OF HORSES. STUDY UP ON THE HORSES, WE COULD ALL USE A COUPLE OF WINNERS ONCE IN A WHILE. THE PROBLEMS YOU THOUGHT YOU HAD ABOUT A MONTH AGO - ARE NO LONGER PROBLEMS. YOUR GOAL NOW IS TO TAKE 1 DAY AT A TIME, WHICH IS HOW I STILL LIVE MY LIFE. FOCUS ON THE POSITIVE, I KNOW AT TIMES IT'S HARD, BUT YOU'RE FIGHTING POISON WITH POISON. REMEMBER - WE'RE FROM THIS WONDERFUL PLACE CALLED "ASTORIA", WE'RE A DIFFERENT BREED. A COUPLE OF HINTS TO YOU: 1.) KEEP YOUR HEAD UP AT ALL TIMES 2.) BE RESILIENT 3.) KEEP YOUR SENSE OF HUMOR - IT'S ONE THING THEY CAN'T TAKE AWAY FROM US! 4.) STAY THE COURSE. 5.) MOST IMPORTANT "KEEP THE FAITH" THROUGH ALL THIS TOM, REMEMBER ONE THING, YOU'RE NOT FIGHTING ALONE. LYNDA + I HAVE BEEN FIGHTING THIS FOR 20YRS. + I WOULD NOT BE HERE WITHOUT HER. THIS IS A TOTAL TEAM EFFORT. ONE OF THESE DAYS, TAKE A TIMEOUT + THINK ABOUT ALL THE PEOPLE THAT YOU ARE TOUCHING RIGHT NOW. AT THIS TIME OF OUR LIVES WE HAVE SURROUNDED OURSELVES WITH SOME OF THE GREATEST PEOPLE IN THE WORLD + THEY ARE ALL ROOTING FOR YOU! THERE IS NO BETTER FEELING!

LOVE ALWAYS,
KENNY HOLLER

*WHATEVER YOU GUY'S NEED- WE'LL GET - JUST CALL!

85
Valiant

Amy: *Astoria Friend*

Of all the years that I knew Kenny, and all the times we hung out, and all the things we did, and all the times we went out to the Island, the big thing that touches me is so much more recent.

I was at Tommy M's wake. I had just been diagnosed with papillary carcinoma of my thyroid. I was talking to some of the people there and I got very emotional, because I was getting ready for surgery in the next few days. Kenny took my hand, took me aside…

I am crying now as I reflect on this because it is so emotional for me…

Again, of all the times I knew Kenny over all those years, that one moment stands out so powerfully in my mind. He took my hand, he took me aside, he looked right in my face and said, "Amy, you have no idea how strong you are. You don't realize how strong you are until you are faced with it."

I knew he was talking to me from his own experience.

He continued, "You have no idea how strong you are. You are going to be fine. This too shall pass. Hang in there, be strong. Say your prayers. I am going to go home tonight and I am going to tell Lynda and we are going to pray together for you." He made me smile. I got such a big hug and such a good feeling from him. That touched me in my heart and my soul. I won't ever forget it.

Thank God, I am fine now, but at that moment, when I got the news, my world collapsed. I was talking to Kenny whose world really did change. In the middle of everything he was going through, and all that he had to face, he took those ten minutes with me. It touched me forever, I can't even tell you.

My one word would have changed over the years. Years ago it would have been handsome or funny, but now I would have to say, after going through everything, it would probably be courageous or valiant, to that end. I like "Valiant." Valiant to me is courageous and determined.

I can't even imagine how much information Lynda has gotten from so many different kinds of people from all through Kenny's life. It has to be so overwhelming, but also wonderful for her. When she is done, we will sit and read it, and it will be heartwarming; I know that I am not the only person that Kenny touched so deeply.

***

When I ride my motorcycle in the rain it is not the most pleasant thing, but when it passes and the sun comes out, I appreciate that sun more than the person that may have been riding in a car in a controlled environment and not gotten wet. I earned that appreciation; suffering is pretty much earning. At least that is the way that I look at it. There is a price to be paid.

Chang, FDNY Special Operations Command

86
Hopeful
Nancy: *Aruba Friend*

I remember very clearly the first time I ever saw Kenny. I was meeting Sue, Amy, and Joann in a Italian-Greek restaurant somewhere in Astoria. We were walking down the block and here came this super-handsome man with this big smile on his face. He started talking to Sue and Joann and they introduced me.

I only lived in New York until 1982, when I moved to Richmond, Virginia. That first time that I saw Kenny was also the last, until I started going to Aruba in 2002. That is when I got to know Kenny better. The relationship that I had with Kenny was one of, unfortunately, illness. It is very hard to explain, but it is kind of like a club; unless you are a member, you really can't understand what is going through another member's mind. It was a one-week relationship a year, but it was one that I always looked forward to.

Kenny was definitely an inspiration for me when things got difficult. He really suffered greatly and I always thought, "My goodness. What I am going through is nothing in comparison." So, it was very helpful to me. One critical thing for both of us, a really difficult part, was that we didn't want our parents to bury us. We used to talk about that; we just didn't want our parents to have to deal with that burden.

Lynda was asking for the one word and I thought about that for a long time, because I really had so many one-words that I could use. I thought about it and decided that for me the word that comes is "Hopeful." Of course brave, compassionate, there are just so many things, but for me it was hopeful, because I didn't have the hopefulness that Kenny had. I really didn't. I would get these really awful thoughts of, "I am going to die. It's not worth it". He was just an incredible inspiration.

It was also always a comfort to know that his family was praying for me. I don't know why particularly; I don't know if I felt that they had a special relationship with God and it was really going to be heard, but that was really important to me. They prayed for me and then I was able to pray for Kenny.

Anything with Aruba, I always think of Kenny. How much he loved it there and how much those vacations really meant to him. The understanding of how difficult it was for him to travel, how difficult it was for Lynda, all the things they needed to bring, making the soup, what's really odd about that is, I never saw that part.

I watched how Kenny enjoyed the mornings so much; that was his special time: taking his little swim and just sitting there on the beach. I remember that as difficult as times could be, his appreciation was for the simplest things: the sunshine and the feel of the water. How the simplest things are the best things. That's all I really felt when I was there. I didn't feel any of the other stuff, the challenges. That is my perspective.

I always knew that it was a struggle, that what he was going through was never going to have a good outcome, but the lightbulb went on the day that Lynda and I spent at the hospital.

I sat with Lynda and kept her company during one of Kenny's serious surgeries at Sloan. I had time to think about it and I was really worried about what was going to happen after that. That was a very scary time right there.

The interesting thing about suffering is that you never realize it at the time, but the experience usually allows you to learn something or see something you wouldn't have otherwise. One thing, of course, that it does is give everybody perspective on their own life: how short it is, how you have to be grateful for everything that you do have, that things can change so quickly and to not waste time, to make sure you are doing the important things with your relationships. Unfortunately, the enlightenment usually happens later when the people are gone. While they are suffering, we can't see the good in it. It can be very hard to see anything.

Through suffering, we really learn and we really see the power of love. I know we can all feel love in our daily lives. I know my sisters love me. I know my mother loves me and my friends love me, but when we are going through intense suffering, there is an incredible light and this love that we feel that is just magnified. When we know someone is in pain and suffering and that we might lose them, our love intensifies and it can be felt; it envelops the sufferer. And it is joyful.

It is really a dichotomy, isn't it? Through this terrible suffering there is also joy. It changes things forever.

For me, I felt so loved and that sustained me. I survived and I feel somewhat special having experienced this deep love of knowing my life really matters. We sometimes lose sight of this. My connection now with family and friends feels deeper and stronger than before my illness. I am changed from it and so are the people around me.

***

We have to take our hats off to Lynda. I think Kenny's strength was also related to her. Let's face it, she loved him and her love was true. That's the power. In life, when people have to face adversity, it's not the strongest, it's not the most intelligent, it is the person that has the love. That is what makes them so strong.

Dr. Herrera, Primary Physician

87
Dignified
Susan: Aruba Friend

I met Kenny on the beach at the Costa Linda, early in the morning before sunrise, as we all came down to reserve our beach huts for the day. I remember thinking he was relatively quiet when we first met, because we had a rather gregarious group on the beach each morning.

The early morning beach group could be a reality TV show in itself. Every once in a while Kenny would interject just the right amount of humor or he would speak up when he felt that the conversation was getting a little too heated. Politics were often one of those topics that brought the best and worst out in everybody.

By the time he was very ill, my husband had had the stroke. So although Kenny's situation was a much more serious situation than Johan's, there were so many parallels.

Kenny lost his ability to speak: "Hello, my name is Kenny, I can't talk."

"Hello, my name is Johan, I had a stroke. I have aphasia, I can't talk."

Many of the messages I got from Kenny, Lynda, and the boys, were gathered from sitting back and observing. I would say to Johan, "If you work, you can get your speech back." That wasn't an opportunity for Kenny, but he was serving as an inspiration.

Kenny wanted to keep living life; he wanted his family to live life! I talked to him a couple times one-on-one; he knew the sacrifices that were made and he appreciated them.

It wasn't until after Kenny's death that Lynda and I ever sat down and had a conversation. I thought, "Here is this career woman, with a young husband, young in their relationship, and they have this event in their life." It is a tragedy, it's something terrible, but it really forces you to examine your marriage vows, your love, your faith, and what it really means to support each other. It goes both ways; I know in my case, there were times that Johan supported me, that I needed his support. Even though he was the one with the stroke, he was able to do that.

When I thought about one word to describe Kenny, what came to my mind immediately was the word "Dignified." He suffered his illness with dignity. It is a hard thing to do. It is a hard when you have an illness not to be angry. Not to be frustrated. You have all those emotions, that are normal, that are natural, but do you deal with your emotions in a dignified manner? Kenny did!

He continues to be a role model. Although in this book he is the focus, I think Lynda and the boys, now young men, are role models too. They are role models on how to learn from their situation. The boys learned from their dad who was a dignified man who taught us all and gave us a family who continues to teach us.

***

Kenny inspired me. Like all of the people, stroke, heart issues, it binds us together.

Johan, Aruba Friend, Stroke Victim

88
Loving

Beth: *St. Lawrence O'Toole Friend*

I met Kenny at a very difficult time in my life. I was out of work and also in the process of a very difficult divorce from someone that was quite abusive. I was a person that had always dreamed of a loving family life. I am very Catholic. I wanted to stay married forever, raise my children, have my grandkids, and share with my husband a love, a bond that was unbreakable. But some people can't love; they have issues that prevent them from treating others with love, care, and respect. I was in a situation like that.

I went into Lynda's house, met Kenny, and it was obvious to me that he had had a radical neck dissection at some point in his life. His speech was impaired at that time, but he could speak. Lynda and I went downstairs and a few other ladies joined us. While we were there, Kenny came in with sandwiches and fresh ice tea that he had made for everyone. I was so impressed with the way that he cared for his wife, the way he was so generous with his time and his energy, and so thoughtful, to bring freshly-prepared food and drink to us when he himself was suffering.

He was well enough to have quality to his life, but it was apparent that his life was not easy. It was apparent that he didn't eat well or at least not the way we do. I was so touched in my heart by the way Kenny behaved, because I didn't know that type of love. I didn't know a man could treat his wife and her friends and his children so gently and with so much kindness. It impressed me to such a deep level that I shared it with Lynda.

When I was divorcing, and going through those months of feeling sad and struggling with the situation, I was searching for the real definition of love. I took St. Paul's Letter to the Corinthians, the passage on love, and I hung it in my bedroom and in my hall and I would read it very often. It's the one: "Love is patient, love is kind…" I remember being so moved after meeting Kenny and Lynda and their boys, and recognizing that's what love is. Being that kind, that gentle, that patient. Kenny is the description of what God meant when he described what a helpmate is supposed to be. In my heart, I said to myself, "I want a man like that someday."

I prayed that I would meet a man that could love me the way that God does; I really feel that Kenny was a man that loved Lynda and the boys the way God loves them, as much as a human man can. That's the impression that Kenny will always have in my heart.

Now, after all these years, God has brought someone with that same level of loving kindness and love of the Word into my life. Mike loves the Lord and is so aligned with my values; he treats me with love, care, trust, and respect. I say to my friends that he doesn't just treat me like gold, he treats me like platinum!

Recently Mike and I had a conversation and I shared with him the story of Lynda and Kenny. I described how the way he treats me reminds me of the loving way that Kenny treated his wife. How special Kenny was that in spite of being ill, bearing the burden of his own illness, he would go over and above for his family. He knew what it was to be a Christian husband and father. Mike is so similar and I feel so blessed, because I feel like I found my Kenny. It brings me so much joy in my heart and I am grateful to God every day for that.

With joy I tell this story, because someday I want Kenny's sons to read these pages and know that their father was the definition of what a real man is. There are a lot of healthy men out there that may put on a big show, but they don't know how to love. Kenny knew how to love and I hope his sons will live that legacy for their own wives and families.

Love is patient and kind;
love is not jealous or boastful;
it is not arrogant or rude.
Love does not insist on its own way;
it is not irritable or resentful;
it does not rejoice at wrong,
but rejoices in the right.
Love bears all things,
believes all things,
hopes all things,
endures all things.
Love never ends;
So faith, hope, love abide, these three;
but the greatest of these is love.

Corinthians 13:4-8,13

SUFFERING

God reminds us about these things, about what it is really like to be alive. That suffering is part of life. Tough thing to say to somebody that it is part of life, but it is. We suffer for people we don't even know. And maybe that is what God teaches us. When we all do something together as a group, all of us gain as a group.[14]

Now that I have a baby, I take all Kenny's suffering and the way he was able to be such a great father with his boys, seeing the way he interacted with them here, I take that, put it into my own life, and say, "I want to be like that." That's not an easy task. It is something that I have to work at, so he is a role model to me in that way. No matter what is going on in my life, I think, "Keep going, keep being strong, keep being brave, and just be happy for your children and try to give them joy." It is amazing how much he impacted my life.[15]

Kenny's suffering came to help me appreciate that whatever misery we may experience, as long as we have our family and are surrounded by people that love and support us, that's all we need. Everything else will either fall into place or we'll get through it. I realize how important family is and how important it is to be there for one another through good, bad, indifferent, whatever.[16]

Sometimes we wonder how much suffering people can take. I see people suffering and growing, dealing and accepting, and using that suffering; then I also see people suffering and just being bitter. Kenny was not bitter. I didn't see Kenny at the end, but I know that he wasn't bitter, just from knowing him and Lynda. Suffering and pain at any level can lead to bitterness if we don't explore that suffering. I have seen that. In Kenny's case he was patient and faithful in the middle of his trials and tribulations. Faithfulness is one of the Gifts of the Holy Spirit and I believe that truly speaks to Kenny's character.[17]

I derive a lot of strength from Kenny, the way he handled himself. He had a tough road. I hold him up as an example of having a cross to bear, if you will, and being able to deal with it. Kenny was stronger than I even thought. So if you asked if my impressions changed over the years, maybe that would be it. I don't know too many people that would go through that ordeal and handle it with the same grace that he did. A lot had to do with Lynda and his and her faith. If you don't believe in a higher power, I don't think you can handle it. I really don't.[18]

I had never been sick a day in my life, then I was walking down the street and Boom! like a light switch, I am on the ground and they are rushing me to the hospital. How can my life change in one second? I am not really a religious person, but lying in the hospital you do a lot of thinking about yourself, and I started praying to God to get me through. I recognize that suffering makes us better people, makes us appreciate life, helps us have empathy for other people who are sick. I definitely feel sorry for other people and what they are going through. You don't realize how it affects a person's life until it happens to you.[19]

14   Dr. Wenick, Colin & Tim's Pediatrician

15   Tara, Lake George Friend

16   Annamarie, Brewster Friend

17   John, Halloran Fund, Speech Language Pathologist

18   Gary, Astoria Friend

19   Freddy, FDNY Engine 261/Ladder 116

89
Memorable

Dr. Morris: *Head and Neck Cancer Surgeon, MSKCC*

Doing what I do, I come into contact with so many different people in such a strange and unanticipated part of their lives. I don't necessarily get to know the real person, but I get to know a part of the real person, particularly how they deal with something that is incredibly anxiety provoking.

I am a surgeon, so I went into surgery because I like doing surgery and I feel satisfaction if I can do a surgery that helps a patient with cancer. But very quickly, I came to enjoy my Mondays in the office, because I build connections with people. Over time, I get to know a little bit about my patients, but I really see them in a very unnatural way. I see them when they are sick. I see them when they are really nervous, really stressed out, worried, and most of the time it brings out really amazing things in people. Not always, but most of the time it does. In many ways, I am seeing the best of people and I glean a lot of inspiration from certain people, of which Kenny is probably at the top of the list. Very memorable guy.

The reason that he is so memorable is that I didn't meet him at the beginning of his whole journey with head and neck cancer. I met him, really, toward the end. So here was a guy, that for decades, had been suffering with multiple head and neck cancers and when I met him for the first time, with Dr. Shah slowing down his practice and me just basically starting my practice, Kenny was someone who we would sort of call an "oral cripple." That is not meant to be a derogatory term, but just a description of what it is like to have had so many surgeries to a part of our body that is so important to social interaction.

My specialty on one hand, in the abstract sense, is dealing with cancer. But in a very personal sense, Head and Neck Cancer practitioners have a huge impact on social interaction due to the damage the tumors cause and then the additional damage that our surgeries or radiation or treatments cause. This is something that we are very aware of in doing what we do. It is very different than taking care of cancers in the abdomen, for example, where a person could have had a similar parallel journey to Kenny and no one would know. It would affect him for sure, but it wouldn't affect that patient's outward appearance, his outward ability to communicate, his ability to have a conversation with his kids, his ability to go out to dinner with friends and family. All of those things were impacted, so when I first met Kenny he was a guy who had already adapted to that.

His disease was something that he was going to deal with the best he could and he wasn't going to let it consume his mental bandwidth. He focused on his priorities, which without a doubt, appeared to be family, appeared to be kids, appeared to be coaching, and just having time to spend with all of the people who were important to him. Not everyone is like that; in fact many people are not like that. I don't know that I would be like that in that sort of situation, because fundamentally it is an incredibly unfair, undeserved thing that happened to him.

So every time I met with him, there was an escalating degree of severity to what was going on. When I first met him, we could have a normal conversation. He could speak clearly; he was not difficult to understand, in spite of everything that had been done to him. He had adapted to all of this. If you looked at him and weren't someone that does what I do, you wouldn't know what he had been through. That changed dramatically in a fairly short period of time, when you consider how long this had been going on. This is the normal progression of things in this small number of patients that we see who have these multiple cancers that keep coming; it accelerates. The whole pace of everything accelerates.

So what was very memorable to me was to watch Kenny go through this transition where a lot of the things about social interaction: family interaction, appearance, all the things that are really so important to how we go through every second of our lives in public, all were taken from him in short order. In his case, with all of the other things that were going on, he also had the problems with his neck. The cancer had spread outside of the head and neck area probably pretty early in the time that I knew him, causing him a lot of pain and discomfort in other ways. He couldn't get comfortable sitting at home in his chair.

I saw this accelerated pace where it just all fell apart, specifically changes to his appearance, changes to his ability to put a sentence together and articulate it well, the tracheostomy, the feeding tube, and other things that he was doing at the beginning, but unable to do soon after, and that was just devastating. It was devastating in a way that cancers in other parts of the body that kill you as well, that take your life in just as unfair fashion, are not as devastating to your family life or your life with your friends, your public life, or just doing the things that are important to you.

So, he went through the process that many patients with oral cancer, head and neck cancer go through, however he dealt with it in a very unique way. And again, I know a piece of him. I only know the medical part of him and the brief conversations we would have about what was going on at home and how the kids were doing. His priorities were not to focus unnecessarily on what was going on with his cancer, his disease, but rather to focus on making sure that he had the time and the attention for other people that were important to him and not obsess about why this was happening to him or the suffering that he was going through.

He was a guy whose suffering I would know about because I would turn to Lynda in the office. She would tell me about it; Kenny generally, other than to be factual about it and help me troubleshoot for him, was not one that wanted to waste time, as he saw it, talking about that stuff. He wanted to get in, facilitate whatever treatment we could offer him, and then get out.

He was not "woe-is-me" lamenting what was going on with him or complaining when he had every right to complain about the suffering and the discomfort that he was experiencing. He never once told me that it bothered him that people didn't understand him as well as they used to. He never once told me that he couldn't get out to coach as much as he would like to, that the darn feeding tube kept him tied to one area for most of the day. He was just going to deal with it.

I want to distinguish that he was not in denial in any way. He was not one of the patients that didn't want to hear about it, didn't want to hear bad news, or didn't want to know details about his treatment. That was not him at all. He wanted to know everything, he wanted to deal with it, but it was not something that he was going to let define him. That is a phrase that you hear a lot with people who have cancer, but very few people are paragons of that the way he was.

I have to say that Lynda was amazing. She was not trained as a nurse and she very quickly became an around the clock, twenty-four/seven nurse and she dealt with some pretty scary situations. In many ways, I hope that she has some ability to talk about her own part of this story, because just like there is a whole spectrum of responses to getting sick, there is a whole spectrum of one's partner or family's response to getting sick. Both in Kenny's journey and his response to things, but also Lynda's, they were very, very memorable people. Melanie and I talk about them a lot. I kind of hope that my wife would be like that or I could be like that.

I am operating on a guy in a week, similar story. Very different guy, international patient, but similar disease. But every aspect of the personal story is the opposite. I see the whole spectrum. He had multiple surgeries; his wife left him. She couldn't take it anymore; didn't have what it took to do that incredibly taxing, physically taxing, emotionally taxing job that Lynda did.

I had to have a conversation with Kenny and Lynda about potential bleeding issues and I remember that Lynda didn't want to hear it. She didn't want to hear it, but who would? There are lots of conversations that we as doctors have, that we don't want to have, because it is hard and scary and it worries people and oftentimes worries them unnecessarily. There is no training as a doctor how to have these conversations, but we have to, because if we are worried about something happening, we owe it to the patient and their family to say, "Listen, this might happen and this is what it is going to be like. It's going to be really scary."

So I had to explain that as tumors in the throat grow they can start to grow into the little branches or into the main trunk of the carotid artery, which is the big artery in the neck that takes blood from the heart to the brain and everything in between. If the tumors grow outwards into the branches, they make a little hole, and then we get a very scary situation with the blood under very high pressure coming out of this tiny pinhole and drowning the patient, basically going into the throat and drowning him. It is horrendous. It is scary. It is often fatal and you can imagine sitting there and without any warning, all of a sudden coughing and all this bright red blood comes out of your mouth. Arguably one of the scariest things you would ever see. So that is what happened to Kenny.

The bleeding potential was one of the reasons why I wanted Kenny to have a trach tube, because it was a safety valve that he could breathe through if something started happening.

This bleeding crisis happens a few times a year with patients from similar situations. So it happens rarely, but it happens enough that we have a protocol at Memorial where we do certain things to stabilize. Generally, we pack it off on the inside of the throat, which we can do if the patient has a tracheostomy tube, because they can still breathe. Then we put pressure on the outside of the neck and a doctor stands there for the whole process with their hands pushing on the person's artery, putting pressure on it.

In the old days, we used to have to rush down to the operating room, open up the neck and tie off the blood vessel. That was never ideal, because by tying off the blood vessel we are cutting off all of the blood flow. What we want to do is patch the hole, not tie off the blood vessel, and the best way to do that is from the inside. So we have a team at New York Presbyterian Cornell Hospital, across the street, and that is what they do. They are on call twenty-four/seven and they take care of our patients. We have to transport the patient in a monitored ICU level setting, so that means getting a Cornell ambulance to drive across the street, park outside; we escort the patient down, load him in the back, go a block away, and into the suite I know all too well. Their phenomenal team of doctors, that is what they do, as well as all sorts of interventions where they go through the groin, thread their way up the artery, and go up into the head.

That is ultimately what they did for Kenny. In a previous era, it would have been fatal. Or if Kenny had been at home when it happened it certainly would have been life-threatening, could have been fatal, and would have been a dramatically terrible experience for Lynda and the boys.

Their options for Kenny still weren't good at first. In the operating room, they recognized that they couldn't patch the hole. If they let it go, Kenny would bleed to death. If they tied off the artery, it would be like having a stroke and he would lose all functions on the communication side of his brain. He couldn't talk at this point, but he still was able to communicate in other ways. Tying off the artery would mean he would no longer be able to communicate at all.

So they did a balloon occlusion where they went up the artery, past the area that is bleeding and they inflated a balloon to simulate what it would be like if that artery was blocked off completely. That is called a TBO, Temporary Balloon Occlusion. They checked to see whether there was blood coming from the other side going across the brain. Many people have that, some people don't. In Kenny's case he had that cross-circulation that doesn't guarantee he is going to be okay, but it makes the chance that he is going to have a big stroke much lower. That makes the doctors much more comfortable to say, "Block off the whole artery," whereas we wouldn't feel as comfortable doing that otherwise.

After that surgery, Kenny never came back to Memorial Hospital. He stayed several weeks at New York Presbyterian. Lynda said that gradually, in the weeks following that surgery, it became harder and harder for Kenny to take the thoughts from his head and write them on his pad. She wondered if it had to do with the blood flow in his brain. I don't think it was from that; I think it was really the process of him dying from the cancer.

It is a really basic question that people ask: "How does this cancer kill me anyway? It is just a thing that is growing in my neck. How am I going to die from this?" Unfortunately, there are a lot of different ways that cancer ultimately kills us, but the bottom line is we basically die of cachexia, which is failure to thrive. This essentially means that all the normal functions of the body shut down, because it has been taken over by this cancer. This invading process sucks up all of the energy, and all the nutrients, and all the fluid, like a cancer metaphorically taking over the body. In some ways, at that stage, having a sudden event like a carotid artery blow-out or dying of pneumonia, because of a tumor in the lungs and lungs getting infected, those are almost the exception to the rule and in some ways more humane ways of going, because something quick happens and the cancer takes our lives in this indirect way. More often than not, however, there is this long period of decline from the cancer metabolically taking over. I think that was what was happening with Kenny.

Coincidentally, I became friends with, not a patient of mine, but a patient of one of my partners. He had a problem in the middle of the night and I happened to take care of it, because I live nearby the hospital. He is a retired FDNY guy named Dan. He asked me a couple years ago, "Hey, do you want to go to the FDNY/NYPD Boxing Match in Madison Square Garden?" I said, "Sure!" I brought the fellow who had helped me that night. I had a great time, we became friends through that, and I have gone to the match every year since then. I hang out with him and a bunch of his vintage FDNY guys who are all Kenny's age.

One night Dan commented that a lot of FDNY guys come through Memorial because they are involved in fires where who knows what toxic fumes were in the air or they had World Trade Center exposures or what have you. I said, "Ya, I have known a few. There was this one guy, Kenny." I didn't mention his last name or anything about his medical condition. I think Kenny had recently died. He said, "Who?!" I said, "Kenny Holler." He tapped all of his buddies on the shoulder and told them, "He knows Kenny Holler!" I think they had known him from Astoria; I forget the details of where they had known him, but everybody knew him. So here I am, sitting in the middle of Madison Square Garden, and this guy is tapping all of these other gray-haired, retired firemen. They all knew Kenny; they all knew Lynda or knew about her. So that was kind of cool. That was kind of cool, because I kind of went up in their respect from being connected to a guy like that.

In response to Lynda's question on if I see good come from suffering, as a cancer surgeon, honestly no one deserves the stuff that we see here. So half of what I do every week is to work here in the lab and try to understand the molecular basis of head and neck cancer better, so that we can find cures and make progress towards lessening suffering. And if we can get rid of it tomorrow and those silver linings of good and inspiration aren't around anymore, I think we would be fine.

However, on a personal level, the way Kenny dealt with the cards he was dealt and the way that Lynda dealt with it, were something that to my whole team was very memorable and inspiring. The many fellows who came through in those years, who now I see in meetings, they still remember Kenny. And I understand that the sacrifices that people make undoubtedly have multiplicative impacts on other people. Sometimes I wonder, "What if no one ever got sick?" Yes, that would be great, but if no one suffered and no one was sick, and we didn't have these inspirational stories, what would life be like? What would we appreciate? How would we act to one another? Would there be kindness, if there was no suffering?

***

Suffering gives a man wisdom and experience. A man who has not suffered, what does he know?

Blessed Henry Suso

***

I pray that Memorial Sloan Kettering will be able to advance their studies and find a cure for this type of cancer, that children do not grow up without their parents, and that couples do not have their lives together cut short because of this disease.

Gail, Kenny's Cousin

90
Purpose
Melanie: *Dr. Morris's Clinical Nurse*

When I first heard that Lynda wanted to write this book, I was reading the notes and talking to my husband one night and I just started crying. I had my husband crying, because Kenny had such a positive impact on all of us.

I used to pray for him all the time. I would go to church and our parish has a little book where we can write all the people's names that we want to pray for. I put all of my patients' names in there, so of course I added Kenny into it. I have a strong belief in prayer.

The way he would laugh with the trach tube was very funny! It was the weirdest sound. And when I saw him laugh, his eyes would laugh. He had such pretty blue eyes. That always stuck out for me.

His attitude made me realize how strong people really are, how every person is different, and how their personalities shape how they do after the procedures and treatments. I realized that it is not a trach, it is not a laryngectomy, it is not a neck dissection, it is not radiation. Each person is an individual and we have to remember that. That is the most important thing that I remember about Kenny and I tell everybody, "We have to treat the person, not the disease." We always know in the back of our mind that each person is an individual, but Kenny helped to reinforce that.

Kenny was such an inspiration. I wish he could be in the room with every patient that walks in here. We should have a "Kenny-on-the-Shelf." Really. All we would have to do is look up and say, "That's my model." This book should be an inspiration to everyone. Not just for head and neck patients: the nails, skin, radiation, surgery, chemo, he has been through all of it. I think he could be an inspiration to any of those patients.

Kenny is the instrument here. He is the one that is helping to facilitate all of the good things that should happen from the model he made. He has taken on the burden of helping other people get to the end of a journey and that end of the journey is a good one. We need Kenny to do that, somebody who has been through it and done it well.

That is what this book is about. It isn't, "I am Kenny and I have cancer." I don't think the message is even, "I am Kenny and I can't talk." It is, "I am Kenny and I am here to help you." That is the important thing. He always wanted to help. What made him a fireman? He is still helping people now. That is still his purpose.

***

That is why, with the severity of his illness, he lasted so long. He had things he had to do; he was here for a reason and his medical issues weren't going to interfere with that.

Margaret, Brewster Friend, Homecare Nurse

91
Trach

Up until the last battle, I didn't think he was going to die. I saw Kenny in the A&P after he had been in the hospital for a while. He looked like a frail Kenny and he had a trach, but even at that point I thought, "Ok, he's out. He's got a trach, no big deal." When I was in college my landlord had a trach and he lived forever almost.

Tino Sr., Neighbor

***

I have a lot of visions of Kenny towards the end with the trach. One that sticks in my head is coming upon him at a baseball game at Markel Park. He was there, kind of inconspicuously over on the side trying to clear out whatever got caught in his trach. I thought about how a lot of people would never even come out at this point, but he was so determined to still see Tim, and the love, and see all the kids, that it wasn't going to stop him. I just think it's amazing how his illness didn't define who he was. It's like he was saying, "Ugh, I've got to deal with this, but I'm going to deal with it, because I still want to be part of this life." I know that I wish, not wish but I hope, that I can someday be as strong as that.

Jeanne, Brewster Friend

***

There was this one day at Markel Park, Kenny was in the parking lot and he was having trouble with his trach. He was trying to get his boys' attention; he really wanted to go. He was waving his arms and trying to yell, but he couldn't yell. I went over to him and I said, "Kenny, do you need help? Do you want me to go get the boys?" He said, "Ya, that would be great." So I walked to the other end of the field and told them, "Your dad really needs to get going." We all walked back and I said goodbye. I'll never forget that. I think that was the last time I saw him.

Kim, Brewster Friend

92
Giving
Eileen: Brewster Friend

I didn't know Kenny before he was sick. I thought there had been some kind of surgery that happened years prior and that was why he spoke the way he did. I didn't know that he had cancer. That was during the calmer years and to Lynda he probably was not really sick.

One day Lynda and I went to the city and she told me the whole story starting with the little sore on his tongue and it just blew me away. Then she told me about the soups. That's when the challenges hit me, when she explained how she had to make gallons of soups to keep Kenny nourished. I was at their house one day and I saw her making the soups and ladling them out into quart containers. I saw her open up their freezer and I thought, "Oh my gosh!" I was just floored by what was normal for Lynda, Kenny, and the boys.

What was normal for them was so not-normal. They made it seem like it was normal, but it wasn't normal at all. It was unbelievably hard. So, so hard. I walked away from them and their house thinking, "How can I possibly complain about anything when they do all this and don't complain?" That blew me away, Kenny's challenges and Lynda's challenges.

Then the challenges got much worse. What was normal, they probably looked back at as a blessing. The part that I thought was so hard, they probably looked back on as the easiest of times.

I remember the morning that Margaret called me and told me how bad Kenny's breathing was. I came over and drove them the sixty-five miles to Memorial Sloan Kettering's Urgent Care. Kenny was so sick in the back seat, but Lynda was so calm. I would have thought that she would have been in a panic; I was in an absolute panic driving. We were talking. I was white-knuckling the steering wheel listening to his awful breathing in the back. I was thinking: "What if we have to stop along the way? Where are the closest hospitals along the way if I need one?"

Then I dropped them off at the front of Memorial Hospital and I had to go find parking, which I really had trouble finding. I just bawled. I just bawled and I think it was partially a relief that he was in someone else's hands now. I was thankful to God that we made it, but sad that they were going through this. So I just bawled and I was glad that I couldn't find a parking spot for a while, because it gave me time to recover before I walked in to the waiting room.

We waited for hours until they admitted him and I went upstairs with them to his room. He had his board and what does he do? He writes, "So how is Danny?" It was like, "That ordeal is done, I am breathing better and I'll have a little conversation." He blew me away with his attitude on things.

I never really saw them as Lynda and Kenny, I always saw them as a team. That is how they fought everything: together as a team. Kenny absolutely inspires me, but more so the family inspires me, the unit. The way they persevered with their faith despite all the suffering. The way they were so humble and giving. The way they were all so bold in their faith throughout everything, the way they brought doctors and nurses in to pray. The way they prayed all the time over

Kenny in his room. How many people they must have touched and brought back to the faith. They'll never know and there are so many, I am sure.

One thing that I loved knowing about Kenny and seeing him live up to that high praise that everyone had for him, was that he was a fireman. My dad was a fireman, so I love firemen and I think that they are the most giving, most wonderful, loving people. Kenny was exactly that. His funeral just brought me to tears. Seeing all those firemen, I was beyond proud to be a fireman's daughter that day. It was just the best.

Kenny's story culminated for me at the community planting day at their house the October after he died. I just loved that. Everyone came together and planted spring trees and daffodil bulbs in their yard. It was such a tribute to the community, a tribute to the Hollers, and it was just a really nice tribute to Kenny's life.

***

It is hard to have hope if we don't have faith and Kenny always had hope.

Jill, Dr. Shah's Clinical Nurse

***

It is really funny how Kenny has lived his life and has built a whole community around being that nice guy. We never caught him on a bad day. If he had a bad day, we never knew it, because he was as happy-go-lucky and charming and engaged whether he had just come out of a stint in the hospital or had a bad loss on the fields or someone had just cut him off on Route 6. It is kind of an amazing gift.

Jamie, Brewster Friend

93
Crucified
Lynda

I had come to realize something about Kenny in his illness, but I wondered if the boys recognized it too. One day, I was alone with Colin and I asked him, "What do you think of when you see Dad sleeping in his recliner?"

He answered, "Christ on the Cross."

You have to envision that by this time Kenny had the trach and acute pain and muscle atrophy in his neck. He couldn't lay flat and could only sleep in his recliner. When he slept, his head would fall forward and the trach would push it to the side, so that his head would hang down tilted in the same exact position of all of the images of Christ on the Cross.

I felt that the boys and I were truly learning to know Christ better through Kenny, through his suffering and sacrifice. Kenny was choosing to suffer for the boys and me, because he wanted to be here for us, he wanted to serve us, because he loved us so much, just like Christ.

Our God, Jesus, chose to suffer the most extreme pain possible, to be crucified, because he loves every single person that will ever live. Kenny tolerated agonizing suffering over the years, but the last six months was truly excruciating. He did it voluntarily, just like Jesus did. He didn't like it, any more than Jesus did, but he did it out of love, just like Jesus Christ.

***

The first time I saw him not in pain was at the wake.

Joe, Brewster Elks Lodge

94
Courage

Dr. Lacouture: *Director, Oncodermatology Program, MSKCC*

Mr. Holler came to me because he was taking a chemo medication that caused his nails to become ingrown; it was an extremely painful condition. His oncologist wanted to hold on the treatments and the only way that he could continue to receive the medication was if we were able to control his ingrown nails. They can become infected and then that infection can become very serious. So we had to remove parts of his nails or the entire nails on many of his fingers and toes. It is an extremely painful procedure.

I inject lidocaine anesthesia with a needle into the skin next to the nail before beginning to cut, but it is essentially still like pulling nails off of someone. Mr. Holler would never complain of pain or scream or say any bad words or anything; he would just bite a paper towel or a hand-kerchief he had with him. Every other person that I have ever done the procedure to, even men, always scream in pain or say things; he just quietly tolerated it. This week in fact, I had a male patient that screamed so loudly that he was heard throughout the whole floor. This shows how strong Mr. Holler was.

Many of the people that I see are couples. It is a wonderful thing to see people come in with their spouses, but in many incidences the relationship becomes a little bit difficult. The spouses want to help so much that they don't let the patients talk for themselves. But I remember how Mr. Holler was always very open to his wife telling me what was bothering him.

It reminded me of my father, because my father was like that with my mother. My father didn't always want to know about his treatment or diagnosis. He would prefer the doctor to just talk to my mother. Sometimes when my father went to the doctor, he wouldn't even say anything; my mother would communicate with the doctor. He would just respond if he was asked a question directly. He trusted my mother so much, the same way that Mr. Holler trusted his wife.

I think it is amazing that a man, who all his life was a competitive sportsman, very ath-letic, head of the household, a fireman—where you have to be aggressive and take charge of situations, will now in these important times let someone else basically take over control of his health, his entire life. That is an incredible thing for someone to do and my dad was the same way.

Mr. Holler's strength was remarkable. He would never say that he was tired of the treat-ment. Many people do. They say, "If I am going to continue to get this side effect, I am going to ask my oncologist to change my treatment," or "I don't want to keep going with this," but Mr. Holler wanted to keep going, he never wanted to quit. That is not common.

A long time ago when I lived in Chicago, I had a patient, a very nice man, and he had cancer of his ear. He also had radiation treatments and took the same chemo medication that Mr. Holler took. He came one day and said "I am tired of these treatments and I just came to say goodbye."

This was one of my first experiences having someone say that to me. I didn't know what to say, because, as a doctor, I always want to do something for my patients. I know people might say, "Why do something if it might not help that much?" But for most people, the one thing they don't want to lose is hope and Mr. Holler never lost that hope. He never wanted to quit the treatment; he put up with these painful procedures just so his oncologist could continue the treatment.

I have been seeing people with problems from this medication since 2002, since before the drug was approved in 2004. Mr. Holler was one of the worst cases, if not the worst case, of ingrown nails from this medication that I have ever seen. I didn't tell him that because it would not be encouraging and he had so much strength. I didn't want to make him feel that this was another thing in which he was special, because of something bad. Most patients never have to have more than one or two nails removed, but for some reason in him this problem was very prevalent. He was very good at following the treatment plan to try to avoid the nail evulsions, but none of the other treatments worked. Not only that, but his nails often got secondarily infected; so his fingers must have been very painful.

He had other skin issues too, particularly a bad rash and a deep pressure wound under his chin from leaning on the trach. He was so generous with his time and he would pose for pictures for us. Who likes to have pictures taken when their nails and skin looks like that? He never said anything and he always cooperated. I think it is amazing that he was never embarrassed by it.

As a fireman on the front lines, no wonder he showed so much courage. He wasn't afraid of me pulling his nails, at all. Most people shake when I tell them this. I do a lot of lectures on the side effects of these medications and this ingrown nail problem is something that I speak of frequently, because it is very difficult for oncologists and oncology nurses to deal with it. When I present a picture of pulling the nail in one of my lectures, you can hear the crowd gasping—and this is a medical audience.

I think of him and one of the things that I say to people is that although this is a very effective treatment, I never thought that I would have someone come back to my office to have me pull their nails out again. Ultimately, I ended up removing fourteen finger and toe nails on four separate visits over a seven month period. Mr. Holler is the only person that would come here over and over, so he could get more chemo, so that he could be alive. That's how much he wanted to live.

Even though all of his medical issues and treatments had taken such a toll on him, he was such a strong and noble man. He would walk around and he couldn't lift his head up much, but he would always be looking up, even though his head was like that. He never felt that his appearance was any problem or that people looked at him differently. He would always walk with his eyes looking up at people, very proud, not shy, not embarrassed at all. He would accompany his wife who looked very healthy and for a man or a woman to be in that situation, it must be very difficult. But he was so confident, that he never showed any degree of discomfort at all.

At the end of our conversation, Mrs. Holler mentioned that her husband was just a regular guy. I think to the contrary. I don't think he was a regular guy; he was a remarkable man, because I have learned more things, not from celebrities or people in the media like that, but from amazing people like Mr. Holler. When people go through difficult things in life, with such courage and compassion, it really teaches me how to come to work and deal with the suffering that I see in people here every day.

I don't think there was anything regular about Mr. Holler. I think he was a remarkable man with a remarkable wife and it was a privilege for me to be part of their lives.

***

When I saw him, I wanted to give him the respect and courtesy of not looking at his trach. I wanted to look at the man, not his deformity.

Will, Colin's Friend, Age 18

95
Determined
Margaret: *Brewster Friend, Homecare Nurse*

Although I officially met Ken on the ball field in 2007, I have a very specific earlier memory of walking out of church, at that front exit, and him holding the door for everybody. It struck me this person, holding the door open, might be the one that needs help. I would later learn he wasn't the kind of person that wanted help, at any time.

In the ball field days, our family looking at his family didn't recognize there were such struggles going on. Which is a good thing, that normalcy was there even though he was constantly dealing with serious medical issues.

Being a nurse, taking care of him, is what stands out most. Some patients, surrender to their medical needs. He did not surrender at all. That was one of the things he hated. Hate is a strong word, but he did not want to be the patient. I never thought of him that way; I came in and he was a friend I was visiting and I think all the nurses probably felt the same way. Ken wanted to be part of the team; we were a team and we were going to figure out with Lynda, the boys, and whomever, how to get him better.

As far as taking care of him, oh my gosh, was he stubborn! I call it "determined" when trying to be polite. He was determined to do whatever he had to do to get better and he didn't want people doing it for him. There were things he didn't want to do, we know that. He had valid reasons to disagree with some of the medical stuff: this takes too long or that is interfering with things he needs to do with his family, but he set his priorities and boundaries.

It is funny, because healthcare right now is becoming more patient-centered. One of the things I am doing more in my job now is considering, "What does my patient want?" Not, "What do the doctors want?" "What do the nurses want?" Or, "What does his illness dictate?" We ask, "What does he or she want?" So Ken was a pioneer in that, because he was doing that all along. It was what Ken wanted that he pushed for, true self-management of his illness. I think that Ken would have loved that we are listening more to the patients. He made us listen even though his voice was hushed and eventually gone, leaving him to have to write his thoughts, but he made us listen. So that is a lesson. You don't have to be loud for someone to hear you. We heard him; I heard him loud and clear.

When Lynda would have to be away from the house for the day, we would have a plan for me to come in and check on Ken. He was always well aware of the plan. If I was going to be there at eight o'clock, he was up and ready by seven o'clock. If I was coming in at seven o'clock, he was up and done by six. He was determined to show both of us and the kids that he was fine and that he could take care of himself.

I want to share my reflections on when Ken had his fingernails removed to treat the infections due to his chemo. If I had to sum it up in one word, it would be "torture." It was torture; it made me angry and sad to see him have to go through that, but he did it with such grace, oh my goodness. How he tolerated that, I don't know, other than redemptive suffering. There is no other way to explain how someone can tolerate that and continue to function the rest of the day and be kind and funny.

On the four mornings after his nail removal procedures, I came to help change the bandages. He had several finger and toenails removed at a time and the bandages would stick to the raw flesh underneath. We would have to soak them and gently pull, trying not to irritate the fresh wound. Usually, when I am giving care, the end result is the person feels better. This wasn't the case. I was changing these dressings and it was terrible to know it had to be done slowly making it more torturous, more painful. We got a little better with experience and different dressing choices, but the fourth and last time was extraordinary. The dressings just fell off. It was a miracle. We didn't understand why at the time; we were all just so very grateful.

Through it all, Ken had a good sense of humor. Sometimes he would say something funny or a punchline to a joke and I couldn't quite catch it because of his voice projection and I'd have to ask him to repeat the punchline. He'd give me a look like, ugh!, and sigh, and then he'd say it again. It was still funny, but it kind of broke the momentum. I mean when you think about that, there are so many everyday things that we take for granted that could have been so potentially disappointing for Ken.

When I recently had braces on my teeth, I needed a bottle of water with me all of the time and I would think of Ken with his bottle of water, because of his chronic dry mouth. So he pops into my mind at crazy times. I think of his radio too—that old transistor radio with the antenna. That thing went everywhere, room to room; wherever he was, that radio was. It was his companion and I think it only played sports radio! He really enjoyed listening to sports shows. They were a good distraction.

There are days I think of Ken frequently. I don't know, as a medical professional for thirty years now, many people that handled what he had the way he did, managing so well his day to day family and fatherly activities *and* his feeding tube, trach, medications, and bandages. I don't know anybody that went to a Yankee game with his sons and went out to his or her car during the game because a tube feeding was due, like Ken did. It doesn't happen. He would slowly type out his text messages with big bandages on his fingers so that he could still communicate with friends and family when he could no longer talk. Imagine trying to click those little Blackberry buttons with bandages that cover your entire fingertips! Touch screen devices would have been impossible.

People give up doing ordinary things with their families to take care of themselves and they give up things that are too difficult. That isn't always a bad thing; sometimes that's what is best, but that is something that was very unique with Ken. He was determined to figure out how to take care of himself and do what he needed to do medically, yet still do the things he wanted to do with his family. For Ken to be able to manage such complex medical issues so gracefully and successfully for so long, it was obvious he was tapping superhuman resources.

A lot of it was due to prayer. Yes, we prayed for him and the family. A lot. Most of Brewster was praying. I don't know that I actively saw Kenny saying, "I'm going to say a prayer," or that kind of thing, but I know he was praying. That had to be what gave him the strength, because I don't know where else it comes from, other than God!

One thing that was a struggle for me to see, and I know for Lynda and the boys to see, was when he had setbacks and had to go to the hospital. There were many times, but twice they had to call 911 and it was awful. I always thought, "What a struggle for the kids to see that." But I realized that they didn't only see the bad part of it. They were allowed to see, and I know they saw, his strength. And Lynda's strength. They knew that his priority was to be home, not in the hospital. It's not the worst thing in the world for kids to see struggle and learn how to deal with difficult unpredictable challenges. Colin and Tim had a really good example set by their dad. It was an opportunity I think Ken recognized and took on, seriously. He demonstrated and passed on to his kids and to all of us that saw his battle, the importance of keeping the faith.

One of my regrets is I didn't see Ken when he was at Rosary Hill. I know he was only there a short time, but I just wanted to see him settled, comfortable. He tolerated a lot and he had constant physical pain, muscle aches and contractures that even high levels of pain meds couldn't relieve over the last few months. I knew he was well taken care of in Rosary Hill, so that was very comforting for me; but it was a selfish thing, I just wanted to see it for myself.

I have learned that to approach suffering with grace and determination, you have to have strength from elsewhere. Ken's powers weren't coming from him. It wasn't coming from his nurses, and doctors, and therapists, and family. That team was important, but he had to be getting his real strength from God. Period. There is no other way to explain it. What made his response to adversity so much different than most people?

It is like looking at a sunset. If you do not believe in God, and you look at a sunset, really, come on! How does that not convince you to believe? It was like that with Ken. How do we look at someone with that determination in spite of those struggles and not believe in God's presence in our lives?

***

I really wanted to see Kenny at the end to tell him how much he meant to me. I felt a relief for him and as much as it was the saddest time, he looked good. He was passing away and I could tell that he was in peace. I think where he was at Rosary Hill was perfect: the peacefulness of that environment and being surrounded by the people that loved him the most. Although it was very sad, at the same time it was happy that he didn't have to battle that illness anymore.

Maria, Brewster Friend

96
Meticulous

Carl: *Nurse, Head and Neck Floor, MSK Cancer Center*

Kenny and I got along very well because he was a retired firefighter and I am a current FDNY firefighter, so we would talk about the Fire Department a lot. When I started caring for him, he was already trached, couldn't speak, and had to communicate with me by writing.

He also had all his fingers wrapped and I had never seen that before. One funny thing that I remember is all the confusion with my first night caring for him: him teaching me how to do the dressing changes and getting frustrated with me because I couldn't get the system down.

He had a very specific system on how he changed the dressings on his fingernails. They were special bandages that were either pre-cut by Lynda or he would spend about ten minutes precutting them and laying everything out, meticulously. I was relatively new; I was just on nights and had only been a nurse for a year. You don't see that on a daily basis, so when I walked in and looked at his fingers and they were all taped up, it didn't make any sense to me. Trying to explain to me what it was and what it was for by writing on the dry erase board was very frustrating for him. I learned how to do it after taking care of him two or three times.

After working here long enough you can tell when you walk into a patient's room the vibe you get from them and the family members and I never got a vibe from him that he had given up. Even if it was something as little as the dressing changes on his fingernails, he took time to do it and the fact that he was so meticulous with it, always stuck out in my mind, because it was something that he had control over. That is why I think it was so important for him to do that.

I think about that to this day, because I was relatively new at the time that I met him and it is something that I picked up on from other patients too. They latch on to something that gives them control. It is good for them; gives them a sense of pride, a sense that they can care for themselves.

Kenny was a big Ranger fan and I was working nights at the time, so I would try and get all the medications done so I could hang out with him and watch some of the third period. We did it a few times—five or ten minutes of the game, him and me uniting. Maybe for just a few minutes helping him forget where he is, just hanging out with another guy watching the Rangers. I got a lot of pleasure out of that too and I felt like I gave him a few minutes of peace, not thinking about his situation.

***

When I was little I didn't see Kenny as sick. When I was older and he had to eat pureed foods, I sort of realized what was happening, but I didn't realize how serious it was until he was in the hospital.

Phelan, Marie's Daughter, Age 13

97

Perseverance
Connor: *Tim's Friend, Age 15*

I have been friends with Tim since kindergarten and I am at their house all the time; it is basically like another home to me. I knew Mr. Holler was suffering, but there was one day when he was in a really, really awful state.

Mrs. Holler called us up; we live right down the road. The ambulance came and a policeman or two. They took him away. I remember sitting in the car, in the back seat, and I saw them bringing him out on the stretcher. I already knew that Mr. Holler was suffering badly, but that really put an exclamation point on it.

I still think of him a lot. When things are hard, sometimes I think, "Mr. Holler wouldn't have quit in that situation, he would have kept fighting." Also, when I hear about hockey players that put initials on their jerseys for someone they are playing for that game, I always think to myself, that if I ever have an opportunity, I would definitely put Mr. Holler's initials on my jersey. It would be an honor to represent him on the ice.

Without a doubt, I definitely see Mr. Holler in Tim. Tim is a funny kid. I always get a good laugh when I am around him.

Also, the perseverance thing: it obviously wasn't easy for Tim, growing up in a house where his dad was suffering so much, but Tim never complained. Just as much as Mr. Holler never complained. Mr. Holler wasn't the only one fighting. Tim was fighting too. Colin I am sure was fighting and I am sure Mrs. Holler was fighting as well.

***

We prayed for Kenny all the time once we knew, hoping for a good outcome, but the Lord had different ideas about him. That's what happened.

George, St. Lawrence O'Toole Friend

98
Devoted
Susan: Brewster Neighbor

As Kenny was declining more and more, I hadn't seen him for quite a while. He was at Sloan a lot and I kept in touch with Lynda and Colin to some extent, but mostly through Tim.

Then the Saturday after Easter, Tim and Connor were scheduled to do their Christian Service project for Confirmation. Chris and I were getting in the car to go pick up Tim and take them to St. Lawrence for the day. And for the very first time in all of those years, since Tim and Connor were in kindergarten, my cell phone rang, Lynda was on the phone and she said, "You have to get here now! Kenny is very bad and we need you." Since Lynda is not one to dramatize situations, I said, "OMG Chris, that is Lynda and Kenny needs us right now." We flew right up the road, and went into the house. We told Connor to stay in the car; Tim came out and we told him to stay with Connor.

Colin had called 911 and a police officer met us in the driveway and came in with Chris and me. He gave us some direction as we waited for the EMTs to show up. Lynda had dialed Margaret and asked that I talk to her. She was telling me what to say as she was taking care of Kenny with Chris. Kenny wasn't coherent. He couldn't breathe regularly, was somewhat flailing a little. He couldn't express how he felt and what he needed. I remember feeling very scared. Although situations may have been bad in the past, I had never been exposed to them; the emotion of the situation and not knowing where this was going was very scary. I was very worried about Tim and Colin having to experience this with their dad and I know Lynda was worried about that too.

The EMTs came and took Ken out. Lynda went with him in the ambulance to Putnam Hospital. She asked us to stay with the boys to make sure that they were okay mentally and emotionally. We were very happy to do that. Tim and Connor went fishing, then we took all of them to lunch.

After that I didn't see Kenny again. He went from Putnam to Sloan and so forth…

Connor who is so close to Tim, just adored Kenny. He really did. He still talks about him. Kenny made a profound impression on Connor from the perspective of his strength and his kindness. And he had fun with him. It was great for him to have experienced a relationship with Kenny.

Lynda asked if my impression of Kenny changed over the span of having known him. It didn't change, but my impression of him got deeper and more meaningful. When I first met him, I thought of him as a kind, gentle soul, but after having seen all the events that had gone on and just knowing him from Little League, how he was with Connor, seeing him as a dad and a husband and a neighbor, everything I thought in the beginning, all those first impressions became more meaningful and were taken to a different level.

What is amazing to me was how great Colin and Tim have adjusted. There is happiness with them. Even last night when Tim was over, I thought how he is just such a well-adjusted, happy kid. You look at kids that may still have both parents living, who live in a huge mansion, who travel all over the world, and they are truly not happy. So it really doesn't matter what material things you have and what image you project on the outside. Kenny and Lynda should be very proud.

It is funny, now that I am driving an hour to work every day, I spend part of that drive praying. I did pray for Kenny back then and from time to time now I think, "Hmm, Ken. Connor could use some help on that Chemistry test!" And when I see Tim laugh, I think, "Ken would enjoy seeing that, knowing that he is doing so well."

***

I remember bumping into Kenny at a fish store in Danbury with Timmy. He struggled to speak. He couldn't speak that well, but I understood him; he made himself understood. I thought about him all night that night; I worried and couldn't get him out of my mind. That's when I realized how sick he was.

Shortly after, my younger son Nico and I pulled out of the driveway and the ambulance went by us. I made a left and we were right behind it. I was thinking, "I hope this is not for Kenny." And almost at the same time Nico said, "I hope this is not for Mr. Holler." Sure enough it pulled into their driveway and I said, "That was for Mr. Holler..."

Carmela, Neighbor

99
Relationships
Kristen: Nurse, Head and Neck Floor, MSK Cancer Center

I took care of Kenny a lot! I have been here since 2009. I actually remember the rooms where I took care of him. He was in 1736. I remember the most recent one was when he was in 1725B.

The most memorable time that I had him was when he had his final episode of bleeding. I came into work at about 6:45 in the morning and no one was in the station, everyone was already back in Kenny's room. I had checked my assignment and saw that he was my patient. I walked into the room. He was awake, he was alert, he was listening to what everyone had to say about what was going on and he was bleeding from the trach and mouth. I didn't report to any of my other patients and Kenny and I had a couple of hours together, just me and him hanging out in that room with doctors and nurse practitioners coming in and checking on him.

He was scared, who wouldn't be with what was going on with bleeding, but he was so calm the whole time. I don't know if it helped him at that point, that we knew each other pretty well, but it definitely helped me. It helped me to know: "Is this how he is acting because he is losing blood or is this how he normally is?" He was a pretty calm person for me. He would write on his white board, "What is going to happen? What are we doing? What is the plan?" Or "I'm having pain." Or, "I'm nervous. Can I have something for anxiety?" So the whole time, even with him having a little bit of bleeding that would stop and start again and stop and start again, he was telling me exactly what it was that he needed. If everyone reacted to his or her life-threatening event as he reacted, we'd be doing okay.

They decided right away that they were going to send him across the street. I went with him down into the ambulance with the doctor. Kenny was put into the ambulance and it did a U-turn and pulled into New York Presbyterian Hospital. I was scared for him, knowing him so well, knowing how long he had been in the hospital, how his disease was progressively getting worse, and how he was getting weaker and having more pain.

A couple days before, his glasses had broken. I tried my hardest to get those things fixed. There was an issue with the screw on one of the arms. I went across the street to Duane Reade and I got a little kit to fix glasses and he said, "I can't believe you did that! Really? You could have just taped them."

I said, "No, you would look like a total dork with your glasses taped!" Honestly, I don't think they held up for that long. We'd find them in different places in the sheets. So for whatever reason, I always think about him and those glasses.

Unfortunately, because Kenny was here so many times with a lot of different issues, Kenny was like a mascot for the floor. A bunch of nurses cared for him and he was someone we remember because … he was Kenny! "Oh, Kenny's back. I'll take care of him."

Lynda had the pictures of the boys up in his room, she was always coming in and well cared for him. We remember very well the patient and we remember very well the family. Even now, it has been two years since he has been here and there are still people on the night shifts and day shifts that will say, "Ya Kenny, Kenny Holler. Of course, I know who he is." Lynda said that they were so thankful for the care and love that the medical staff here showed Kenny. He gave it back to us too. He was so thankful and appreciative to us for caring for him.

Kenny put his faith in us as a health care team and he put his faith in God, saying without words, "You are looking over my life and Thy will be done. You are going to be with me the whole time and I am going to be a follower of Christ, follow You, and follow Your Word." Kenny was living his life how it was meant to be lived. He showed that to others too.

***

To what length could we go for the people that we love the most? Kenny was our example of that. I have heard people talk about the trauma they have gone through and their experiences, and difficulties, but I had never really witnessed someone so close actually going through it.

Doris Ann, Lake George Friend

100
Compassion
Jack: *Astoria Friend*

With Kenny having two sons, I often thought about how they saw their father deteriorating. I wondered what Kenny thought about, when he thought about what his boys might be thinking. How he would have liked to have been able to do things with them, but wasn't capable. I think about all that psychological stuff, I don't know how we handle that. It's one thing when people die, you kind of get beyond it, but when it is long like that…

We go through our life, our time on earth and I guess we are supposed to learn things, experience things in this life. We have to do that by different means, so if Kenny was here for me to have compassion for him, then he fulfilled that part of my life, because I needed to know and to feel compassion. Without him, maybe I couldn't have felt it completely.

In a strange roundabout way, maybe we are all here for some reason for each other. So that somebody else can say, "I know Jack, he did this … and that was good because without having experienced Jack, in some way my life wouldn't have been complete." If it is God's plan that we are here to experience life and all its ups and downs with everybody teaching us something, it shows that we are all connected somehow, even though we don't understand it. That this is just a step towards the next life. Our time here feels long, but then when we look back it seems like the blink of the eye.

I was in church one time, my mind wandered, and I experienced a spiritual event. I felt like everything—it's tough to describe—everything in the universe and how everything is connected became perfectly clear, for around ten seconds. I remember thinking, "Oh man, now I get it! This is great!" And then realizing that I was coming back down to earth. I was trying to hold it, but it was gone. It was complete bliss. That is the only way to describe it. Just the peacefulness of it. The completeness of it. It was overwhelmingly wonderful.

Kenny certainly suffered here on earth, but he impacted everyone around him and now that is what Kenny is experiencing: an eternity of what I had for only ten seconds. He is part of that perfect bliss. No pain, nothing, just bliss.

***

After Kenny passed away I was diagnosed with cancer from 9/11. I have lymphoma; I am in remission, thank God. I thought about my kids and my wife which made me think about what Kenny, Lynda, and the boys went through. The horror of thinking that I am not going to be there for them. I think about that. I think about that a lot: what Kenny had to be thinking about knowing that he wasn't going to get better.

Little Murph, Astoria Friend

101
Witness
Victor: Lynda's Friend

Witnessing people like Kenny, I realize that it doesn't matter who you are, how old you are, what color skin you have, where you work, cancer can affect anyone. We have to accept that. We have to take each day as it comes. It is a good thing to be realistic. Cancer knows no boundaries or age limits or anything like that.

Of course we ask the question all the time, "Why, why, why?" It is no good saying it is God's wish—I mean simplistic terms like that. I am sure it was His wish, but we don't want to hear it like that.

Someone can say, "God is good." We know God is good, but we still say, "Why in Christ's name is he putting me through this?" I don't have the answers; nobody has them. I would hope that it has made me a stronger person looking towards life.

Most truthfully, if anything has come out of Kenny's suffering, I don't really fear death myself. I've never thought, "I'll be 66 next month, I'm getting older." Of course, maybe when He comes knocking on the door, I might be screaming my head off, you know, but I don't worry about it. It is inevitable. If we worry about it we will just go crazy. It has just solidified my opinion that we need to just take life as it comes and make the best of it.

***

When we are hit with some small situation, medically or personally or whatever, we can turn around and see what Kenny and other people have been through. That makes us stronger, makes us say, "If I can't deal with this, how did he deal with that?" It's that type of stuff that has an impact. A big impact.

Mike, Kenny's Cousin's Husband

I only met Kenny because of Lynda. Lynda was a huge, positive person in my life when I first met her. I had left my job, my career, and was a first-time mom. Lynda taught my Adult Education sewing class. I still have the window curtains and shower curtain I made hanging in the boys bathroom. I had my first baby boy, Brian, and Lynda was pregnant with Timmy.

Then, I didn't see her for a few years until Pre-K at St. Lawrence. My first memory of Kenny is meeting him downstairs in the cafeteria when we were picking up the boys. I remember I was excited to finally meet Lynda's other half and I was happy that our boys were in school together and that they liked each other. Then I found out that he was a fireman; I love firemen.

I went to the Holler's house and I could see how proud Kenny was of his career by his pictures on the wall and Fire Department memorabilia, but I never saw pictures of Kenny when he was younger until the wake. Those brought him to life so much for me. I got to see him healthy; I got to see him fooling around. I got to see him without a shirt on and just being Kenny. It was very surreal for me. I loved that moment of seeing his timeline; seeing what he used to be like.

He was so happy that he got to receive the Eucharist, the Body of Christ, at Church, with his water. That made an impression on me. A couple times he told me how Father had given him a little piece of the host and he would use water to wash it down. That was so important to him. Lynda told me this story:

Kenny had gone quite a long time without receiving the Eucharist—a few years, because of the repeated surgeries in his mouth, the long time that it took for his mouth to heal from those surgeries, and he was also afraid that with his dry mouth, he wouldn't be able to swallow the dry host. He hadn't been able to eat solid food either and they had been praying every night for Kenny's mouth to get better, so he could eat with them as a family again. So a couple months before Tim was to make his First Communion, the four of them were driving in the car, and Tim said something like, "Daddy, maybe your mouth will get better and you will be able to receive Communion on my First Communion Day!"

Kenny and Lynda told Father Doughty that story soon after and he said, "That's the Holy Spirit speaking through Tim. He wouldn't think of that all on his own." He continued, "I haven't thought of this before, but what we can do is break off a tiny piece of the Eucharist and give it to you. It is the same Body and Blood of Christ." So Kenny waited until Tim's First Communion Day and he walked up and received; they called it Kenny's "Second First Communion." He continued that way for a long time.

Lynda also told me that he had needed water for years because of his dry mouth, but only recently had they been able to buy those small bottles of water that he could stick in his pocket. In the early days, he would take those little liquor bottles that you get on an airplane and put water in them. He'd have that in church. They always kind of wondered what people were thinking when he was swigging that down!

I had never orchestrated a prayer service before. I knew there were a lot of people in the community pulling for Kenny and his family and wanting to do something, anything for them. Anything to lift all of their burdens. In the end, I thought that it would help for everybody to get together and pray for Kenny. I felt that prayer was what we had to offer. And we were looking for a miracle. Lynda had written something prior to that about praying for miracles and I was really praying for a miracle that Kenny's health would turn around.

I remember that Lynda had a really hard day that day. She came to the service with the boys, but at the end of it, she said that she was angry. I had never really seen her angry. Kenny was in the hospital and she was afraid that he was going to get pneumonia. She said, "On top of all of this, now he is at risk…." And I said, "I am surprised that you are surprised, because you have been faced with everything." It shocked me. Lynda was vulnerable.

Organizing the prayer service and setting up the meal train were kind of just automatic to me. This is what you do; this is what it is all about. It's helping people. And as a mother, feeding our children is so important as a nurturing thing. I love it when my boys are happy with their meal. I try to make them nice meals. Lynda was trying to keep that normality to their family life.

I didn't see Kenny very much when he couldn't talk. One of the last times that I talked to Kenny was at the Brewster Bear Classic Cross Country meet in October. Both of their boys were running. Kenny had the trach. I know it was difficult for him to talk, but what he always said was, "This is great! This is great to be here." He was so supportive and there for the moment. If there is anything that people should learn, it is to be present and enjoy the moment. I took a picture of Kenny, Lynda, and the boys on the field after the boys ran.

Kenny was accepting. That is a good word. I think some people that are suffering need to verbalize every ache and pain, but Kenny didn't need that. If I have physical things going on with me, I am not very verbal about them either, because I don't like to put that burden on other people. When my husband Jimmy comes and says that his back hurts, he verbalizes it. I internalize it; I try to fix it. So maybe Kenny was saving us all from trying to fix things all the time.

I talked with my son Brian about a single word to describe Kenny. The first word he came up with was "Tornado." He said, "You know Mom, he is the center and everybody is just gravitating towards him. Everybody wants to be with him and he is in the middle of it." Kenny stayed as the calm in the middle of the tornado too. He stayed very calm through all of his challenges.

A while ago, I talked to Father Gill and we talked about Kenny. Kenny's wake and funeral made a big impression on me. I listened to everything; I didn't want to miss anything. I came away from his funeral thinking, which I had never heard before, but I liked: "Christ suffered, but because we have free will and people still continue to do sinful things here on earth, there are other people that are suffering and carrying that cross as well for us."

That made Kenny's suffering so much bigger. I know that I thought of Kenny's suffering as a very big hardship, but that made me understand that he was doing it for us. Because of Kenny and Lynda, I get that now. Lynda has impacted my life in many ways too, not just Kenny. Their message is being heard; their message is helping.

Somehow, how Kenny suffered, how they dealt with it as a family, has been uplifting for the community at large. That level of suffering is so deep. There is a strength in their family that is awe inspiring. I still think of them as family and they're all still a part of him. How proud Lynda must be that he was her husband and these are her beautiful sons. He lives on.

Carole, St. Lawrence O'Toole Friend

103
Healing Prayer Vigil

When our parish got together and had an evening of prayer for Kenny, it was amazing. It was very powerful and that was probably the first time that I really experienced the Body of Christ in this parish, in that way. It was totally voluntary; it wasn't a Mass that people had to attend. I began to hear the love in our parish, see the community of our parish. It was blossoming.

Jean, St. Lawrence Friend

***

Kenny was a unifier of our community. Coming together to pray for him, that was very powerful. When we had the prayer vigil it was packed, packed with kids and adults and older people, younger people, people that never went to church, and they were all there. Around then I really started thinking about the power of prayer.

Denise, Brewster Friend

***

I am not a religious man at all, but when they held the Healing Prayer Vigil for Kenny at the church, I said that I'm definitely in, I'm going. I went with the family and I was blown away by the support and the number of people who were there in the church that evening. It was so moving for me, touching. Wow!

Chris, Brewster Friend

***

I remember Deacon Mark and how moved he was emotionally at the strength of Kenny's family and the sense of passion and urgency that he had in his voice. I had never seen or heard Deacon Mark, or a priest for that matter, talk like that. Whether it is the joy of the Christening of a new baby or the joy of a marriage or whether it is the sadness of a funeral, the priests and clergy are always even. I remember praying and hearing Deacon Mark speak and that impacted me a lot.

Tom, Brewster Baseball Friend

211

When they had the special Healing Prayer Vigil for Kenny, it was just so nice to see the turn-out of friends showing how much he was loved. It was truly, truly remarkable to see the love that he received from one town and I can't imagine other places, other friends that he's had. I am sure that he has touched the hearts and lives of so many people. I am so grateful that he was able to touch my life and those of my family.

Kathy, Brewster Baseball Friend

104
Email
Brigid: *St. Lawrence Friend*

Hi, Lynda,

I know we didn't get much of a chance to talk last night, and maybe you wouldn't have wanted to anyway.

I have been praying for you, of course, but I added a new intention for you and Kenny after we talked the last time. I'm asking the Lord—and Mary—to reveal to you the purpose of your suffering. I don't claim often to know much about God's ways, but on this I am sure: there is no suffering without purpose for God. There is no such thing as just bad luck, just the short end of the stick. If that were true, then there would be no all-loving, all-good God. If there is just bad luck, then someone is being forgotten and forsaken by God, and that is not possible. When Jesus said those words on the cross, "My God, my God, why have you forsaken me?" He did not say them because He had been forsaken. He said them so that we know that, even in great suffering, when we feel forsaken, God hears us, and we can cry out. And we can have confidence that he will, at the proper time, make us new again.

Lynda, I am sure you and Kenny often feel alone, even with so many praying for you, because what you experience can't really be shared. And yet it is shared by so many. So many saints! So many good, innocent people who suffered so much! And, yet, their suffering was never in vain, was never for no reason, was never just tough luck. No, it always, always had a purpose. And so does yours.

No need to reply unless you want to.

Love,
Brigid

July 19, 2012

105
Redeemer
Lynda

I was born into a devoutly Catholic home where praying and attending church was as natural as eating and sleeping. I remained faithful to God and the Church in college and adulthood, continuing to attend weekly Mass, praying, and trying to remain obedient to my parents and my Heavenly Father. I chose to fall in love with a Catholic and we received the powerful Sacrament of Marriage before God and our friends and family at Our Lady of Fatima Church in Jackson Heights.

Eight months later, Kenny was diagnosed with his first of many tumors and the praying intensified, but I didn't really recognize any results, any satisfaction from my prayers. I felt a real spiritual darkness; I would cry myself to sleep praying and wake up still feeling lousy. For a long period of time, I felt as sad about God's seeming distance, as I did about Kenny's illness. In retrospect, without the prayer, the invisible graces that we received through the sacraments, and the focus outside of ourselves, we could never have survived those two decades. By that, I mean not only physically survive, but our marriage might not have survived either.

Of course, we taught our children to pray. We prayed in the traditional ways, but we added our own personal touches too. For instance, I am not someone who feels content praying for masses of people. Praying for the souls in purgatory feels too impersonal, like praying for everyone in Yankee Stadium—no connection. So in addition to loved ones, at bedtime the boys and I would pray for specific strangers in purgatory. For example, one of us would be inspired with a description like: an old black man that played the saxophone, had one daughter, and lost his wife early in their marriage. We would ask God for our prayers to be the extra boost that man needs to be in Heaven with Him that day. We were confident that someone there fit that description.

When we pass a cemetery, we bless ourselves and ask God to boost the next soul buried there. These forms of prayer give us the feeling that we are helping specific strangers, one real person at a time, and it feels good.

The suffering that Kenny endured was unlike anything I had ever seen or could have ever imagined. I would speak with my priests and enlightened friends about God's purpose for suffering and they would mention Redemptive Suffering.

Redemptive suffering in its simplest form, is the "offer it up" technique that we learned as a kid from our mothers when we didn't want to eat our cauliflower. But it goes much deeper than that. Christ dying on the cross was redemptive suffering. He could have chosen any other way to save us, but he chose to suffer an excruciating death on a cross. The worst form of torture known in the ancient world or even in the world today, for that matter. So I understood that suffering had to have value. If Jesus chose that method to prove that He loves us unconditionally, to redeem all of us from sin, and bring us to the Father, it must be very powerful indeed.

So throughout our darkest periods, I was told that Kenny's suffering, and my own suffering, was being used to help souls, to bring them closer to Christ. This was still a tough concept for me to comprehend. I could kind of understand how Jesus' suffering could help us, but how could Kenny's suffering make the world any better? No one could describe it in any more concrete way, so it was too abstract of a teaching to bring me any comfort.

Of all of the horrific experiences that we endured, one of the worst, one that I will never forget, is when Kenny had to have his finger and toe nails removed. He had a total of fourteen nails removed over four separate visits. For the first one or two, we were rather innocent, but the last visit was very different. We had tried to treat the latest infections topically, but to no success. We made an appointment to see Dr. Lacouture and they fit us into a crowded schedule.

They brought us into a small examining room and for some reason I didn't think Kenny was going to have to have nails removed that day. When the doctor announced that he was going to have to remove several more, I was devastated. I felt that my heart would explode with sorrow. Normally, I had remained in the room behind the curtain for the procedure, but this room didn't have a curtain. I would have left the room and waited outside, but Kenny couldn't talk by this time and I needed to stay there for him.

A French doctor was observing and saw my silent distress. He positioned himself between me and the table as a block. I pulled out my rosary beads, closed my eyes, and started saying the rosary in my head, but I was bumbling my way through my prayers. I couldn't even say a complete *Our Father* or *Hail Mary*. So at one point, I put down my rosary, clenched my fists with my head bowed and eyes closed, and I silently prayed:

"God please use this suffering for something enormous! Save a lot of souls, bring people to you, or whatever, but please don't let this be for nothing."

Then I picked up my rosary and continued those prayers as best I could until the procedure was over. The kind nurse, Pat, carefully wrapped up Kenny's fingertips, we packed up our stuff, and went home.

The next worst thing to removing the nails was removing the bandages the next morning. They would stick and we'd have to soak them, so that we didn't tear any of that sensitive skin where the nails used to be, but that morning the bandages just fell off. I didn't attribute it to my prayers, I was just thankful and we went on with the rest of our daily challenges.

Fast forward a few months and Kenny has had the carotid artery surgery and is at New York Presbyterian Hospital. I visit him about every other day by train. I am too tired these days to drive there anymore. I try to leave him by four o'clock so that I can get home, serve dinner, and be with the boys in the evening. This one day, Kenny was sleeping most of the day and I was just keeping him company bedside. At four o'clock, I woke him to tell him I was leaving and he held up his index finger, signaling, "Wait." Occasionally, when he would start to write something on his notepad, I would jokingly ask him if he was writing me a love letter. He never was, that wasn't his thing; he would just write that he needed pain meds or his trach suctioned or something like that. But this time he was writing a letter to me, telling me how much I meant to him.

I was not going to leave until I had that letter.

The problem was he kept dozing off. I would gently shake him and say, "Kenny… finish my letter…"

The other obstacle was that he couldn't take the words from his head and write them properly on paper. For instance, if he was trying to write, "I like you." He would write something like: "IIIIIIII IIiiiiiiikkkkkkkkeeeee yyyyyouuuuu," and it would extend across several lines. The other thing that he did that day was write from left to right across the top of the paper, like normal, but when he got to the right side, he would turn the paper ninety degrees counter-clockwise and continue writing down the side of the paper. These things could leave the meaning of his thoughts a bit open for interpretation, but his meaning that day in his note to me was very clear and I wasn't leaving without it.

So, he would write a few words, doze off. I would wake him; he would think about it, write a few more words, and doze off. Two hours passed as I waited for my note. Finally, he wrote perfectly in the center of the page: "To be continued." It never was.

I thanked him for the note and kissed him goodbye, but he held up his finger again, "Wait." He took a fresh sheet of paper and wrote, "Tell the kills I love."

I walked out of that hospital across Sixty-Eighth Street toward the subway with those two precious notes in my bag, my arm protectively holding the bag secure, and feeling that my heart had been hit with a hand grenade. I felt like I was suffering as much as Kenny was at that moment. I had sun glasses on, crying, sure that my heart was splattered all over my insides, and without realizing it I prayed the same words I had back in Dr. Lacouture's office several months earlier:

"God please use this suffering for something enormous! Save a lot of souls, bring people to you, or whatever, but please don't let this be for nothing."

And a revelation came to me from God. The words were spoken to me from within my heart as clearly as if they had been whispered into my ear.

> God told me that we are suffering for people that do not suffer well: for people that are turning away from God because of their suffering instead of toward Him. That we have continued to grow closer to God through our suffering and we are helping real individual people. We may not know them or we might. It could be Felipe in the Philippines, Doris in Denver, or someone in our own family or community. That is God's discretion, but our suffering is valuable, it is accomplishing something, and it is very, very important.

When the message was over, I realized that I didn't feel any better. It didn't alleviate the pain, the sadness, the disappointment one little bit, but it gave it purpose. God explained Redemptive Suffering in a way that I could understand and appreciate it. Remember how we had been praying for individual strangers? We are called to be disciples and there is nothing more important that we can do than to bring more souls to God.

Most people that I have spoken with since have never even heard of Redemptive Suffering and the few that have cannot describe how it works. When I discussed it with my Baptist friend, she lit up and said,

"That explains why bad things happen to good people! We feel so bad for those good people that have very challenging lives, that seem to have one bad thing after another happen to them. Their suffering is being used by God to save others!"

When I discussed my revelation with Father Gill to make sure that I hadn't misunderstood the divine message, he said that Victim's Souls will meet up with the souls that they saved in heaven and will rejoice together. Imagine celebrating with complete strangers because we saved them from eternity in hell. Wow! Kenny must be surrounded by an enormous community of new friends!

I feel that was part of God's purpose in revealing this simple definition to me, that I would share it with others and help them understand. So that all of us can make the conscious effort to offer God our suffering for his service, to put it to good use, to give it purpose, not to feel that it is getting in the way of the life we were supposed to live. It becomes key to our purpose on earth.

Redemption can come from daily inconveniences like a broken washing machine or flat tire, a headache or a poor test grade. Or it could be major life disappointments and sacrifices like job loss, financial problems, divorce, serious illness. The list goes on and on. Every day we deal with life's challenges and know others that are fighting even bigger battles. We can continue to blame it on an unfair world or we can put it to use, unite to Christ's suffering, and make the world a better place.

I had the opportunity to explain it to Kenny and he understood it. He couldn't talk or write a response back to me at that point, but I am sure that this man that would give the shirt off his back for a complete stranger, found comfort in knowing he was helping them on a more eternal level.

I explained it to the boys and they "get" it. I wish that I had understood it at their age: that I could have taken my life's challenges and disappointments and felt that there was some good coming from them. I trust that God did it for me back then, but now I will consciously try to remember to offer my suffering to God for His good, at His discretion.

***

I think about Kenny and Lynda and what they did with their kids, praying for someone else in purgatory. Hoping that their prayers will be answered and somebody will be set free up into heaven. I am going to cry … I do that now. One thing I do differently because of Kenny is the way I pray for souls in purgatory.

Emily, Brewster Friend

106

Inspirational

Deacon Mark: *St. Lawrence O'Toole*

I preach on marriages when I do weddings and I preach on what a true marriage is that accepts sickness and health. Not just at the moment of happiness when we are exchanging our vows, but long-term, because that's part of life. When sickness strikes, I have seen couples go their separate ways. They become so angry, so anxious. I never saw that in Ken and Lynda. Never. They grew closer because of it, bonded more deeply, worked as one. Ken and Lynda's marriage reflected their love. Just like the snow cannot permanently cover the spring flowers, no amount of pain could cover the love the two of them had for each other.

As time went on, I got to know Ken even better. The only thing that to this day leaves a knot in my soul is thinking about him receiving Communion. He started from receiving a full host, then smaller and smaller and smaller pieces until it was barely, barely a crumb. It was beautiful that he still desired to receive Christ in the Eucharist, but I just felt so terrible, because I saw him declining everyday more and more and more. He took his sickness with such deep faith. I've seen people get so upset at God.

Lynda told me about her revelation on Redemptive Suffering. I don't know if she realized the power of those words, "God please use this suffering! Save a lot of souls, bring people to you, but please don't let this be for nothing." God gives faith to all of us the day we are baptized, but it is up to us what we do with it. The gift of faith that she received manifested itself at the most difficult moment in her life. She said that she felt like a grenade had exploded in her heart, but she didn't cry, "Oh please God, why me?" She said, "Do it for others. Use it for others."

It doesn't come naturally for most people to accept suffering. God gives us life. That is a gift. He wants us to fight for that life. That's what I saw in Ken. A month before he died he wouldn't sign the DNR (Do Not Resuscitate) papers in the Emergency Room of Yale New Haven Hospital. He wanted to fight it to the very end. The way I saw him, he never looked at his suffering as a punishment. That takes a lot of faith, takes tremendous faith, because sickness can be very discouraging. It can bring us to our knees in many ways.

To me that was so beautiful, to suffer that way. I discussed this with my wife, when Ken was suffering, and also when I blessed that tree that was planted in his honor on the Little League field. I said, "No one prays for death to come, but seeing Ken suffer, almost silently, without complaint, and with so much faith, it took the fear of death away from me." Honestly, I do not fear to die. I came to the realization that it is a process, it is part of my life. Obviously, I am not going to volunteer to take the cross upon me. Even Jesus said, "Father if you are willing, take this cup away from me; still, not my will but yours be done." That is what Ken did. He went through his agony in the garden. He accepted his chalice of suffering and he really suffered very bravely.

Ken's life here was a superb example, not just for his wife and boys who shared their lives with him, but for us who were privileged to have met him. I was definitely, personally, positively influenced by Ken's life, by his suffering and death. To see his suffering, I consider that a privilege. That I was able to witness that, it influenced me, how I look at life.

Christ took away our sins on the cross; Ken's suffering took away my fear of death. I honestly believe that God put Ken in that position to influence other people, gave him that sickness and suffering, so others could see how to suffer.

*****

The reason why God exposes his chosen servants to so many grave dangers ... is his burning desire for the salvation of sinners.

Saint Lawrence of Brindisi, Doctor of the Church

LIVING

I think it is a miracle for me to get to meet a family that's able to be so functional in the face of such difficult things. It is not about, "Is it fair? Is it not fair?" It is about the ability to hold on to our lives and what is important to us. For Kenny and Lynda as a family, it was so important to them to maintain normalcy and for Kenny to never be alone. That was so much about Lynda too and so much about mobilizing their entire community. I remember that there was a community upstate that was involved bringing meals to the house. Then with Kenny's tracheostomy, not being able to speak, being in the hospital and never being able to be fully as kept and as neat as he would want to be, he still remained so elegant. And as a family they remained so elegant. They rose above difficult circumstances.[20]

---

20   Dr. Adams, Palliative Care Physician

107
What Cancer Cannot Do
Anonymous

Lynda found this poem in Kenny's hospital toiletry bag after he died.

Cancer is so limited…
It cannot cripple love.
It cannot erode faith.
It cannot eat away peace.
It cannot destroy confidence.
It cannot kill friendship.
It cannot shut out memories.
It cannot silence courage.
It cannot invade the soul.
It cannot reduce eternal life.
It cannot quench the spirit.

108
Gentle-soul
Deb: *Kenny's Hair Stylist*

I cut Kenny's hair for about twelve years. I had the chance to really get to know Kenny. Sometimes he would ask me, "Can you hear me? Can you understand what I am saying?" I guess a lot of people would question him and ask him to repeat himself. I could understand every single word he said. I got to know him so well that I could actually read his lips.

I remember going to his house for the first time years ago. I had been cutting Kenny's hair in the salon, but he had a very serious operation where they had to cut into the jaw bone. Lynda called and I went to the house. He was ecstatic that I took the time to come over. I said, "Kenny, if you were in my shoes you would do the same thing." That's the kind of person he was. I felt that I needed to return that back to him, because he would have done it for me or anybody else.

He would ask me if I was okay to shave the side of his neck, because sometimes it was very hard to do with the contour of his neck and texture of his skin; I didn't want to cut him. He would say, "Don't worry about it." In other words, if it was going to bother me to do it, don't worry about it. I would do it anyway, because it would make him feel so much better. Then when I finished cutting his hair, he would say to me, "I feel like a new person." So I knew it made him feel really good to get all cleaned up.

Appearance was very important to Kenny. He didn't want people to feel sorry for him. He wanted people to look up to him. I think having me do his hair and shave his neck made him feel better, more presentable, because he didn't want people to think he looked sick. He wanted to look as healthy and normal as he possibly could.

I went to Putnam Hospital to cut his hair a couple days after he had been admitted after the second 911 call. At that point he was really planning on going home, I remember that, but he never went home again. He couldn't speak to me, but he wrote down on the paper that he was going to get better. He still, in his mind, was going to get better. He was even writing and making jokes with the nurse. He made a comment to her, "Don't worry, we'll clean up the hair!"

I think that was the one and only time that I started to question myself, "I wonder if he is going to make it?" But he was like a cat with nine lives. I would push that thought away, "He's going to bounce back!" I think a lot of people felt that way.

I left there giving him a big hug and kiss thinking, "I am going to see him again; he is going to come home." I walked out the door and he gave me the "thumbs up" like, "I'm going to be okay. I'm going to make it." He wanted me to leave the room and say, "I'll see you at the house." It was the last time I saw him.

Good memories. Very, very good memories. I miss him terribly so when the boys come in, I see him in their eyes. I do; I see him. I almost feel like he is sitting in the chair with them because of their mannerisms: the way they talk, the way they act, now that they are getting older. I see Kenny in Colin. I see Kenny in Timmy. I see the maturity in the boys and Dad coming through the boys.

They have so much of their father; they carry on that legacy that he created with them. It is wonderful. I would rather have something good for a shorter period of time, than something not-good for a long period of time. So many things remind us of him, because he was such a gentle soul.

***

Kenny, no matter what, had this cross to bear. It wasn't like, "I had cancer, I went through a hard treatment, and I am cured." He had a significant lifestyle change that was there on his face every single day.

Jamie, Brewster Friend

109
Resilient

Jack: FDNY Chief Special Operations Command

This place here, what we call SOC Island for short, is a clearinghouse for a lot of guys getting out of the job with disabilities. Most of them are here for a year, year and a half, and then they leave. There are some guys who are here for longer terms with their disabilities. So in my eighteen years here, there have been hundreds and hundreds of guys who have passed through SOC. As I would love to remember all of them, I don't unfortunately, but Kenny I never forgot. He was just that type of individual that had an impact on me.

What impressed me the most about Kenny was he was always in a good mood, always had a smile, always had a joke to tell. He was obviously a big practical joker. I didn't work with him as a fireman and I probably would have dreaded working with him as a fireman, because when I was a fireman I was the type of guy that people always said, "He's an easy mark."

By this time as a chief, I was kind of immune to that. He never picked on me; but if I was a fireman, I could tell I would have had to sleep with one eye open.

One story that stands out, pertains to a guy that tended to leave early. He worked days, so he didn't have to be relieved by anybody else. There is a back door to this firehouse. It has a sliding bolt, then a series of stairs, and then a chain-link fence. He did it every day; this guy would always leave five minutes early, a half hour early, whatever. Everybody but the chiefs knew exactly what the guy was doing.

One day, Kenny went out and zip-tied the chain-link fence gate. When the guy went to leave, Kenny followed him out and slipped the bolt on the steel door behind him, so that once he got out, he was trapped. There is a ten-foot chain-link fence around the enclosure he is in, it is zip-tied, so he comes back, but he can't open the door. Kenny is just chuckling, watching him like a gerbil in a cage. That is one of the top stories I can remember, but there were always so many little types of things. We had to be on our toes with Kenny.

That being said, Kenny is the type of guy I would have liked to have been a fireman with, meaning as a boss I am friendly with people, but not friends with them. I never went fishing with Kenny. I never golfed with Kenny. I didn't play basketball with Kenny, all the things that I know he loved to do. I wasn't the brunt of his practical jokes either, so that part was good, but I was always the fly on the wall watching the interactions between the other firemen. I don't want to call him the life of the party, but he was the type of guy that when he walked in a room, the room lit up, because he always had the smile and the jokes. People with that kind of personality are people we are drawn to, especially if their jokes are good-natured, all in good fun.

One of the types of impacts Kenny had on everybody at SOC is still part of the culture here today. When we have dinner, there are typically fifteen people eating together. They spend two hours making dinner and they eat it in ten minutes. Most firemen grow up that way, because you never know when the bells are going to go off, so we have to eat quick. We don't want to come back to a cold meal. One of the problems with Kenny was, because of his condition, it took him a long time to eat his meals.

When I first came here, everybody was eating pretty fast; they'd be clearing their plates right away, and Kenny would hardly have started his dinner. After a couple minutes, Kenny would look around and see that everybody was scraping their plates, and getting ready to clean up. He would just stand up and start to scrape his almost full plate into the garbage.

He never complained, but one of the smarter guys here finally was able to make the connection that this was uncomfortable for Kenny. We didn't say anything to Kenny; we all just decided on our own, and came up with what we called the, "Twenty-minute Rule." It was really the "Kenny Holler Rule," that everybody would wait until Kenny finished his meal before anybody would get up and scrape the plates. Kenny had that impact that everybody wanted to make him feel comfortable. We still have that rule here. Nobody knows why we have that rule, but we always just stayed with it.

It was obvious from the surgery on Kenny's face that he had gone through some tough times, but I never really knew how bad it was for him. I knew he suffered. I knew his prognosis was iffy because of his disease, but it was almost like we said, "Kenny is going to beat this, no problem. He never complains about it. He seems to be able to do everything he wants to do." The unfortunate part about that, is people that are not the immediate family who understand exactly what he is going through, think, "Oh, that is not a problem. Kenny will be fine."

I don't know the suffering he went through. I am sure it was great. I had a brother that died of brain cancer; he lasted two years. Those two years were a blessing for him, but if he could have had twenty-one, he probably would have sold everything. Kenny was able to be with Lynda and his children for that much longer. That is awesome.

I am choosing the word "Resilient." It is one of the things that impressed me about Kenny. I am fifty-eight years old. When we get to be fifty-eight, unfortunately we know a lot of people that got sick and I have seen how everybody handles it differently. Some people climb into a shell and don't come out of it, just withdraw from everybody. Other people get angry. Maybe Kenny did those things, but while he was here, I would never know that he was ill at all.

I am fairly religious and I go to church every week. I would pray for Kenny when he was sick and whoever else here who is sick. That is probably another reason why I remembered Kenny for as long as I did, because I tried to include him and guys I knew that went through what he went through. It is one of the ways that helps me remember them, by praying for them and their families. I am not sure how much it helps, but it is something that I feel is important.

Like I said, we were not good friends. What I tried to impress before, was for Kenny to have his condition and to continue in his personality, was impressive. For a person that is the jokester, the guy that is always making people laugh, making sure everybody is having fun, to have that kind of sentence on him. Not that it was a sentence at the time, but knowing that he was going to have a rough time down the road, and to not let it bother him, at least in front of people, that's to be admired.

We read all these crazy things, but when we meet somebody like Kenny, it sticks to us. He is the guy that you read about in Reader's Digest or somewhere that has had great challenges, and you think, "Oh. I don't know anybody like that," but it turns out I did.

110
Brilliant
Karen: Steve's Wife

In Puerto Rico, that's where I got to know Kenny. That was the trip when he flew as Pete's girlfriend Carol! He was just so much fun, crazy and quick witted. OMG, so fast with the comebacks. Somebody would say something and he was on it in a heartbeat! We were there for the Super Bowl and they almost won the big pool. At the last minute, at the very end of the game, something happened and the box changed, so they didn't win. Kenny went out on the patio and I said to Steve, "You better go out there with him. He might go over the edge!" We were only on the second floor, so we figured he wouldn't get too hurt! He was down, but then five minutes later he was back to himself. Those memories stick out.

Kenny was in our wedding party. He pulled up to my wedding in his car. I really wish I had a picture of this, but I don't. On the back of his car was a sign that read, "Just Married," with the streamers and the cans on the back as if he were the groom! There is a video of him getting out of his car, putting on the jacket of his tuxedo, ready to go, I thought it was hysterical.

I remember Kenny and Lynda's wedding. It was hot, it was May; it was a beautiful wedding. I remember Lynda's dress, she made her dress. Lorraine and I said, "She made that dress!" We couldn't make anything. Kenny was so handsome, OMG! They were so beautiful, so young. So carefree.

Then nine months later for Kenny's fortieth birthday, Lynda had a party in their apartment in Jackson Heights. That party was only two weeks after Kenny's first surgery. He turned forty on February 27th and he had just had a piece of his tongue removed around Valentine's Day. Lynda had somebody making all this delicious food, but that was the beginning of Kenny's challenges with eating.

Lake George is really my main memories of Kenny. The way he would make his comments or call, "Lynda!" His voice; I'll never forget his voice. He had the best voice. He really did.

I always felt bad that he couldn't eat. We'd all be eating. He'd be cooking for us making those chicken legs. It made me feel terrible, but Lynda said, "His kids have to eat," and that was true. That was part of it that I didn't think of, but Lynda had to deal with it every day. And their kids had to deal with it every day.

I just remember Kenny quietly getting things done. If somebody did something over here, he would tidy it up. Or if there was something that had to be done, Kenny would take care of it.

I prayed for Kenny all those years. Prayed for him; prayed for Steve. Steve's dedication to Kenny … I am a nurse. I knew that Kenny was going to die and Kelly, Jack, and I would talk about it, "Daddy is going to be a mess. It is going to happen and he is going to be a mess." When it happened, Steve was devastated, but he had seen Kenny deteriorate so much and it was a relief to him to see his friend out of pain. It was definitely not as bad as we expected it to be, because Steve knew the fight Kenny put up and how hard he tried. It was time to let it go.

I know Lynda struggled with that. I remember three or four weeks before Kenny died,

Lynda met us at the beach. She wanted her husband back; she wanted her life back. I don't know if she even knew it was coming that quickly. I knew it was coming. I knew the end result was going to be what it was. We go through all this and we try and we hope and we pray, up and down, roller coaster. Lynda did that for how many years for God's sake? It is a testament to the faith that they had.

Another thing that sticks out in my head about Kenny is the faith. How they went to church and went to see the Pope that time. Steve got his faith back too. Maybe watching what Kenny went through and having gratitude that he never had to deal with that. I think Steve saw that there was something to it. Now it bothers him when we don't go to church. There are times that we miss, but for the most part we try to go every Sunday. I think him seeing Kenny go, and Shorty go, when we are in Lake George, that kind of made him feel like, "I can do this too. There is nothing wrong with this."

Over the last few months Steve was able to take some of the pressure off of Lynda. He had retired by then and it gave him a purpose. It made him feel like, "If I am not going to work, at least I can help and do this." And the guys would be on the phone.

Steve would go see Kenny and maybe Tommy would go with him or Carole would go with him. When Steve got home he would be on the phone. He was absorbing what was going on with Kenny and then dispersing all the information. It made him feel better. It made him feel like he was doing something useful and helpful.

Then at the end he knew, he knew that Kenny was going to die soon. He wanted to make it as easy for Lynda as he possibly could. If he could help her in any way, he was happy to do it. And Carole too, he was happy to drive Carole back and forth. They had a lot of laughs in the car, so that was good for them. The day that Kenny died, it was early enough in the morning, Steve got in the car and went to her house. They had bonded over that.

We didn't know what to do. We weren't even going to go on vacation. Then Steve said, "No, we are going to go. What's the difference if we drive up to Brewster from Long Island or down from Lake George?" I let him decide it. I didn't tell him what to do. I said, "Whatever you want to do, we'll do." Lynda had the wake for two days, so we went the second day and stayed overnight and went to the funeral.

Think about the meaning of Kenny dying on the first day of our Lake George vacation. He died when I was off work, so I was able to mourn him, to think about him, and I was able to be in a place where I would normally see him. If I was home and he died, if it was January, it wouldn't have really affected me, because I didn't see him at home. But having him die the day I was on vacation, I think that was God's way of saying…. I don't know what it was God's way of saying, but for me, it helped me to understand Kenny's death, to accept it, because I had the time. It was sad for everybody, that whole week and I don't know if it made it different for anybody else, but I didn't have to deal with work, so I was able to deal with Kenny's death.

I would like to use the word, "Brilliant," because Kenny was very smart in how he dealt with people, how he talked to people, how he would bring people together: "You know this guy from this guy," and everybody was intermingled. He would kind of work a room in a way. He would be able to talk to everybody and made each of us feel like we were the most important person on the planet when he was talking to us, yet he could be talking to three different people at the same time. Kind of entertaining. Like a stand-up comic in a way. Sometimes I would just sit back and watch him laughing, making everybody laugh around him. The kids especially; he made the kids laugh.

I remember him with Colin and Tim, he would poke them, then give them a big hug. He would walk by them and hit them on the head, on their baseball caps, then he'd hug them. I just thought he was very brilliant, the way he interacted with everybody. He was open and honest and himself.

He was just Kenny. When I say he was "just Kenny," everybody would know what I mean. He was just a funny, happy-go-lucky guy, until he got sick. Then he wasn't a happy-go-lucky guy anymore.

Brilliant, I think the way he handled life, the way he handled his death. He suffered, and unfortunately he died way too young, and his family had to go through so much, but just going to the wake and the funeral showed a wonderful legacy of people that loved him. He did a lot of smart stuff; marrying Lynda was one of those things. Having those boys, maintaining his friendships with the guys. He lived a nice life. He lived a good life. It was short, but it was quality. I could cry right now thinking about him. We miss him. We talk about him all the time at home.

***

Come now, my brothers and sisters, we're Christians; we all want to make the journey; even if we don't want to, we're still making it. Nobody is permitted to stay here, all who come into this life are forced by the turning wheel of time to pass on. There's no place for sluggards; walk, or you will be dragged along.

As we were making our way along and found ourselves at a kind of fork in the road, we were met by a certain man—not a man in fact, but God who is man for the sake of men. He said to us, "Don't go this way; this route certainly looks easy and smooth and delightful, well-trodden by many and broad; but this road in the end leads to doom. Since you aren't permitted to stop and live here, nor is it in your best interests, you will have to keep on going; but go this other way. You will be proceeding through a number of difficult places, but no sooner are the difficulties over and done with than you will come to a vast field of joys, and you will have avoided those traps and ambushes which nobody can avoid who chooses to proceed along that way."

St. Augustine, Doctor of the Church

111
Bond
Maggie: Shorty's Daughter

I remember at Kenny's funeral I cried like a baby. The biggest reason is because I had never seen my dad like that. My dad is a very put-together person and to see him fall apart like that; I know how much he loved Kenny. We all love Kenny, but to see the way that Dad and Steve and all those guys reacted. I could see how much they truly missed him. It broke their hearts. It takes a very special friendship and bond to dedicate yourself to other people like that.

Another thing that is unique within Kenny's situation was his illness causing him not to be able to speak. To still have that bond—that, "We are such good friends, we don't even have to speak to each other. We can just be in each other's presence." That is a very strong bond.

***

So that was probably the biggest impact that Kenny had on me, showing how that whole Astoria neighborhood, when one of their own people hurt, stand behind him one hundred percent. One thousand percent. They are all very impressive those guys. They all have great hearts, they are hard-working, and their generosity just amazes me.

Mary, Lake George Friend

***

It is great that my dad and all those guys are friends from early on and they were able to carry that into their later years. I hope that Colin, Tim, Jack, and I all end up staying friends like that and hopefully going to Lake George every year when we are that age too. I think that is a great thing that they have, especially that Kenny was surrounded by all of his friends. Steve especially was there for him and Dad as well. That was very good.

Patrick, Shorty's Son, Age 18

112
Light
Rachel: *Brewster Friend*

My son Rory and I used to go pick up my younger son Shane at CCD and we would go into the church, light a candle and we would sit and pray. We would pray and try to send light to Lynda and her family, to know the support that we were there. Not really knowing how to help.

Then, when I was in nursing school, I was working at Putnam Hospital. This is such an amazing memory that I'll always have. Kenny had a 911 call at the house the day before and they took him to the ER at Putnam Hospital. He was admitted and sent up to MS2, the second floor at Putnam, which is a step-down from ICU. That just so happened to be the floor that I was on as a nursing student. I hadn't seen Kenny in a while, because he had been so sick and it was too hard for him to get to games and things. I would inquire with other people about going to his house, but I don't think he wanted a lot of people to go see him at home. So of course that day, I wanted to see Kenny.

I didn't know how long Kenny was going to be there, because Lynda was trying to get him moved to Sloan. So I went to my instructor at seven o'clock in the morning, and I said, "A dear friend of mine is on the floor. I would like to see him." The instructor said to me, "By no means are you to go to his room. You are here as a student." As nursing students we are not allowed to be assigned to somebody we know.

To explain nursing school, every bend along the way, if we step out of line, they threaten that they are going to fail us. I was in my last semester, my last clinical, and my nursing instructor at that time was very nice, but she said that there was no room for movement on this. They said that when I was done at two o'clock, I would have to go home and change and come back as a visitor. I was thinking, "I cannot be here for six hours, on this small floor, and not see him!" She went and reported to the head nurse that I knew this patient and I was not to be assigned to him. I remember seeing Lynda in the hallway and her saying, "Come say hello to Kenny." And I said, "I'll try, I'll try."

On that floor there are only twenty rooms, so each of us had a nurse and a nurse had five rooms. The nurse I was working with at the time was phenomenal and all of the nurses on MS2 already knew and loved Kenny. She said, "We're going to get you into that room. We're going to figure it out." We did our rounds and as we were walking by, she said, "I think the light is on in that room. I think they need help. No one else is around; you really need to go. I am going to go get coffee." I went in and Kenny was asleep and I was not going to disturb him. I don't know where Lynda was at the time, because she wasn't in the room. Later on, the same thing happened and my nurse said, "Go in."

I went in and his eyes … Just to see that he was so full of light. He couldn't talk, so he had the white board. I gave him a big hug and we just stepped right into line to where we were last.

I said something about the Rangers being up in the series 2-0. He wrote down that it was 3-0. I had the series wrong! I had the series wrong and the first thing he writes to me is correcting me! It was hard for him to write, but it was such a tension release.

He was really exhausted and then he got a tear in his eye and started writing about Colin and wrote asking me to thank Tom for Colin and his internship. And I thought, "Is he kidding? It is always about everybody else." I looked at him and said, "That was Colin. Tommy gave a reference of what a great kid he is, but this was all Colin." He said, "No, no, no. You thank Tom."

That was really the last time that I got to see Kenny. I may have been the in the room ten, fifteen minutes and I left with such a memory of him that I'll never forget. There was somebody who was in major pain, who couldn't speak, knowing it was towards the end, and he still was all about everybody else. And still had the way to know what the Ranger series was …

I left thinking that I wanted to do something for him and I couldn't. He was never about that. He just gave and gave and gave in so many ways. Such a great example of how to live our lives.

I find that whenever I get caught up in silly things, something bad happens with the kids or if I am having a bad day, he is quick to come to my mind. "Get over it. This is so minuscule."

Kenny always had it right with his family, friends, and faith, he just radiated that. And to have that feeling for someone who expressed very little about himself.…

I think about Kenny all the time. So many things, watching the Rangers, the Giants, things happen like Tom Coughlin no longer the coach. That would be what we would talk about. Being on the sports field, seeing his kids, and Lynda. I think about him all the time.

Kenny's light. I think that is why people were drawn to him. He had such a way, even when he couldn't speak. When I reflect back on it, it is something that was there when I first met him. We are drawn to people for certain reasons. After everything that he went through, he still had the light. He still did.

***

It's almost like Kenny knew something that we don't know. I can't explain it. There was a calmness about him that made you feel better.

Anne Marie, Neighbor

113
Gentle

Bill: *Nurse, Head and Neck Floor, MSK Cancer Center*

Prior to my taking care of Kenny, I was already expecting something beautiful from him, just by the way that the nurses talked about him. When I first saw him he just looked calm. True, we were giving him a lot of medicines which would give the appearance of calmness, but there was something that transcended that and said that he was a calm type of personality.

As I continued taking care of him for a few days on and off, I fell more and more in love with him, just because of the gentle way about him calling us for assistance and writing little notes to make his needs felt. He really had a beautiful way of waiting for us to take care of his needs. Some people when they get sick get very anxious and we have to do things their way and so forth, but with him there was always a gentle way about things. If we were busy doing something else, he was always polite and would wait for us, never give an attitude or anything. So I always wonder, "Would I be as gentle if I were in his shoes?" I think I learned that from him, the ability to stay gentle when your world is crumbling down around you. His body was toning down and dwindling away, yet he was able to keep the gentle way about him.

I often pray for my patients. When I used to work at night it was much easier, there wasn't as many calls and stuff; daytime is a little bit tough, so it is on the go. Oftentimes, I am just running around and I have my thoughts toward Heaven, but sometimes when I have the peace and the quietness, that's when I have time to reflect.

I had Kenny all together four or five days. I can't say that I stay thinking of him, but he falls under the category of the few patients that made an impact on me. Some people stand out for certain things and we categorize them for those things. Kenny, I categorize for being pleasant, gentle, and no matter how badly he felt, he always treated us well. That's a rarity. That's a select group that happens in the hospital setting.

I see character that shows out of suffering. I think a person shows who they really are, his or her true colors come out. When you reveal who you really are under dire suffering, then it shows the character that has been developing your whole life.

***

Having taught religious education for years and years, Kenny to me is the definition of a Christian. These are some words that I use for Christian-like: goodness, prayerful, holy, faithful, family-first, helpful. We talk so much in religious ed about our goal to live our life the way Jesus lived His life and how He wants us to live our lives. Kenny was that good person. He was the holy person. I never heard him say anything about anybody else in the small little world that I knew him in. So many people are just jaded and don't have their priorities right. We need to live our lives in a holy, respectful, God-loving way. Christian, that's my word.

Kathleen, Brewster Friend

114

Communities

Dr. Adams: *Palliative Care Physician*

I remember caring for Kenny at Weil Cornell Medical College/ NY Presbyterian. I got Lynda's email and it took me a moment, but then I totally remembered who Kenny was, who Lynda was, who their family was. I don't remember the first moments we met, it was a few years ago now, but sort of snapshot images and a very good energy of coming into the room, meeting Kenny and at different times meeting Lynda. Then at times I met friends. I don't remember a time going into the room where I wasn't really greeted with warmth and appreciation. I think what really resonated with me was at Kenny's heart, what was most important to him, was his family. It wasn't just words; it was sentiment, warmth, love….

Lynda and I started talking one day, because I remarked that Kenny was really an exceptional person. I was noticing my reaction, what a pleasure it was to work with him, and I realized that to be something that he was doing for me. I take care of a lot of people and with some people, it can be frustrating to be involved in their care. It can be frustrating because it can be hard to treat their symptoms. It can be frustrating because they are so frustrated, so angry. It can be frustrating because sometimes personalities are not the right match with one another.

What I noticed working with Kenny was it was the opposite. It was a real pleasure to work with him, even though his pain was very hard to control, even though it was frustrating to see that he couldn't speak, even though it was sad that he was a dad that was so in love with his wife and so in love with his boys and so in love with his friends. And while he was continuing to very much be alive, it was clear also that things were getting worse.

All of those things were sad and frustrating, yet caring for him and being around him and being around his family was uplifting, which is something that I don't think people always understand about palliative care. People always think that what I do is sad; I think it is wonderful. I get to meet people and see extraordinary things. I get to sometimes be welcomed into a patient's life and a patient's family and I get to see some exquisite teamwork, family, community.

I had an epiphany with Kenny. He was somebody that made me think, "This person makes me feel good, and not just as a doctor, but as a human being. Going to see this person uplifts my spirit. It gives me a lift in my day and it feels healing for me."

So what is it about different people, where some people make us feel sad or down or unhelpful, while someone else makes us feel uplifted? With Kenny I started trying to understand that better.

The other thing about family, and that is true about the Holler family, is that there is the traditional family of wife and kids, parents, sisters, and brothers; then, there is extended family. Kenny was really part of the 9/11, fireman, and public service community, the childhood friend community, the neighborhood and church communities. Childhood friends would be there when Lynda couldn't be. Kenny and Lynda were committed to having their boys live a normal life, participating in their sports activities, being around their friends, around family. That whole family of communities was what allowed them to make it all continue to work and Kenny and Lynda were able to welcome that help.

That was the conversation that Lynda and I had one day. Lynda said that she was surprised herself to see that Kenny was willing to accept help. He had had an evolution himself, where I think he realized that it was important for him, important for Lynda, important for his kids, but also important for all of those other friends. That being able to offer that help to Kenny and his family was so very helpful to his communities. I think that was what I was feeling that day when I made those comments to Lynda, that it was such a pleasure to work with someone that made me feel good. I was his doctor and yet he cared for me too.

Kenny was part of a fabric of community. In palliative care we also have a community and that is something that I have been thinking about a lot myself, because it is something that people really benefit from. He was Kenny, dad, and husband, but he was also a firefighter, a coach, and a parishioner. Being part of that larger thread, the sum is greater than its parts, is something that was so important to Kenny. It was also something that their family used so effectively to keep themselves intact as a family. And keep Kenny intact. Those were probably a lot of the reasons that he did so well. People always say, "He did all of these things right. Why did he develop delirium? Why did things get worse?" I think that things would have been a lot worse if it wasn't for all of the things that they did. It was a terrible disease, but having those types of communities is really impactful.

Lynda mentioned that she is hearing all these stories about Kenny from different parts of his life and they are bigger than him. They are bigger than him in part because we give and we get when we are a member of a community. Being a member of a community we learn a lot from other people and we pass along a lot to other people that are in our fabric as well. So we can never see ourselves as just "Me." That is humbling. It discourages a culture of just, "Me, Me, Me," and when we are able to let go of the "Me," it makes us better and makes us more proud of our community allegiance, than we could be as solo practitioners.

It is something we talk about a lot in palliative care. Among physicians there is a history for the tendency of sort of one man for himself—or herself in my case. That creates something that is not healthy for any individual and actually doesn't provide best care either. That would be an obvious point to a firefighter who knows that he can't fight a fire alone. That they can only do it with others and there can't be just one hero.

The founder of palliative care is a woman named Cicely Saunders who was a nurse, a social worker, a physician, and eventually also a dame for all of her fine work in England. There are a number of things that she talks about that I carry with me. One is that we live until we die. The way I interpret that is I don't think of anybody as a dying person, I think of him or her as a living person. We are all dying and we are all living people; that is true for everybody.

Another principal that she talked about a lot and I think about every time I am managing symptoms, is the idea of total pain. That pain is not just physical. It can be emotional pain. Pain associated with all types of loss: loss of roles, loss of fatherhood, loss of professional roles. It can be financial pain; the thing someone might be suffering the most with is the pain of financial worries or leaving others with financial worries. Or spiritual pain, spiritual distress.

Kenny suffered, but many of those types of pain were managed for him so that he suffered much less than some people do. He had physical pain, but he had pain that was treatable. His family was targeting the other pains in many ways; they kept intact his role as a dad, his role as a husband, his role as a friend. They kept intact his connections to his community of firefighters and probably even some of his mentoring roles, so while he was no longer actually fighting fires, he was still supporting the work of others. That might be as relevant, if not more so, because sometimes our reach is even broader. Certainly his involvement in spiritual community and his own spiritual faith is something they brought from the community and something that they as a couple brought to each other on a very consistent basis.

I'd also like to comment on the fact that they were a very spiritual family, how grounding that was for them, and how grounding that is for a lot of people. I have worked with a lot of people of a lot of different faiths and I continue to be deeply impressed by the power of faith. It's not just about what you have faith in. It is about that community structure, about belief, and about love. It's not faith versus what is going to happen. It's not faith versus serious illness. It's not faith that is in denial of how serious things are. It is faith that allows us to keep going and allows us to remain alive and be present with all that we have. That is what I saw a lot with the Holler family.

I share, not specifics of their story, but that story of the miracle of the family when I remind other families what that miracle looks like, because it is sometimes hard to see it in the moments of suffering. That is the reality of the circumstance. Despite all of that, Kenny was suffering, Lynda was suffering, and she is still suffering. But that goes parallel with love, with life, with hope, with, "It's going to be okay." I think of Kenny on a fairly consistent basis and by him, I mean all of them.

Kenny's family was really wonderful about bringing in a lot of things from home that created a home-like environment in the hospital room. That helped us all to get to know Kenny. He had a professionalism about him, which is not something one should need to have as a patient. Lynda said that he was a patient for so long, there probably were certain strategies, certain demeanors that he took on. Yes, I think patients have to adapt to their situation. I think it is actually part of the key; I think it makes them better survivors and I think recognizing that does help them as patients. In as much as Kenny didn't have a speaking voice, he had a voice. He always had a very powerful voice.

For me as a person, apart from being a physician, he is a role model that way. Life is complicated. Bad things happen. Wonderful things happen. If we can be present for the wonderful things, we are doing pretty well. They can be big, they can be small. We actually don't know when we will impact someone or when we are going to give somebody a lift. One day it might be really important. It might be the words that keep someone going through some much harder moments. I think Kenny was really aware of that.

***

I would like to hope that people learned to appreciate and take Kenny's insight out of all of this. Especially our community, but I am thinking of it very narrowly. I am thinking that Kenny is a Brewster guy. I am sure there are a lot of people in Queens that will say the same thing for being on the basketball court or on the playground. Or being at a party and him making them laugh, having a good time, making the party more enjoyable. Or the Fire Department, the whole brotherhood in itself. Every group took the collective of who he was to them and Kenny connected us, weaving us together into a larger, stronger, more courageous community.

Anthony, Brewster Baseball Friend

115

Accepting

Dory: *Palliative Care Social Worker, Weill Cornell/ NY Presbyterian*

Rather than memories, I am better with emotions, I guess that is my job as a social worker: dealing with people's emotions.

So my emotions, how I felt about working with Kenny: just very grateful, inspired, and also lucky to be able to be in his presence. I want to underscore that that also means Lynda and the boys. I remember thinking, "Wow, these kids are amazing and they are very lucky." They are going to grow up way before their time, but what a gift for them to be so proud of what their father did and how he responded to such a difficult challenge. What a role model for those kids.

I can see Kenny's face. He was struggling with all the machines and barriers to communication, but with his facial expressions and the light in his eyes, his spirit came through in spite of all the difficulties that got in the way.

And family and friends, it is so important for us to know families. It was really important to keep that connection with Lynda and support her too. She was very strong and very available. How she handled everybody, how she managed to organize all the support and help the kids. Her role was so multi-faceted, so to me that was also a big piece of what I remember about Kenny.

We talked about crying and Lynda said that she didn't cry much, that she feels it was a gift that God gave her or she could have been crying all the time. That is not unusual. People have to rise to the occasion and they cannot fall apart. She had to take care of everybody and that was her coping mechanism.

When patients have loved ones around, it makes a huge difference in how they cope. An important part of life is our relationships, a very big part, and to have people there to support you, what is more important than that? Honestly?

I can think of a patient right now who has a rare disease, a neurological disease, a bit like ALS and Parkinson's. He is losing his functioning and his wife is not able to rise to the occasion. She is not able to help him. He feels abandoned and very, very, very sad. He feels that life is not worth it anymore. It makes me very sad. I am not judging. There are lots of reasons why people are not able to manage, but when they do, it is an amazing gift. It is strength: strength in numbers, strength in partnership. For people to stay together and work together, there is strength and when people can't, the strength isn't there for either one of them.

Kenny wasn't the only one that benefited from their partnership. Lynda gained so much by sticking it out with Kenny. She knows that; she is inspired. She is inspired to do this project and she is inspired to live her life in a certain way. Her kids are the same.

I am Catholic and we are ingrained that suffering has value. I don't think that people should suffer with pain, but suffering is part of life. It is part of the human condition, so people learn from suffering. People gain from suffering. I am sure Kenny gained from his suffering. People become transformed from suffering. Lynda became transformed from watching Kenny's suffering, and she suffered too.

There is value at the end of life when we are suffering and when people try to cut off those opportunities, they are not doing themselves justice. They are missing opportunities, as are the people around them. There is a lot to be accomplished when people are at the end of life. A lot of healing that can take place. A lot of repaired relationships, a lot of appreciation and gratitude, and expression of what is important. It would be a shame to miss that.

I have a patient right now that is newly diagnosed with terminal cancer. He is a young man in his early forties and he understands that his illness is very life-limiting. He hopes that he will have time to heal some of the relationships in his life. He feels that he hasn't done right by his wife, by his mother, and by his siblings. He wants to have some time to repair those relationships and he feels that is very important; I hope he will have that opportunity. It is a reminder that we are all here for a little bit of time, so we have to really use all the time that we have to do the best we can.

Kenny is an example of somebody with faith, somebody with support, somebody that had meaning, somebody that had something to be proud of—a life that was well lived, even though shorter than it should have been. A life well lived, doing what he loved, a family that he loved, somebody to pass something on to. That is huge. It is bigger than all of us. We can't control certain things, so when we try to control them we become very, very frustrated. Obviously Kenny wanted to be able to control his environment and make the most of it, but in the big sense of control, he didn't feel the need to control it. Whether it is God or something bigger than ourselves, whatever it is that lets us let go of things we can't control, it is a lot more peaceful when we are able to do that.

We talk about reframing hope in palliative care, because we all hope for things. We hope that we are going to have a good day. We hope that we are going to see sunshine or we hope that we are going to talk to somebody that we haven't talked to in a long time. We try to help patients reframe hope. Having hope doesn't mean that you are going to get better, if you can't get better. Everybody has to look at hope in a different way and we try to help them do that. Hope is important. There is a poem by Emily Dickenson which I think of a lot. The title is "Hope" is the Thing with Feathers. It is a short, really beautiful poem.

"Hope" is the Thing with Feathers
Emily Dickinson: 19th Century American Poet

"Hope" is the thing with feathers—
That perches in the soul—
And sings the tune without the words—
And never stops—at all—

And sweetest—in the Gale—is heard—
And sore must be the storm—
That could abash the little Bird
That kept so many warm—

I've heard it in the chillest land—
And on the strangest Sea—
Yet—never—in Extremity,
It asked a crumb—of me.

116
Faith
Elizabeth: Brewster Friend

Kenny was on the prayer board down at Maryknoll where I work as a nurse. I put on the request and I had a little explanation that this was a fireman who lost a lot of friends on 9/11. That shook him up more than having cancer. We all were stunned at 9/11, but it was the friends he lost. He didn't talk about it to get pity or anything, but we knew where his heart was all the time. So anyway, when I put his name on the prayer board explaining that he was a NYC fireman who had lost many friends and was deeply affected by the 9/11 tragedy, the nuns really did pray for him.

Because of Kenny's attitude, I thought he was going to keep on fighting until the very end, just like he did. He was a person with some inner spirit, inner belief, inner faith. I have seen people with worse disease processes fighting to the very end. I have a nun now that had three broken hips. Can you believe it? She only has two hips, but she broke them three times, plus liver cancer and she is still hanging in there and fighting. I have to believe that there is a purpose, an overall purpose in this.

I think that Kenny's presence here on earth, for the little of it that I knew him, for the joy and fun that he gave the people that he worked with, lived with, hung out with, I think those are all positive things and we can't put a negative thing on it just because his life ended earlier than we wanted it to. It's not our call.

It's funny, I think of Kenny when I go into Kobackers Market. I would run into him there an awful lot. Do I think of him in relationship to cancer? No, I don't. It was visible, but I never thought, "Oh, God, he got cancer." I never looked at him that way. Just saw him as Kenny.

***

Kenny handled his suffering by putting more love out into the family. He extended, he pushed more love out of him, because I know inside of him he knew it wasn't going to last. So I think that is what it was all about. It forced him to love even more. Not just his family, everybody. I believe he was thinking, "It's not going to be a long trail. It is going to be a shorter trail, so I am going to give it everything I got." And he gave an abundancy of love and he compressed everything into a shorter life. He was successful. I give him credit. It worked.

Pete, Queens Friend, Owner of Suspenders

117
Dignity
Chuck: Astoria Friend

I have known Kenny since I was nine or ten years old.

Having gone through the exercise of planning to talk to Lynda, I thought, "How do I take the different strands of when we were kids and teenagers and adults, all the different relationships, and bring them back together? The thing that stuck with me, is that I believe that there was a silent space inside of Kenny, like a secret space, that kept him going through the good, as well as the tough times that he had to endure, and the suffering he had to get through. That is what gave him the strength to keep going for his family, friends, whatever.

As he got older, his personality started evolving; the person who loved having a good time. Kenny had an incredible sense of humor in a way of dealing with crowds, but my impression was that Kenny had a mask on. He had a mask that he put on to entertain, to project, but deep down he was a very quiet, strong person, who for whatever reason was hiding something, keeping something inside, or just maintaining a sense of dignity with a reserved nature to him.

All of the joking around, the games and the fun, he would love doing that, but it was away from his real self. I think his real self was where his strength was. He was able to find it within himself to deal with the adversity and the suffering that he had to go through. I am probably not explaining this properly.

It's like being an actor who can play all these parts, but in the meantime the real person is who the real person is. At the end of the day, Kenny's real person was very reserved. He didn't want attention on himself, which was a crazy thing when you hear some of the stories of him on the boats or in the firehouse. He liked projecting his personality as a "this" or a "that." When Kenny was in the center of the party, it was as a different person, as a mask.

When he first got sick in '93, I went to visit him in the hospital, me and the two Tommys. While we were there another patient named Patty came into Kenny's hospital room. He was a cop and lived in the Poconos. He saw us sitting there and he said, "I'll leave." Kenny said, "No. Come on, talk to my friends." We started talking and the guy was hysterical. He was so funny that for twenty minutes we did nothing but laugh. Guy leaves; guy dies six months later. He had the same doctor as Kenny, same disease as Kenny. Kenny said, "I am the luckiest guy in the world." Kenny couldn't go to the funeral. It hit him hard.

Kenny thought he was lucky. To me, I am saying, "That is a crazy perspective!" He didn't deserve the disease, but he didn't gripe about it; he didn't say, "Woe-is-me." What he had now, a certain strength and dignity, was present when he was younger. That silent place inside him was there as a little kid all the way through.

They say that adversity gives us character? No, adversity shows our character and his character was shown from way back when. It was quiet; it was varied enough and strong enough that he could be a funny guy, the clown, the person everyone said, "Let's hang out with Kenny," but that was just an off-shoot of the real strength inside of him.

When he was real sick in New York Presbyterian, I went to see him. Steve was there, Carole was there, McCormick may have been there too. Kenny fell asleep and we talked amongst ourselves. I hung out for a little bit, but he was sleeping, so we all decided to leave. Steve called me and said, "If you are around next weekend, we are not sure who is going to be covering for Kenny." So I said, "Sure," and I went in by myself on Sunday morning.

Kenny was sleeping. The pen was in his hand and he had written, "So this is morning," on the pad. There were some doodlings and it was pretty good penmanship. I said to myself, "Did he write that or did someone else?" but the pen was still in his hand and he was sleeping. So I just watched him, and I watched him, and I was going to wake him up, but I remembered Steve telling me that he doesn't sleep very well. I just watched him and watched him and he had the pen in his hand the whole time.

I was trying to think; did he mean: "I made it another day."

Or, "I am not sure what to expect."

Or, "Is this something that I should acknowledge, that this is another morning?"

Maybe: "So this is morning. It's a miracle. A new dawn. It's a new day."

I never really calibrated it in terms of what it meant to him.

I didn't know what to do. I didn't want to wake him up, knowing that he would recognize me, but that I couldn't talk to him. So I just watched him. And watched our whole childhood, from the first time I met him back in 1961 or 1962 and I thought, "This is where we come to." I kept thinking when he said to me twenty years earlier, "I can't believe how lucky I am," when he saw his friend Patty die. Different perspective. Then I just got up and left, and that was the last time that I saw him.

My mother died of a long illness too. She died at home. I think of her almost every day. I think of Kenny almost every day. Life goes a thousand different ways; we don't know what hand we are going to be dealt, but that is the one we have to play. Not a word of complaint from my mother; not a word of complaint from Kenny. It's a certain strength that is inside of us. Are we born with it? Do we learn it? I don't know. Lynda had it, because she dealt with it too. Kenny dealt with it every day and who was by his side? When they were five or six years old was it in there and it just got reinforced, got stronger, did they get more committed?

I don't think we learn it when we get thrown into a situation. I think it is inside of us. God puts it inside of us, but we can develop it and use it, or we can say, "I'm not big enough to handle this. I am not strong enough to handle this. God, take it away from me." Lynda dealt with it, Kenny dealt with it, my mother dealt with it. Will I deal with it at some point? Yes, maybe. Maybe it is inside of me since I was younger too, and my brothers and sisters also, but we never know how we are going to react until we are actually faced with adversity.

Kenny's kids also have had to deal with, on a daily basis, something that their friends probably would never understand. Probably ninety-nine percent of what Lynda and her children went through I don't know about. I can imagine it. I know what happened to my mother, but the people that are closest are the ones that deal with it every day.

Me, Gary, Mike D, and McCormick have an understanding that we have given up the right to complain about anything that ever happens to us, because of Kenny. How he dealt with it; how he accepted it. How the whole time he lived with a certain strength and handled himself with dignity: "This is me and this is what I do and I don't have to complain and tell you about it. It is just something I have to deal with." And that is how Kenny dealt with everything.

God, I wish I had spent more than forty-five minutes with that man. I know I would be a much better person than I am today. All of you that had him more than that are truly blessed.

Dennis, Retired NYPD, Septic Driver

118
Patience

Corinne: *Lynda's Niece*

The memory of Uncle Kenny, although not a particularly happy one, that sticks with me the most is from the days towards the end of his life when he was at New York Presbyterian Hospital. I was volunteering at the Hospital for Special Surgery right next door and would stop over from time to time and sit with him. I would just sit reading a book or talking to him when he was awake. I would tell him about what was going on with me.

At this time, he was only communicating with paper and pen, but he was still conveying very important things like level of pain and the effects of the medication on him. From time to time, I would see that he was getting frustrated or feeling helpless, because he wasn't always able to accurately take his thoughts from his head and transform them to words on a page. Between the effects of the pain meds, the cancer's progression, and the vascular brain surgery he had just endured, now his communication limitations expanded beyond oral issues. So it was very rare for people to completely understand what he was trying to say and he would try again and again to keep expressing himself—choosing different words and writing them on different parts of the paper, trying different routes to get his message across.

I think about this a lot. One of the aspects of my personality is that I get very frustrated when I hear someone ask me, "What?" or if I have to explain myself again. You see, I talk really fast and it is a gut reaction for people to say, "What? I need to hear it again."

But recently, I have been drawing back to that time with Uncle Kenny and thinking that I am lucky to be able to have the opportunity to express myself again. I am able to just take a breath and try it in a different way, in a better way, knowing that I can get where I need to go and say what I need to say quickly and effectively. So every time I have that train of thought and I find myself getting frustrated, I think of Uncle Kenny. Although it's not the happiest memory, it is an important one, because it makes me a little bit more patient, a little bit kinder in my day-to-day life, and a more pleasant person to have a conversation with.

We have great family memories. My family never lived close to Aunt Lynda and Uncle Kenny, so a lot of my memories revolve around holidays and beach vacations. He was always such a good host. He always wanted to run out and get us something; he would go out for bagels, taking everyone's orders, even when he couldn't eat himself. He always asked questions about what we were doing, what was new with us in school, staying up to date with sports. He was so good that way. Kids change so quickly; he worked so hard to know each of us personally, when I am sure that there was so much going on with him. But he didn't allow his own issues to take away from enjoying the time he had with us, getting to know us, and staying up to date on our lives.

I played very competitive basketball throughout middle and high school and that was a nice connection that we had. Uncle Kenny and I would go out and play HORSE a lot and he would always appreciate me telling him a new story about a game. In high school, my brother

Sean helped coach and that was a good bond that we all shared.

Although I never really knew a young, healthy Uncle Kenny, that never affected the quality of the uncle that he was for me. He always seemed really happy, always cracking jokes, content listening to stories that my brother, sister, and I were telling him. There must have been times when that was really difficult for him. I sometimes have headaches and can't bring myself out of them enough to interact normally or pleasantly with people. The older I got, the more I realized the magnitude of the pain he must have had. That helps me appreciate the fact that people are always going through something and although it might not be written all over their faces, they can be suffering or experiencing something really big.

So an important thing that I gathered is to try to scale the difficulties that I have going on in my life with the worth it has for ruining a moment, an hour, a day, a month, a year of my or anyone else's life. Uncle Kenny had some extreme difficulties and that could have ruined a lot of things for him over the years. Instead, he chose to do everything in his power to enjoy those moments and create those memories for everyone around him, but also for himself, to make his life better and not to be victimized by the hard parts.

That is a huge lesson that I learned from him: not having the difficult moments ruin life and trying to keep tabs on my attitude. It is usually just little things, like if I am going shopping and my shoes are a little bit uncomfortable, I choose not to let that ruin my entire day. The conditions of our life affect us, but our choices are what decide if we are going to be happy and pleasant to be around.

I think that the first time that I really realized the intensity of Uncle Kenny's struggles was when they removed his fingernails. Not that I hadn't felt sorry before, but he was always such a strong man and I didn't recognize the sufferings he was enduring. This treatment, however, just seemed like pure torture. I am sure that many of the others were too, but I just hadn't known the details. This was the switching point where it just seemed that everything he was going through was so brutal.

I prayed for him all the time when he was sick. Now I pray to him for guidance. If I am being impatient or struggling with the way to say something, I believe that he is someone that can inspire me. I am sure he struggled with that even when he could talk. I never remember his speech to be perfect; it wasn't what it used to be before the cancer. His communication slowly diminished throughout his life and his strategies must have been constantly evolving: "What is the best way that I can get my message across now?" So when I am looking for a way to communicate my message, or how I need to say something right, I pray to Uncle Kenny and I am sure that he is listening as intently as he did when we were together—always interested in my life and anxious to do whatever he can to help.

***

This book is Kenny's story, but it is Colin's, it's Aunt Lynda's, it's Tim's stories. It's everybody who speaks for this book; it is my story.

Sean, Lynda's Nephew

119

Amazing

Pete R: *Astoria Friend*

Kenny is three years older than me. When I was in sixth/seventh grade, he must have been in ninth/tenth grade and I recognized that Kenny always did his own thing. Kenny was not a follower; he was a leader. He had this gesture of waving his hand away and doing his own thing, never just following the crowd.

One of the things that I always remember about Kenny from that time, was that his clothes always fit him perfectly. Like his Lee jeans, they always looked great. I'd think, "I want my jeans to look like Kenny's jeans." He had, back in the day, a half-bleached jean. They weren't dark blue, they weren't light blue and I would think, "Man, where does he get those clothes? How does he wear those clothes?" I would look up and admire him for stuff like that. He was a cool guy and everything always fit him perfectly.

I wound up going to college and into the Marines. Later on as an adult, I had another friend named Ed and he had the same type of cancer as Kenny. I was really tight with Ed; he was a Marine too. Ed fought his cancer for almost twenty years. I never said anything to Kenny or Lynda, I never brought it up, but about two years before Kenny passed, doctors told Ed that he had some time left, but he was going to have to go on a feeding tube. He decided that he wasn't going to deal with that, so he took his own life.

Ed was the kind of guy that had fought it so much and he had been on the brink and he came back, then he had been on the brink and he came back, then the surgeons would always go in and take more. Just like Kenny. Same frickin' story. Always more, always more, always more. He lived on the Upper East Side, he was in his sixties or seventies, living with his girlfriend. He asked his girlfriend to go down to the bank. He locked the door and shot himself. I went through the whole thing with the family. Then once that happened, I started getting the calls from Steve and Hut and guys about Kenny.

I had another friend from baseball, same exact thing because of the chew—the chew and the snuff. He passed away about a year or two before Kenny. He had been fighting it and fighting it and fighting it. All these guys that I knew had the same frickin' disease, the same frickin' thing. I thought, "This has got to stop."

So by now my friend Ed had shot himself and my other friend passed away; Kenny started getting bad and I went to see him at the hospital. What is on the wall, but a picture of Jesus! Here is this guy lying there in so much pain and living through this, and he is still believing. He is still loving. I watch this. I am sitting there the whole night; the nurses are coming in and suctioning his trach, caring for his wounds, giving him his pain meds. This guy is probably in pain up to the wazoo, yet I look at Kenny and he is looking at the picture of Jesus. He keeps looking at Jesus.

Do I pray? Yes, I pray all the time. I pray all the time, especially after I saw something like that. For a guy like that to continue to believe and with all of the issues that I have had with death, that made things a lot easier for me. It really made things a lot easier to believe and to stay with my beliefs. That helped me an awful lot. Like I said, I saw two guys go of the same thing, and one guy couldn't handle it—a Marine. A Marine! He couldn't handle it, but Kenny stuck it out all the way through.

The first two or three times that I went to visit Kenny at New York Presbyterian Hospital, he was doing pretty well, considering…. I met Lynda's niece Corinne in the room and I explained to her who I was. We sat and chatted and Kenny was going along with the conversation. Kenny is pointing to me, giving the thumbs-up, writing to Corinne that I am a good guy.

One day, I got an urgent call from Steve that Lynda needed help with Kenny. He had been texting her crazy messages that the hospital staff was trying to hurt him and he had to get out of there. She was too far away to get to the hospital; I was nearby and was able to get there quickly. I expected him to be like he was in the earlier visits, but this time it seemed like he was hallucinating, like he was seeing things, and it was hard for him to calm down.

I think when I came in and he saw a familiar face, he was happy to see me, but maybe a little embarrassed to see me at the same time. I had to compose myself when I was outside his room, because it was hard for me, never mind him. I wanted to go in and show strength to him so he could be strong. He calmed down once I got in there. Even the nurse said, "He's a lot better now." I just remember Kenny wanting to hold my hand, hold my hand, hold my hand. There was anxiousness there and I kept telling him, "Kenny, the meds are going to work and it's going to get better."

That night McCormick stayed the night and had a bad night, Steve came in the morning to relieve him during the day, and I came back that night to sleep over. They were trying to balance his pain and anxiety meds at the time and it was very complicated. They never knew why it started or why it stopped.

All I could think about was my first night at boot camp. I wanted to get out of there. I didn't know where I was, I didn't know what was going on, I was disoriented, people were yelling in my ear.

I would say, "Kenny, we're going to get through this; we're going to get through this. This is not going to last. You and I have been through worse together. You and I have been through worse alone. You have been through a lot worse. Relax. Relax. We're going to get through this."

He kept grabbing my hand, grabbing my hand, grabbing my hand. I would look at the picture of Jesus and say, "Let's pray. You want to say a prayer?" He couldn't even sit still for that. He couldn't sit still for a long while, but eventually he calmed down. I guess he fell asleep for a while, at about four or five o'clock in the morning.

But even when he was in pain, all he would do is motion or write a note or push the button, never kick or thrash around or get angry. None of that stuff. Never, never ever! If it was me, I'd be all over the place; I'd be pounding on the walls. My footprints would be on the ceiling. But he maintained his cool the whole time. I couldn't believe it. Going back to sixth or seventh grade, this is that cool guy from Steinway Park. He was always cool to the very end.

Do you know what was weird though, really weird? When he came around in the morning, he asked me in a series of cryptic notes, "How did you get here?"

I told him I drove.

Then he wrote me, "Where's your car?"

I told him it was in the street."

Then he wrote out, "T-I-C-K-E-T."

I said, "Are you kidding me? I can afford the ninety bucks today, don't worry about it!"

He said, "No, no. Go get your car." One of the other guys happened to walk in at that point, Tommy or Steve, so Kenny did that wave with his hand signaling, "Get out of here," so I wouldn't get a ticket. It was so weird. I thought, "Why is he even asking that? After a night like that, his first concern is about how I got here and if I would get a ticket?" That was very weird, very cool, and very Kenny.

***

My child, I have need of victims, and strong victims, who by their sufferings, tribulations, and difficulties, make amends for sinners and for their ingratitude.

Jesus' Words to St. Gemma Galgani

120
Brotherhood
Larry: FDNY Lieutenant

Our friendship started out just casually. We were part of the same brotherhood being New York City Firefighters and we had the bond of this special job and wanting to have some fun and hang out. We probably met in Suspenders on a payday cashing our checks and going out for a couple beers.

Then for a time we went our separate ways, both moved on with our lives and got out of the bar scene. We met women, fell in love, had families, and life went on. We would run into each other on Memorial Day or Medal Day or the St. Patrick's Day Parade with the Fire Department and say, "Hey, how are you doing, Buddy?" Quite casual, but it was good; I enjoyed his company and the mutual friends we had.

We reunited after 9/11. A very close friend of ours, another FDNY brother, Vinny Halloran, got killed that day. We both were very close to the Halloran family and we were both there in the beginning when we hoped that Vinny would be found alive. We both got involved with the family, trying to ease some of their pain and suffering, and to just help them out in any way we could.

There is a picture hanging in their house of Kenny holding onto his dress hat with the Mass card of Vinny and Chief Raymond Downey inside it. It was taken by a reporter from the Rocky Mountain News at his friend Tommy Kuveikis' memorial service. To me it is a very iconic picture. Most of us carry Mass cards of our fallen brothers in our helmets, in our uniforms, in our pockets.

In the last couple years, his cancer became a lot more serious and we could see the physical effect on Kenny, but we never saw the mental effect. He would always be laughing; he would always be talking. Every time I had a conversation with him, the first thing he would ask is, "How are your boys on Washington Avenue?" That was my firehouse in the Bronx. He always wanted to know how the brothers were. "How's this guy? How's Tommy? How's Red?"

Tommy, his buddy from college, ended up being a firefighter also, and together we visited Kenny at his house to check on him a few months before he died. Kenny said, "Come, I'll make lunch." Kenny probably hadn't had solid food in ten, fifteen years and Kenny was cooking us lunch. I guess like any firefighter, lunch and cooking and preparing food was always a big thing, so besides having some cold cuts, he had hamburgers, hot dogs, salads. We were having a beer and talking and Kenny was busy making sure that Tommy and I had enough food and that everything was okay.

Then Kenny went into the kitchen, came back out on the porch and asked, "Do you guys mind if I join you to eat?" So he lifted up his shirt, had a feeding tube, had a can of liquid nourishment, and Kenny poured his food into his feeding tube. When he got done he wiped his mouth and said, "Um! That was delicious!" Tommy and I said, "Look at this freakin' maniac!" He didn't even put anything to his lips and he's telling us it's delicious.

249

The frustration that man had to go through by smelling food and not being able to taste food, was something that struck me that day. Again, he never complained and he made a joke of sticking a bottle right in his feed tube. I give Kenny credit for keeping his sense of humor when the chips were down.

Later on when he got sicker I stopped to see him in the hospital a few times. Once was in New York Presbyterian on May 5th; it was my birthday. My birthday happens to be on Cinco de Mayo and I had a big, big Sombrero. Kenny couldn't speak at this time and he took out his board and the first thing he wrote was, "How are the brothers on Washington Avenue?" We talked about that, then I told him it was my birthday and I had the big Sombrero to celebrate. Kenny grabbed the hat out of my hand; he barely could lift his head up, but he put that Sombrero on, looked up, smiled, and gave a "thumbs-up," as if saying: "Happy birthday to you. Everything is okay. This is just another little set-back."

The strength and determination and dedication it takes to put out a fire is pretty remarkable and Kenny was part of that. So we have that bond, and then when one of us passes away due to line of duty, non-line of duty, or causes related to the department, it is a fitting tribute that NYC Firefighters honor their fallen brother by standing Honor Guard. Since I was a good friend, I was honored to be part of the Honor Guard for Kenny.

With the Honor Guard, two firefighters stand beside the casket in uniform at the funeral home and every ten to fifteen minutes they rotate. We give each other the hand salute and we salute our fallen brother in the casket.

At the funeral, we line up outside the church. NYC Firefighters want to show the family and their relatives that this guy was special. It is like that movie, *A Band of Brothers*. We are a special group and we want to honor them the best way we can and at the end it is by standing Honor Guard or standing at attention and giving a hand salute when the funeral is over.

Another big tradition of a New York City Fire Department funeral, is getting the pipe and drum band or in Kenny's case, where he was retired for a couple years, a bagpiper. I had a bagpiper there from the New York City Fire Department in his dress uniform. The Fire Department Bagpipers represent the whole tradition of honor and respect and dedication, almost like a Viking funeral; we want to send our brother off in the highest tradition in our eyes.

For the last couple years off and on I was teaching at the New York City Fire Academy and I would get 116 Truck and Engine Company 261 in the classroom for the day. I would ask, "Did you guys work with Kenny?" That's my calling card when I meet a guy from 116: "Did you know Kenny Holler?" By now there is probably only one guy left there that worked with Kenny, maybe two.

When I ask young guys they say, "Oh no, but we heard about Kenny," and they say that they have seen his picture on the wall. That means that his name or his stories are still living on at that firehouse. We're not the type to brag or talk about ourselves, but I think we all hope that we have left our mark, a positive mark on the firehouse where we worked, either through friendships or through something that we did during our careers. It is a great tribute to a fireman to leave his mark on his firehouse. My brother Kenny definitely left his.

The Fire Department's support at Mr. Holler's funeral showed us a very intense brotherhood. When all of the firefighters marched into the church it showed a comradery among such a strong group of people. On a lower level, all of our friends in our grade were there to support Colin and his whole family. It was a very cool thing that all of us guys were willing to put everything else aside to be there in order to help. That group of guys is a good group that would be there for any of us, at any time.

Kyle, Colin's Friend, Age 18

Steve's birthday party - November 2012

Fishing in Florida with Sandy's husband Rich
December 2012

Kenny's birthday - February 2013
Just returned home from rehab after getting the trach
Notice the Welcome Home sign

Supporting Tim's summer team - June 2013

Fishing on Pete's boat in the Hamptons
July 2013

Yankee game - September 2013

Lake George Beach - August 2013
McCormick, Jim, Steve, Kenny, Shorty, Marty

Brewster Bear Classic Cross County Meet
October 2013

Larry's sombrero - Thumbs up
Cinco de Mayo 2014

Memorial window for Kenny in
St. Lawrence O'Toole Adoration Chapel

Remembering the Rugged
Cross that Kenny carried

Brewster Community Planting Day
at the Holler home - October 2014

Brewster Little League Tree Dedication
Markel Park - Opening Day, Spring 2015

253

122
Brotherly
Rich: Lynda's Brother-in-Law

We live six hours away from Lynda and Kenny, but Sandy and I went to see Kenny at New York Presbyterian Hospital within the last month of his life. Of course we didn't know that then. That was really a hard time. It had been somewhat of a challenge communicating with him for a long time, but because he could use hands, and because of where we were and what was going on, there was always a context to the conversation. So even if we couldn't understand him well, we knew what he was saying.

But when he was just lying in a hospital bed, it became really hard to know what he was thinking: "Is he thinking? Does he know totally what is going on? Can he hear us?" That was really scary, because it just didn't seem like Kenny. It became very evident how hard that was. He couldn't even write that well. We weren't sure what he was "saying" and we weren't sure if he understood what we were saying.

We went to see him a couple days in a row. We stayed with Corinne and came back the next day. We actually helped Kenny pack up. He was being transferred to a specialty rehab facility in Connecticut. It had been put off a few times because he had a little bit of a cold or something and they wanted to make sure he was strong enough to make the trip. It was a long ride, two or three hours in an ambulance.

We got his clothes and his sneakers out of his closet and took down and packed up all the letters and cards and pictures on his wall, things the boys had made for him. We talked with the ambulance drivers, the ones that were going to be taking him up there. I remember thinking that they were good guys and they were going to take care of him. Kenny seemed okay, but we were very fearful and really felt that this was the one that he probably wasn't going to come back from. At least not come back to the Kenny he had always been, where he was able to get up and around and put on sweat pants and sneakers and go off to the store and function.

He got in with the ambulance crew heading to Connecticut and Lynda was going to meet him there. We left and went on home. Sandy and I had a pretty quiet car ride, at least for the first few hours, because it hurt. We really felt his pain. And just wondered if we were going to see him again. As it turned out, we didn't.

I just see so much of Kenny in the boys, so much respect, so much good-naturedness, all their friends, and faith. The boys have good faith; they really have sound faith for kids their age. I think there is no doubt it will stick, that it will be a part of their lives. That would be the silver lining in this, what they learn from it, dealing with it, and how they will remember their father, because of their faith. I think it made them keenly aware of the time they did have with him. And the things he did, which was amazing that he could still be such a good father both physically and spiritually for the boys. To still go out and work on the baseball fields and coach the sports and take them to the games, to make sure they got that part. I am sure they will never forget those times.

His battle impacted all those people that knew him. Giving everybody a reason to pray. Everybody just really felt that they had to pull out all the stops and pray in church and pray at home for God to help him. It drove us many, many times to pray together, where I don't think Sandy and I openly prayed together before, until we really, really started praying for Kenny. Hopefully, now that he is gone and they are back to their lives, some of that carried on. I am very confident that with us it did.

This all makes me think about a few years earlier when Colin was preparing to be confirmed; he asked me to be his sponsor. I hadn't been confirmed and I decided it would be a good time, so I could fulfill my obligation to Colin. One of the reasons that I had put it off for so many years was because I travelled so much and I couldn't commit to going to class every Tuesday. So what I decided to do was join up with RCIA (Rite of Catholic Initiation for Adults) classes wherever I was. We were living in Hollywood, Florida at the time, so my home parish was there, but throughout that year I attended RCIA classes in Las Vegas, Phoenix, and Edmonton, Canada.

The teachings became very real, very relevant. Many times going through those classes I would hear something and think of Kenny's battle and think of the suffering. One class in particular was about suffering: how Jesus suffered and how life on earth is considered to be suffering. With Kenny's battle, I know that we all have to pay our dues sometime and I hope that getting into Heaven will be so much easier for him because he has paid his dues with his suffering.

If anything can come out of this, I sure hope it is that. That his journey is going to be easier getting into heaven. And if his battle drew the rest of us closer and gave us cause to pray more for him, then maybe he has made our battle, our road easier in getting into heaven too.

***

There is no doubt in my mind that Kenny made an express trip to heaven. I don't happen to believe that everyone goes right to heaven. I know some people do, but I don't think everyone does. I think that most of us have work to do in purgatory before we get there. I don't think Kenny had that; I think he paid for his express ticket with all his suffering, but more so with all of his good works and being who he was in choosing to use the graces that he was given by God.

Loretta, St. Lawrence O'Toole Friend

123
Time
Mike: *FDNY Ladder 116, SOC, Golf Partner*

Kenny used to come stay with Debbie and me at our house in Brewster when he was single. He was my Fresh Air Fund kid. I would take the underprivileged kid out of the city and bring him up to the country.

He used to love to come up here and go fishing. He absolutely loved it. Kenny was Kenny. Up in the morning, out the door. The next thing we knew he was coming back with a bag of rolls and the newspaper. I'll never forget those times.

Kenny and I worked together at Ladder 116, then he got me over to SOC. That was a big favor for me. During that time he was getting sicker and sicker, but he was always a dependable person. If you needed anything, he would be the one to jump up and do it. No doubt about it. People would ask him for a favor, "Can you do this for me?" He would be immediately there. That was something that impressed me.

Then we went into the bad times.

I am referring to the last two years, but the early years had their extreme challenges also. I'll never forget being down by the lake during the summer of '93 and Kenny showing me the inside of his mouth. It was burned from his radiation treatments. You know when you get a white blister from a burn? All over the inside of his cheeks and his tongue were covered with them. He did his best to drink from a straw for a while, but by the end of the treatments he ended up dehydrated and had to spend two weeks in the hospital to recover. And the pain from it was terrible.

The saddest thing for me was the fact that he would get to that five year period and something else would come up. Get to another five year period and Boom! something else would come up.

The biggest letdown was when he couldn't eat after the big surgeries where they removed teeth. It took a year or two to heal completely from each and then everything seemed good. He told us, "We're doing okay. I am getting my teeth." We were out on the golf course and he was taking potato chips and saying, "Look, I am going to be able to do this!"

Then it didn't work. He had the teeth but they couldn't get them adjusted; they were giving him problems. Before that got fixed, a tumor came back. That meant another surgery, removing more teeth and no way to anchor a future bridge. That was sad. That was very, very sad. We used to go out and have lunch, have beers. We would go out to play golf, but golf was only part of it. Hanging out, breaking each other's chops, stopping afterwards, getting something to eat, getting a couple of beers, just hanging out for a few hours. So we couldn't do that part of it. That got taken away.

But that being said, even though we couldn't go out to eat afterwards, we still had a lot of fun golfing together. I knew that there wasn't a lot that he could do, but he could still do that; so, I thought, "Let's go do that." He was the first person that I called if I wanted to make plans.

If he couldn't go, a lot of times I wouldn't even bother.

That was like the last third of it, then the final part of it was just horrendous.

I was retired and able to help Lynda with Kenny during those last two years. My helping them was nothing that Kenny wouldn't have done at the drop of a hat for me. I told her, "The phone. Pick it up. I am not a coffee-klatch guy. I am not going to come over and sit there and say, 'Hey, how are you doing today?' I am not going to pick up the phone and do that, but if you need something, call me."

When they had the incidents at the house and Lynda was afraid to leave Kenny by himself, that was when I knew that he was deteriorating and not coming back to the way we had known him before. He was coughing up blood. There were many trips to the hospital, many incidents, day after day after day. It was at a point that it was getting worse and worse and worse and worse.

How do you watch somebody that you know, you like, your friend, just deteriorate in front of your eyes? I'll never forget; I don't know how we got on the conversation. Lynda must have seen this in Kenny's notebook:

I came over to hang out with Kenny because Lynda had to go out for a couple hours. We were talking about things and what his future medical plan would be. I said, "Listen, it always seems that the longer you are here, the more things doctors come out with, the better it might be for you." It was just a conversation between two guys and I said, "I don't know how you are doing it. If it was me, Kenny, I don't know if I would last as long as you did. Or put up that kind of a fight."

He wrote down in the book, "I don't want to die."

That just sent me. I had no response. I think a big part of that was the boys. To be able to be around and do the things that he wanted to do with them. That I could understand. But it was tough to think about. That was the toughest five words I ever read in my life.

The other killer was the rehab place in Connecticut. Kenny had just been transferred from New York Presbyterian and I went to visit him the second day he was there. This was the place where they were going to get him up and get him moving again. I got there and the room was shut down. Curtains were drawn. I grabbed a nurse and asked, "What is going on?" She asked, "Who are you here for?" Then, "Oh, we have some problems." That's when I called Lynda and learned that he had just been transferred to Yale New Haven Hospital's ER. I said to myself, "The one day, Lynda got a break to do whatever she needed to do and I was going to go up there and hang out with him and it didn't work." Now he was back in a hospital and still more than an hour away.

I went to see him a few times at New Haven. At that point, it was really sad. He was so wiped out. He was clinging, and clinging, and clinging, but he was just wiped. He was probably ninety-some-odd pounds at that point. He was skin and bones; it wasn't him. You could see the expression of pain in his face, constantly. I was talking to the doctor, nice guy, young guy and I said, "He is complaining about the pain." He said, "The amount of stuff that we gave him would knock you and me out for a month." I said, "Oh, man…"

At that point I would just talk at Kenny. He would smile, but he couldn't respond.

It was no big deal for me to drive Lynda to Yale early that Wednesday morning so she could take the ambulance ride with Kenny to Rosary Hill. The doctors were afraid that Kenny might not survive the trip and after all they had been through, Lynda did not want Kenny dying alone in an ambulance. It was kind of good; I got to see him leave there with Lynda. That was the last time I think he was cognizant of people around him, because by that night, he was kind of out of it.

I went to Rosary Hill the night he passed away. Kenny was completely and totally peaceful at that point. That was comforting.

Spending time with Kenny and Lynda at the end was a good time for reflection and a good time for trying to get an understanding and a grip of what was going on. We reflected on some of the good times. We did laugh a little bit here and there from the stories of the good times. We always manage to think of those.

But I chose the word "Time" because there was just not enough. Knowing Kenny through the years, I wish we could have had more time, more years to know each other and more years with better circumstances. The years that we had with the good circumstances were great, but not enough time. There is never enough time for anybody.

***

I saw the transition from week to week. I saw it. There was no question in my mind what was happening. Even the nurses don't want to tell us, but when we really asked, they knew, because they deal with it all the time. Even when I was talking with other guys, friends in that group, they would never use the "dying" word. I said, "Guys, he is dying. You have to deal with it."

Gary, Astoria Friend

***

When we first moved to Brewster Kenny would visit and he and Mike would go fishing. Michael still loves to go fishing and he loves to go now with Timmy. He tells Tim stories about when he went fishing with his dad. He really enjoys that.

Debbie, Brewster Friend, Mike's Wife

124
Legacy
Maureen: St. Lawrence O'Toole Friend

Believe it or not, I met Kenny, probably about 1970. One day, my older brother Michael let my mother know that he was bringing home for dinner a couple of Queens boys that went to school with him at Power. Kenny Holler walked through the door and I have to say, he was one handsome man! I couldn't believe his crystal blue eyes. They were piercing. He had a smile that lit up the whole room. After high school, Kenny went his way and Michael went his.

More than thirty years later, I was living in Brewster with my husband Ed. My son Michael, my last little guy, was in St. Lawrence O'Toole's PreK4 program. There were a lot of cute little kids running around, but there was one little boy named Colin Holler that definitely caught my eye. I had a fleeting moment, "Maybe? Could it be? Kenny Holler's son?" I went over to Kenny and asked him, "Are you Kenny Holler?" and he said, "Are you the little Hanvey?"

I am a woman of prayer and we have a prayer group at St. Lawrence called the Prayer Warriors. We went to his house and prayed over Kenny. We truly, truly prayed for a miracle. I was hoping that if there was a big miracle to be had here at St. Lawrence, that the miracle would be given to Kenny. He so deserved it.

It was unfortunate that the big miracle wasn't to be had, but God's mercy was. I have to say that the whole parish, for a number of years, got behind Kenny, Lynda, and the boys. We were all a family supporting this wonderful man that deserved every bit of our attention and help, caring and prayers.

On August 1, 2014, Lynda called me at home. They were at Rosary Hill Home, which is a beautiful Catholic hospice facility in Hawthorne, NY. She told me that I might want to come down and say goodbye to Kenny; she didn't believe that he was going to last much longer.

We prayed over Kenny. He was so peaceful. After all the pain and suffering he had gone through for a number of years, he was finally comfortable. It was so hard to know that he was going to be leaving this earth, but we knew that it was only a matter of time that he was going to be in the arms of the Lord that he loved so much.

I left there that day having peace. I knew what Lynda and the boys were going to go through after Kenny died; I knew that journey was not going to be easy, but I knew with all my heart that Lynda knew that she did all that she was capable of doing for this man that she loved so much. There is peace and acceptance in that.

St. Lawrence Cemetery is where Kenny is buried, so is my husband Ed. When I go to my husband's grave, I see Kenny's tombstone diagonally across. Kenny's headstone is a rugged cross. It is so fitting for him to have that for a symbol, because Kenny carried that cross for most of his adult life. Jesus told us all to pick up our cross and follow Him and Kenny did that with a much heavier cross than most of us have to bear in life.

Kenny's legacy will be left here at St. Lawrence O'Toole parish forever. After the renovations of the church in 2014, we reopened our doors on Divine Mercy Sunday, the Sunday after

Easter 2015. In the renovations, they built the Divine Mercy Chapel that is used for Adoration. In that chapel, there is a beautiful stained glass window of our Blessed Mother, the Apostle John, and Mary Magdalene at the foot of Jesus on the Cross. At the bottom, are the words: "In Loving Memory of Kenny Holler." Lynda and the boys donated it to the chapel. The Divine Mercy Chaplet was a prayer that was very important to their family; Lynda, Colin, and Tim prayed it many times over Kenny when he was sick. Now Kenny is a part of every prayer that is said in that chapel.

What is so significant about the stained glass window with Jesus on the cross surrounded by the ones that loved him the most, is that is how Kenny's life was at the end too. Kenny was in excruciating pain; he was the one being crucified. Kenny suffered deeply on all levels of his body from head to toe. At the end, he was surrounded by his wife, sons, and closest friends. When I see that stained glass window, I will always remember how brave Kenny was and remember the suffering that he went through that few of us knew about. He united his suffering with Christ's suffering, something that all of us are asked to do. So now, whoever enters that chapel to pray, for whatever their needs are, that window is there to inspire them to unite their suffering to Christ too. May we all strive to make that our own legacy.

***

I know Kenny is watching everybody in St. Lawrence, and that every Sunday he is around with us in the church. That is pretty nice.

Luis, St. Lawrence O'Toole Friend

I only have one working vocal cord from thyroid surgery back in 2003. My voice is a lot better, but whenever I get stressed it gets squeaky and quiet. I felt Kenny's pain when Lynda told me that she found the note where he wrote, "My name is Kenny, I can't talk." It reminded me of all the little things that we take for granted.

I remember going for cold cuts in the summer and it was always an eighteen year-old behind the counter. I would say, "A half-pound of turkey." And he would look at me and say, "What?" I would have to lean over the glass, and repeat, "A half-pound of turkey." Other people that wouldn't bother, but I would come home and cry, "Oh my God, this is awful!"

There was a friend in my neighborhood whose husband was dying. I wouldn't even knock on the door; I would just open the door, say "Hello," and pull up a chair. She would say, "You know, he won't let anyone else do that." I have always felt that way. I just want to help. And I always, always had this feeling that nobody should ever be alone in a hospital without an advocate.

Knowing that communication was an issue, it inspired me to start visiting Kenny regularly in the hospital. I started going after the carotid artery issue when he was in New York Presbyterian. Probably in the back of my head, I thought that he probably wouldn't feel so bad if I went in talking like this too.

There are certain things about Kenny's illness that I will never forget. The first one was when I was in New York Presbyterian one day with Steve and the nurse; and Kenny wanted something. It was like a game show. "What do you want?" "What?" "Do you want this?" "Do you want that?" "This?" He was struggling with the pen. I never saw him frustrated before and I thought, "Wait, he has to pee." Then I said it, "Wait a minute, he has to pee." And he took a pen and he wrote, "I love Carole!" I will never forget it. Steve and I just looked at each other. I don't know how I knew it, but it was like a game; it was hysterical. I took the note and put it in my pocket and I have it upstairs by my computer. These are the little things. I will never forget that.

Then there was the soccer playoffs. The first bed was empty; I was sitting in a chair, and like four employees were in the room, because we had the soccer game on. They were watching the soccer game, I was just sitting there, and Kenny was reading the paper. It was like, "Give us a couple of beers and some peanuts and we'll all be fine."

The doctors and nurses were so helpful at New York Presbyterian. The palliative care doctor, Dr. Adams, was the sweetest thing ever. Kenny was such a complicated case with so many issues: pain, trach, wounds, nutrition, potential pneumonia.... They would say, "I can't give you that. I can't give you that." He would ask, "When can I have pain meds next?" We were biting our nails, because what else is there? They really gave him everything they had in their power and it didn't even make him sleepy. Usually you give people morphine and they are in a comma, at least for twenty minutes or so.

I was very impressed with Yale too. I really was. They were another one. The nurses didn't seem like they were overwhelmed with work and they were receptive to our suggestions. Their actions and compassion conveyed: "I wish I could do something for him, but I don't know what to do. Do you have any ideas? How can I help more?"

It was in Connecticut, when his face blew up, and I realized that Kenny was not going to pull out of this. Even after the carotid artery, I had hope. He was up, he was in the wheelchair; they were walking him with the walker. We were making jokes because his butt was sticking out of his hospital gown. I would say, "Okay, now I am not Carole, I am a nurse. I just want to look at your butt and make sure your skin is not breaking down or anything." He would grumble, but I would say, "Sorry, I got to do it. You know how it is."

But when we got to Yale, the doctor had a meeting with us. In the way that doctors talk, he was trying to tell Lynda that they couldn't control Kenny's pain, so he was not going to be able to go to therapy. So what is going to happen from here? Not much....

I thought Rosary Hill was great. I have always said, "There is nothing like a statue of Jesus and a nun to make you feel better." And better yet an old nun, because they were taught differently. Sr. Edwin worked to get Kenny's neck positioned better, because when she moved his neck a certain way he wouldn't be as purple. She took the little humidification mask for his trach and she cut it and they padded it. I remember telling my friend that that was the way we were taught in nursing school in 1973, how to make do with what we had. And sure enough she put it in place and he was okay. And Kenny's male nurse was so respectful, so sweet, not rushed. He treated it as an honor to care for his patients.

Another beautiful story was at Rosary Hill, when they told me and Steve to go downstairs because they were having a little barbeque outside. A man was playing the piano, patients were around in wheelchairs, and he was singing the Frank Sinatra song, "And now, the end is near..." Steve and I just looked at each other and said, "What! How could he sing that song here?" It was like everything was funny; we had to find humor in it. This is how people survive I think. Lynda found comfort in her faith; Steve found humor in a lot of stuff.

I am a prayerful woman, always have been. And honestly, I prayed for God to let it cease. I did. I said, "Enough already." By now I knew Kenny wasn't going to get better, so I couldn't pray for him to get better. I prayed for his family and just to let him go.

If I could give Lynda a break for a day, that was all I was looking for in the beginning. Did I think it was going to turn into every other day going to see Kenny, so she could take a break and take care of her children? That was fine with me too. It just really turned out to be ... how do I want to put this? In someone else's suffering, it made me feel good about myself. I think I am going to cry now thinking about it .... I don't know if a lot of people will understand that. And I grew closer to Steve in the process. We used to meet for coffee and a bagel for a while afterwards.

And probably by me being comfortable with doing that, because I was a nurse, I was able to allow Steve to be part of this, which he would not have been comfortable with otherwise. I am sure he was glad he was there, but we had different roles. Men see things differently than us chicks. He would sit there and read the paper and get up and come back. He'd get up and he'd come back. They are not meant to be coddling like we are. They are just not, but Kenny benefited from that relationship with Steve sitting there too, because of the bond that they have had for so many years. The male thing.

I thanked Lynda for letting me be a part of that, because it was very important to me. I always thought too that if Kenny's mother Mary or my mom were there, they would have picked up the phone and said, "Carole, do me a favor." So they kind of did, from heaven maybe, "Go. Do it. Help him and see what you can do."

***

I cried very, very hard when my dad's name was brought up at the funeral. It was sad and I was upset for Lynda, I was upset for her family, I was upset for my dad, but then after everything that the priest read and what Lynda had written, I think that set me at peace a little bit. I do. That was a very good thing that Lynda did, because I think a lot of people felt that way. No one wanted to see Kenny go.

Kelly, Steve's Daughter

126

Coffee
Steve: *Astoria Friend*

I first remember spending time with Kenny up in the park, in Steinway Park. Then when we were older we hung out in McGivney's. A lot of silly stuff up there.

We rented houses out in the Hamptons. I remember I would go to work and Kenny was out there and he didn't have a car. He would drop me off in the morning and I would take the train to work. I would tell him which train and he would pick me up. It was like we were married. He would work a mutual and have three days off. We didn't have much money; I remember we used to live on English Muffins. We used to put butter on them in the morning and we would make English Muffin pizzas at night.

When I think of Kenny I think of a lot of laughs. A lot of good times. A lot of silly stuff, but a lot of fun.

For my one word, when I think of Kenny, I think of coffee. Me and Kenny used to meet every morning in Lake George, six o'clock. Either I would be outside of his cabin or he would be outside of my cabin. We would drive down to Bolton Landing and go into that Stewarts. We would have coffee; we would sit there; we would pick out the losing horses for the day. We would spend about an hour or so, just me and him. Then we'd head back. He might go back with sandwiches for the boys, then he would have breakfast, and his whole day would get started with his family.

Even at night, we would all be hanging out and my cabin was the Coffee Cabin. He would come down and say, "How about a cup of coffee?" He'd come in and we'd watch the Yankee game or something, have a cup of coffee, and hang out before we would call it a night. After all these years and all these experiences, "Coffee" is definitely my one-word memory.

Going back ten years or so, I remember there was one or two times where Lynda had stuff going on with the boys and Kenny was getting out of Sloan after one of his hospital stays. I drove into the city and drove him home. His mouth was all filled with the padding. He couldn't talk much, but sitting in the car for an hour, hour and a half with traffic, I got to really see what he was going through. Those couple of trips in the car, just me and him, right after he had his surgeries and stuff, they hit home pretty good. I realized how serious it was.

It worked out great, me and Carole going together to visit Kenny in the hospitals over those last few months. I was going up there with a nurse. If Lynda had stuff to do and couldn't get there, you couldn't ask for a better person to be there than Carole. She would call and give Lynda her report. I would go up there and visit with Kenny and I was her driver. I was so glad that I was able to get the other guys to come up too, because I think Kenny liked seeing everybody. Hut went up there, McCormick went there, Pete R, Stove, Lombardi, Shorty, Gary, Pete and Sue... I think that everybody that Kenny wanted to see and everybody who wanted to see Kenny made it there. I think we took care of that.

Kenny died the day we were checking in at Lake George. I remember I got a text from

Lynda at three o'clock in the morning. Karen was sleeping. I didn't wake her up. We got up at seven o'clock in the morning to get ready to go and I told her.

I prayed for Kenny when he was sick; we all did. It was hard for me; it was hard on all of us. Between spending all that time together in Lake George and in the hospitals, Lynda really got to know the Astoria guys. They are a great bunch of guys. Really tight group.

Kenny is a big void in my life, you know that. We all have to go on.

***

That is one of the things about the guys, all of the Astoria guys, when something happens they are on the phone; they are all over it. When Louie died, when LaPierre died, when other guys died, on 9/11, everybody is on the phone back and forth, talking each other through it. These guys don't isolate. They talk to each other; they support each other.

Karen, Steve's Wife

127
Confident
Sean: Lynda's Nephew

When I see Uncle Kenny, I see a strong firefighter, comic relief, athlete, sportsman, and competitor. He was confident, because for him to have all those other attributes, he couldn't do them without confidence.

- You can't be a good father, without being confident.
- You can't be good at your job, without being confident.
- You can't be a good husband, without being confident.
- You can't just light up every room you walk into, without being confident.

When asked to share my memories of Kenny, I used the weeks leading up to meeting with Aunt Lynda to write down one word descriptions or short sentences describing my uncle. The process was neat, because not only did it get me thinking about what I see every day that reminds me of Uncle Kenny, I noticed that I would think of my Grandma Eileen (Lynda's mom) and Grandpa Ed (my dad's stepfather), both of whom have passed on, and also of my dad and mom, and all the little stuff. I went about my days, like I normally would, and every time I thought of somebody or something, I wrote it down on little Post-It notes and stuck them all over the inside of my truck. Some memories were broad, and others were the littlest, weirdest things. It was kind of neat to go at it from that perspective. I ran out of Post-It notes.

Here are three small examples of what I'm speaking of:

Fourth of July, 2016, we just got our house painted and we were decorating the front with bushes, flowers, and mulch. Last thing to go up was our American Flag. As soon as I placed it and stepped back, I instantly thought of Kenny. Being a first responder himself and with the many brave men and women Kenny knew who lost their lives or had their lives drastically changed during the 9/11 attacks, I immediately made the connection.

The first time I went fishing with him was in Montauk when we caught the stripers. I have the picture and the grin on his face is just as big as mine and I'm the one that caught the fish. So that is nice. Dad and I liked to fish, but it was Kenny's connections and he got us into doing that. I went deep sea fishing, and Dad did too, years later when we were in Florida. Who knows if we would have ever gotten into doing that if Kenny didn't start that whole thing. That is one of those broad things that I mentioned, like an American flag; a fishing pole, I think of Kenny.

During the early 90's, the Buffalo Bills had their four years of Super Bowl appearances. Being from the Buffalo area we are all Bills fans and Kenny, of course, being from the city, loved the Giants. Being the competitor and athlete that he was, you would think there would be some joking and teasing back and forth. I'm sure there was to some extent, but he just loved to talk football with us. One Christmas, he even had on full Bills gear; I have the picture to prove it. Kenny didn't do it because he was a Bills fan; he did it to have a connection with me. He tried and succeeded to be a part of my life whenever he had a chance. How many of us can say that?

Kenny got to become a dad, and until 4 years ago, I didn't know what that meant. Now,

266

fully aware of the responsibility and joy of being a good dad, it's comforting knowing that a man, who in my eyes is a tremendous role model, was always thinking of others, who had a great temperament and was extremely funny, would father two men to take his place. It's fitting, and in that regard, God's scheme seems to be without fault. But there is missed opportunity for a lot of things, for a lot of people. His version of a grandpa, would probably be pretty darn cool, you know? Or his version of a great uncle, which he got to only experience a little bit with my daughter Jo.

Back-track with me a bit: I remember climbing out of my parents' car and running to see my Grandma at her house. This was well after the death of my Grandpa John. She would be there, in the living-room by herself, just sitting there on the couch. No TV. No radio. Sometimes a book close by, but if she read that much or not, I'm not sure. No sewing or crochet needle. Nothing. It didn't resonate with me when I was young, but it started to as I got older and I got curious. I would always ask her, "What are you doing Grandma?" Looking back now the answer is obvious, she was praying.

I can't help but compare her to Kenny and Lynda. Although Kenny had a great support system, towards the end he couldn't communicate well. Were the quiet days where Uncle Kenny couldn't communicate the same opportunity Grandma had? For him to give prayer for his family, to give them the strength to fight the next fight; the one he wouldn't be there to see?

That leads me to Aunt Lynda and Grandma's connection. Both are devout women who leaned heavily on their faith to help them through the loss of their husbands. So this scenario plays through my head:

"Did Grandma's suffering give Lynda the initial toughness to cope and help Kenny through his fight; knowing full well what may lay ahead?"

"Were those silent prayers, Grandma was sending alone in her living room giving her the strength to prove to Lynda that you can fight through the loss of your best friend?"

I'd like to think so.

As I juggled all the thoughts and memories that preparing for this interview produced, one of the most emotional was reflecting on the fact that Uncle Kenny couldn't speak at the end. I thought how that had to be the most frustrating thing in the world. He probably knew the end was near and what is more essential than to be able to tell people his last and most heartfelt thoughts? He couldn't.

But Aunt Lynda told me how peaceful he was. He wasn't frustrated, which even surprised the medical people that cared for him. He was accepting. He had many friends and family members visiting at his bedside over the last few weeks and he never showed a need to share any last words.

As we reflect on that fact, it can only mean that Uncle Kenny was satisfied with those relationships. There was no need to tell Aunt Lynda, the boys, and his friends that he loved them one more time. He had said the words and shown the evidence throughout his whole life. He had no bedside reconciliation necessary; there were no long-held grudges that needed to be purged. He had lived his life flat out, loving and giving and serving and laughing, nothing else was needed. He was confident of that.

The Lord Himself will fight for you; you have only to keep still.

Exodus 14:14

***

I still do think of Kenny now. Every time I see Colin, Colin reminds me of his dad. My son Christopher and Colin roomed together freshman year. When they first moved into their dorm at Manhattan College, Colin hung a large American flag on the wall. I asked Colin, "Is that your dad's flag?"

Dee, Brewster Friend

128
Lovingness
Sister Edwin: Rosary Hill Home

A lot of people are "face cases" as we call them. They do not have any friends; well, they have friends, but they don't come around.

First of all, men, boys do not usually want to come to visit here. It is ridiculous! They will say, "Oh, I can't go visit. It hurts me more than it hurts them!" Baloney, baloney, baloney! They are too cowardly to admit it. But all these people came to see Kenny in all his swollenness and holes and drainage and nobody cared. It was obvious how much they loved the family and how much they wanted to support them and be there. The friends were there for Lynda, Lynda was there for them, and they were there for the boys. It was just so impressive talking with those people.

When Kenny came, he was in such horrible shape; his trach was all crooked and we couldn't get it in right. It was really a challenge. There was so much swelling; he had so much edema. Lynda was not afraid of him, the kids were not afraid of him. Lynda was the most assertive person I ever saw with a trach, because a lot of people are just so afraid of trachs. I guess Kenny took care of it himself and he showed her how to do it.

Lynda was very prayerful. She had the Divine Mercy picture of Jesus and a picture of Our Lady, which had touched the image of Our Lady of Guadalupe, hanging in Kenny's room. They left them here and I saved them for a whole year until they came back to visit.

The kids were very loving with their dad. They were not distant at all. Do you know how unusual that is? With somebody that is that sick, number one. With kids that age, number two. They could be very distant or very emotional, but Kenny's kids were loving and supportive also. They talked; they didn't just sit there. They talked to the staff and I remember one time they were looking for a Coke or something to eat and I brought them over to the Coke machine; they were so present.

Kenny must have had a wonderful funeral. I hope some of those guys still come around for the boys.

129
Father
Colin: Kenny's Oldest Son, Age 18

Now, more than two years after Dad's death, I have started thinking more about when Dad was healthy and we were in Lake George and in Aruba, stuff like that. It is kind of the opposite from when he first died, where I couldn't remember the good memories. Now it is like I am forgetting the bad memories, but it isn't anything that I am doing on purpose; it is just the way that my mind is working. Mom says that it is the same with her.

I was thinking today about how Dad used to take Tim and me out to lunch in the summer. He couldn't eat, but he still wanted to drive us and get us burgers and ice cream. He did a lot for us when he didn't really have to and it must have been hard since he couldn't eat himself. That's another thing with food, he would still make ribs, he would still make chicken legs, he would still make his pasta sauce. He would still make us the firehouse recipes that he loved, even though he couldn't have them himself.

I don't remember him eating solid food or eating anything with us at the dinner table. I do remember a couple times him trying to eat soup at the kitchen table and me and Tim being too loud, him getting mad, and taking the soup into the dining room. Then we would be quiet for the rest of the dinner. Same with oatmeal for breakfast. That is why when I was younger and I would go over to my friends' houses and their dads would be eating regular food at the table with us, it sounds stupid, but that was weird for me. I thought, "Why…?" I am a male myself and it sounds stupid to think that one day I will not be eating regular food, I'll be eating soup like my dad, but I was younger and it just didn't make sense yet.

Dad always did goofy jokes when we were younger, but now I would appreciate more of his adult humor after hearing all of these stories. He would draw funny caricature pictures and say funny stuff that we would laugh at as young kids, but I would be able to appreciate the things he had done with his friends and the pranks more now. There were times when he would tell me something and then say, "I can't really tell you what so-and-so said when we did this and that." And I would say, "Why? Why can't you tell me? It sounds funny!" He would say, "I don't know. You are too young." So I feel like now there would be a lot more stories that he would be able to share.

I feel that now that I am older too, I would have a better relationship with him than when I was younger and kind of just casually thought, "Oh that's my dad." When I was younger I would sometimes think, "Oh, I don't want to do things with my dad." But now looking at it, I would love to play golf with my dad or just watch sports. When I was younger, I didn't want to sit still long enough to watch a game, but now that I do, I wish he was around for me to watch sports with. It is the "grass is always greener" kind of thing. If he was still here, maybe I still would think, "Ah, it's only my dad." But after doing this book and hearing everybody's stories, I feel that I really didn't know him as well as other people might have, even though I spent every day with him. He was just Dad.

But there are patterns that I recognize from people's stories. One thing that I specifically remember happened one day when we were driving down the road. A woman who had been riding a bike was by the side of the road; she had fallen. We didn't know her, but Dad stopped the car. He put her bike in the back of the car and we drove her to her house. She was pretty banged up from the fall. Tim and I were both with him and we were young, but it was a good example. None of us knew who she was and I'm not sure if we ever ran into her again.

Another important thing that I recognize is that I think that he always respected other people no matter what they did as a job, or the choices that they made, good or bad. He was nice to everybody, even strangers. For instance, to have such a personality that he could spark up a friendly conversation with a supermarket cashier, Dad was able to make an impact on people that he really didn't spend much time with.

Dad didn't take life too seriously. That is one thing that I have been thinking about too. We hear about how he would go on vacations with his friends and he was a co-owner of a boat. He wanted to live life and have a lot of fun. It is something that I realize is important.

I prayed for him from the moment that I learned how to pray. I said that same prayer every night for so many years that sometimes still I find myself praying, "Please help Dad's mouth to get better..."

Thinking back on those last two difficult years, like I said in the beginning, I don't really remember that much from that time. It sounds weird that I was still doing my homework and still just going about normal life. I think I just wanted everything to be normal, so I just acted like it was. It was "our normal," but it felt normal until Dad was all over the place at different hospitals and Mom was driving around all day. That wasn't so normal, but that even got to be normal, a new normal. It's not like I ever talked about it; I didn't really want people to know much.

I can't forget the emergency calls I had to make though. Mom was telling me to call 911 and at the same time in my mind I was thinking, "Do I really have to?" I was hoping that Dad stopped having the fit or whatever it was and that Mom would say, "Oh, it is fine. You don't have to call." So I hesitated, with the hope that I wouldn't have to actually make the call. That wasn't fun.

And it was hard on me when he had the trach, now that I think about it. Being in public with Dad and him having to cover it to talk. He had that raspy voice and people couldn't understand him and I would have to talk for him. I was thirteen, fourteen and that was uncomfortable for me.

I feel like my story and Mom and Tim's stories are different than everyone else's in the book. Even though they saw that he was visibly sick, he was still kind of like the same guy around them. But it was different here, because we saw more of the struggling than everybody else, with him using all the machines and spending most of his time at the end just taking care of himself. It was a full-time job. He wouldn't always be in the best moods, which was understandable. It wasn't his fault; he was going through a lot.

When I see or hear about other teenagers who have to take care of sick parents, I really feel empathy for those kids. The sacrifices that they have to make in their lives in order to help a parent at that age isn't a common thing. I feel bad for people that have to take care of somebody at any age. When I see middle-aged parents, one taking care of the other, I feel for them, because of what Mom had to go through. Knowing how hard it was for her, but also feeling for the kids, because I know what they all have to go through as a family.

I saw two people in the restaurant today: a girl who was probably twenty-one-ish who was with her sick mother. Some people would see that girl helping her mom at that restaurant; I see behind the scenes, which is more than helping her cut up her food or something. There is a lot more to it in their own house. There is a lot more going on medically and it is a lot more complicated. I also know that it might not really get better for them until her mother either heals or eventually passes away. It is going to be a hard process.

I guess after Dad died, it was kind of a relief for me, like a heavy backpack had been lifted off of all of us. Obviously, that doesn't sound that great and I was obviously sad, but the last couple years with him suffering were terrible and we all felt relieved in a way. At the time, I couldn't really remember a lot of happy memories, or earlier memories. I think that was a good thing, because it made losing him not as sad at first. I thought about how we had done everything we possibly could to help him and make him happy, but now that we could do no more, I was confident that he was in a better place and life would be easier for Mom and Tim and me too. It really was the best for everybody.

Yes, I lost my dad when I was only sixteen, but that is only one side of the story. The way I look at it is I had my dad for sixteen years. And he was retired and able to spend a lot of time with us. He taught me so much, lessons and skills and how to live life with his words and with his actions.

It makes me sick to hear people talking about assisted suicide. If Dad had chosen to give up from the beginning, I would never have been born. Or if he had given up along the way, we might not have had Tim, or we would have had less time with Dad, and he wouldn't have met and influenced as many people. I would be a completely different person if he had decided to end his own life instead of letting it unfold the way it was meant to be. It is quite an amazing story the way Dad's life became intertwined with so many people. It was hard at times and it is probably not a life we would have asked for, but I am proud to be part of it. Proud to be Kenny Holler's son and proud that he chose to live, even though it mean suffering for him and for us, because we are all better and prouder for it.

One thing that was comforting then and still stands out the most for me now, was when Dad was in the hospital and he couldn't talk and Mom asked him if he was talking to God. And he nodded. Then she asked if God was talking to him and he nodded again. That was very impactful and that hit me pretty hard. It reinforced that there was good coming out of his suffering. It wasn't like he was able to tell us what God was saying, but we got a good feeling that he was living out his life the way God wanted him to.

Dad's suffering did a lot for the community and everybody that he knew. By reading and hearing people's stories for the book, it shows us the impact he made on those groups. Hopefully, this book with the memories people have shared, will allow Dad to continue to help people and influence an even bigger community.

I have probably grown from these experiences too, but it isn't something that I can really recognize. We don't recognize when we get taller or heavier or older-looking until we look at old pictures. Other people notice our changes more than we do. People have been asking me for years, "Did you get taller?" I never notice it until I remeasure myself. But there is no way to measure how I have grown mentally from everything; it isn't something that I would recognize, but I probably have. It is the same thing when you get a haircut or change your hair style, you don't really remember what you looked like before that haircut. Do you know what I mean? I don't really remember what I was like before I had to go through all this. But I am pretty happy and content on a day-to-day basis; so I guess I am doing okay.

One time Kenny told me that for the longest time, his kids didn't know he had cancer. They just knew Kenny the way he was; that was his physical appearance. They didn't know that he was suffering and hurting, fighting this disease. I give him and Lynda a lot of credit for not wanting to burden their children. They just wanted their children to have a normal life and not worry about their dad until the point they could adjust and handle it. I give him all the pats on the back to deal with life that way.

Larry, FDNY Lieutenant

130
Son
Lynda

About a week before Kenny died, I was sitting alone with him at Yale New Haven Hospital. He was hooked up to tubes: feeding, pain, with steady beeping from monitors, but Kenny lay there serenely. Some visits we would find him very tired and he would sleep most of the day; others he would be fidgeting in pain. As I sat by his bedside and we looked at each other, I wondered what was going on inside his head. He had long ago given up trying to write his thoughts to us on a white board or notepad. This man, this communicator with all the quick wit, street-smart wisdom, and faithful insight, I couldn't imagine that inside his head he wasn't still talking and being heard by someone. So, I asked him:

"Kenny, are you talking to God."

He nodded, "Yes."

"Are you praying?"

He nodded, "Yes."

"Is God talking with you?"

He nodded, "Yes."

Finally, I asked, "Is God proud of you?"

And he nodded, "Yes."

131
Competitor
Lynda

I remember years ago Kenny telling the boys that when he played basketball, he thought of it as his ball. That no one was going to take his ball, and if another player had it, he was going to get his ball back. I saw that he approached his fight with cancer the same way. Cancer was not going to take his life. He was not going to lose.

A few years ago, Kenny tracked down Brendan Malone's address and sent him a Christmas card. He has always respected his tough high school coach who taught him discipline and excellence through the game of basketball. He had known Mr. and Mrs. Malone well and he wrote telling them about his epic clash with cancer. The life-long NBA coach wrote back and told Kenny that it was his athleticism that would help him now.

As I ponder Kenny as a competitor, I clearly see that it was not just the championship that he had to win; he had to overcome many accomplished rivals along the way. Any defeats, anywhere in the season, would have weakened the team that made up the whole of the athlete. The competition was fierce and unforgiving, but Kenny was stronger and more determined to win.

Hunger—Since 1993 when he had his first surgery and a piece of his tongue removed, eating became challenging. Radiation dried out his mouth and he never again had adequate saliva to help wash down his food. After his 2003 surgery, he was never able to eat solid food again. In 2012, he needed a stomach tube and by the end of 2013 he could no longer even swallow. Kenny adapted to all of that by learning to be the master of his hunger. He used his mental toughness to subdue the physical demands. Many times over the years, if we were away from home, Kenny would go hours without eating because it wasn't possible or convenient for him to feed himself. Most of us struggle to go three or four hours without food.

One example is from 2012, before Kenny got the feeding tube. Tim was eleven and playing summer baseball on a fabulous team. They made it to the championship in West Nyack, about forty-five miles away. Their games were at night, but with bridge traffic and warm-up time factored in, we would have to leave home about two o'clock and not get back until around ten. Kenny loved everything about this team and this season. He was an assistant coach, working with the boys, sitting in the dugout, throughout these hot summer evenings. When Kenny ate, he would have to give eating and swallowing his full concentration and there was no place at the ballpark to do that, so he would eat before he left and not eat again until he returned home. Hunger was an enormous rival that could have defeated him, had he not been determined to dominate it.

Loneliness—Over the last two years, the nights were very long and hard for Kenny. He could no longer lie flat, so he had to sleep in a recliner in the living room. Drainage, breathing issues, and ultimately the demands of a trach meant that he couldn't sleep for long stretches, so he would be awake and alone for much of the night. He missed the boys and me while we were sleeping and the opportunity to snuggle with me through the night like we used to.

When he could no longer talk there must have been a different type of loneliness. He could be surrounded by people and yet be unable to interact with them. At first, he could clearly write or text his thoughts and messages to us, but after the carotid artery surgery that ability slowly diminished. Over much of his last two months, he was only able to use body language to convey simple ideas, yet he didn't show very much frustration. Again he was able to control his opponent and maintain the upper hand.

Pain—Pain is a very cruel adversary and a team that defeats many of its best opponents. Kenny experienced pain as long as I have known him. As a veteran athlete, he had arthritic pain in his knees and shoulders from the wear and tear those sports demanded. But the pain that he experienced from the oral and throat cancers and the surgeries and treatments that followed, demoted the arthritis to barely a second thought.

We all know how much it hurts when we bite our cheek or have a cold sore; it doesn't take much imagination to conjure up the pain one can experience from oral surgeries and burning radiation treatments. He had pneumonia, wounds that wouldn't heal, and pain in his neck from sleeping in a chair with the weight of his head falling forward. The skin around his finger and toe nails became infected from the chemo medication and they were very sensitive to the touch. If he even tapped an infected finger on a table or doorway it would send piercing pain through his hand and he would stop dead in his tracks, shaking his hand and clenching his teeth from the pain. Then, because he didn't respond to other treatment options, he would have to have his nails pulled off. Considering that was a torture treatment over the course of history and the medical procedure hasn't advanced much, you can imagine the pain that Kenny endured with this.

But as with Hunger and Loneliness, he would not let Pain prevail. He would not let it dictate how he would live his life or determine its value. It fought relentlessly to the very end, but it was Kenny's mental and physical toughness that was Pain's downfall.

Sorrow—Sorrow was a word that Kenny used one day after his carotid artery surgery at New York Presbyterian Hospital. It surprised me; he had never referred to it before. Somehow, I had undervalued it in the lineup. This is where his battle had to become a team sport; he couldn't handle this last rival alone. Over the years, he had never wanted friends and family to visit him in the hospital; it was too complicated and distracting when trying to recover from radical surgeries and other issues. But at this point, he started to allow it and he enjoyed the visits. Friends that are actually brothers and sisters of different mothers, now became his teammates to defeat Sorrow once and for all. They weren't rookies either and the love, laughter, and loyalty of Team Kenny showed no mercy to Sorrow and ultimately vanquished it forever.

Only a true competitor could have gone toe to toe with the biggest rivals on earth and pulled from his life's playbook the right strategies and tools needed for each. It takes years, decades, of practice and real-world experience to win the big one and be remembered as a champion.

***

I can remember watching Tim run and knowing he was running for his dad. Kenny was cheering for Tim. They were there for each other, supporting each other, and it impacted all of us that witnessed them.

Michele, Brewster Friend

276

Inspiring
Kathy: Astoria Friend

I think of Kenny when I see people that are really sick. Yes I do, and I pray. I pray for the dead all the time so he is definitely in my prayers. I think people got strength from his suffering. Looking at the way he handled it, yes. You know where he is because of his faith, his strength, his everything.

We know he is in heaven and if we want to go there too, we have to do what we need to do on this earth. Whether it be suffering or daily life struggles or whatever it is. We have to be able to cope with it and he gave a good example to everybody of how we do it.

And Lynda did too. She definitely did, yes she did. I have spoken to so many people and they have all said the same thing, "How did she get that strength?" I know it was definitely her faith. That's what got her there.

The words that Lynda wrote and her niece, Corinne, spoke at the end of Kenny's funeral Mass were just so touching. They touched so many people. They did, they really did. I am a true believer, so I knew what they were saying was true because of what I believe in, but there were quite a few people that have no faith at all and they were very touched. I think those words brought them back. I really, honestly think they did, because there wasn't a person there that didn't say that they didn't believe, after Corinne spoke.

To me that was the most touching thing, to think that all these people, that didn't believe, are going to come back to the Church. Or just have some kind of faith, which they had lost along the way for whatever reason. There are many reasons that people said it, but Kenny and Lynda brought a lot of people back. So many people walked out of church that day and said, "How could I not believe?"

In fact, when Corinne finished, everyone stood and gave her and Lynda a standing ovation. When have you seen that in Church? When have you seen that at a funeral? It was just so beautiful to see.

Kenny touched a lot of people. He really did. So many people were touched, but this book will help even more. The world needs that. Definitely.

***

The speech that Mrs. Holler wrote for the funeral brought almost everyone to tears in the church. It made everybody feel sad, but it also brought hope that everything would be okay. That got everybody focused on what they are going to do with their life. I think Mr. Holler would be proud of that.

Ryan, Tim's Friend, Age 15

Kenny's Funeral Homily
Father Richard: *St. Lawrence O'Toole Church*

August 5, 2014

Mark 15:16-21

The soldiers led him away inside the palace, that is, the praetorium, and assembled the whole cohort. They clothed him in purple and, weaving a crown of thorns, placed it on him. They began to salute him with, "Hail 'King of the Jews,'" and kept striking his head with a reed and spitting upon him. They knelt before him in homage. And when they had mocked him, they stripped him of the purple cloak, dressed him in his own clothes, and led him out to crucify him.

They pressed a passerby, Simon the Cyrenian, who was coming in from the country, the father of Alexander and Rufus, to carry his cross.

They brought him to the place of Golgotha, which is translated, the place of the skull.

You may remember the scene from the movie, *The Passion of the Christ.* For me, it was the most memorable scene of all: Jesus was carrying the Cross, barely alive after a brutal scourging and after a night of abuse at the hands of drunken soldiers, after spending the night in an underground pit. He was dragging himself along and collapsing, in real danger of dying along the way. That was intolerable, for the Roman soldiers were charged with strict orders to have him die by crucifixion.

So they grabbed a passerby, someone minding his own business, going about his life, who was near the procession to the place of execution, someone who simply happened to be in the wrong place at the wrong time.

Simon tried to protest saying he wanted nothing to do with this execution, nothing to do with this Jesus who was condemned. But the soldiers were not asking for his cooperation; they forced him to carry the Cross with Jesus. So Simon begins carrying the Cross, resentfully, perhaps cursing his bad fortune. He has to leave his own son behind and get with the task he has been pressed into.

In the film, as they limp along together under the weight of the Cross, shoulder to shoulder, Christ's face is bloodied and beaten and he looks at Simon helping him. Christ collapses from the weight of the Cross and the soldiers gleefully beat him until he gets up.

Veronica rushes to wipe his face and offer him a drink, and the soldiers kick the cup of water from her hands.

As the death march proceeds, you can almost see the transformation in Simon, who grows in sympathy for Jesus, recognizing that whoever this is, he is an innocent man suffering unjustly.

Jesus falls again. As the soldiers beat Jesus, Simon screams at the soldiers and demands they stop. Surprisingly, his words have the desired impact on the drunken soldiers and they stop beating the Lord. Simon helps him to his feet and resumes carrying the Cross with Jesus.

Now, you can see the transformation in Simon—not only is he shouldering the Cross, but now that Jesus is thoroughly exhausted and near the point of death, Simon begins supporting Jesus himself, carrying on his shoulder the cross and holding Jesus up with the other arm. He is looking at Jesus, the truly innocent one.

Then they reach the small hill called Golgotha and Jesus cannot even lift his leg to climb. Simon says to Jesus, "We are almost there," encouraging Jesus to step up to the place of his execution. Now why would anyone encourage a condemned man toward the place of his death?

Something subtle and profound has happened inside the soul of Simon. He has grasped something he did not know before and was not even interested in. He knows now that this death of Jesus is something necessary and has redemptive meaning in God's plan.

And he has a role to play in it.

Some twenty or so years later St. Paul would famously write, "I make up in my own flesh what is lacking in the sufferings of Christ for the good of the Church," touching on this same mystery of redemptive suffering.

Lynda asked us to read this gospel today, because over time she and Kenny have come to understand his long illness as a sharing in the redemptive suffering of Jesus. That deep and mysterious teaching of our faith, that all of us in our sufferings, whatever they may be, are mystically united to Jesus's death and resurrection—that as one Body in Christ, we all suffer and build up the Body of Christ, the Church, in time.

To the world, to those without faith, it seems unfair and unjust. And to be perfectly honest, we people of faith struggle mightily with this mystery. That this happy-go-lucky firefighter, a popular young guy without a care in the world, the joker and prankster, a man in love with life … should have to suffer. That this friend of everybody, who spotted a pretty girl named Lynda in a bar and tried a corny pickup line: "Hi, my name is Kenny; how do you like me so far?" should become a Simon of Cyrene.

But to those who believe in the power of redemptive suffering, there is meaning in all of it.

Because that moment in the bar started the miracle of a love story that lasts today and forever … and which we have all seen in Lynda and Kenny.

- Twenty-one years since the diagnosis, and all the years of struggle and pain
- Two boys he saw grow to be wonderful young men, of whom he was rightly proud
- Love which has grown stronger, forged in a crucible of suffering
- Consequence of the "I do," given one day when these two promised unconditional love, "In sickness and in health, till death do us part…"

Thank you for teaching us, Kenny, Lynda, Colin, and Tim, that without suffering, love can be superficial and weak. That only suffering tests it and makes it strong, something that lasts to eternity … that only suffering out of love can heal this broken world.

And let us all, as people of faith, embrace this mystery of redemptive suffering, when it is our turn to unite ourselves with the suffering of Christ.

134
Thank You

Kenny Holler's Funeral ~ August 5, 2014
Written by Lynda Holler, Read by Corinne DePue

I am so thankful that all of you are here today. It is so comforting to see the impact that Kenny has had on so many people throughout his life. You have been sharing stories of his humor, compassion, friendship, loyalty, bravery, and determination, but this is my chance to honor you for all that you have done for Kenny, and therefore for the boys and me too.

As you know, twenty-one years ago, eight months after we were married, Kenny was diagnosed with tongue cancer. Things were never the same again. Since that time, he endured fourteen very complex, serious surgeries, weeks of radiation, and months of chemo, but no one, even me, ever heard him complain. He never said, "Why me" or "What did I do to deserve this?" Or "This isn't fair." He just accepted and fought.

Our strategy was to try to be normal. We both grew up in very happy homes and wanted to have a life together that would focus on life. We never talked about what if he didn't survive. Each new occurrence meant a new obstacle, but Kenny bravely accepted the challenge and always overcame it. We didn't realize, until maybe fifteen or so years into this, that Kenny was quite miraculous. One doctor mentioned that no one has seven head and neck surgeries. We looked at each other in the doctor's office, talked about it later, and started to absorb the impact of that statement.

When the boys came along it was even more important that we try to give them a solid, happy, normal childhood. Our solid, reliable roots gave Kenny and me the foundation to deal with these challenges and we were determined to give the same to Colin and Tim. We did not want cancer to take away their childhood.

A few weeks ago, one of Kenny's childhood friends tried to comfort me by saying that God doesn't give us a cross heavier than we can bear. What came to me at that time is, "No! That isn't true! He definitely gives us crosses too heavy to bear, but then he gives us family, friends, acquaintances, and even total strangers to help us carry it." We could never have been able to carry this cross for 21 years if it wasn't for you.

Our Astoria Friends—You are the most amazing group of friends I have ever seen. Your friendship and loyalty is unprecedented. You have stood by each other for over fifty years, through all the good times and bad and you are closer brothers and sisters than many family members could ever dream of being. Kenny was so thankful for your friendship and support and we literally could not have carried this cross without you. Especially, over these last few weeks as you sat by Kenny's bedside and held his hand, spent hours on the phone helping me figure out the best course for Kenny, and then hours more updating the others on his status. Can you imagine if I was doing that alone? I can't. Thank you!

The New York City Fire Department—What can I say about a company of men that are already known as the Bravest? The bonds that you brothers form when you put your lives on the line every day for total strangers are unbreakable. You have driven us in snow storms or the middle of the night to emergency rooms, driven us back and forth to NYC for doctor appointments and surgeries. Fixed our garage doors, helped with benefit information, and so much more. Just knowing that you are a phone call away has been a great comfort to Kenny and me. Many of you, in the honor guard at the funeral home on Sunday and Monday and here today, worked with Kenny at Ladder 116 or SOC, but many of you didn't even know him. You answered the call to support a brother and show him the respect that is just natural for this revered fraternity. I don't know how to thank you enough.

The Brewster Community—Our school community, Brewster Little League, Rec basketball, the Elks, neighbors, and friends. Twenty-two years ago when we were looking for a home in Putnam County, something drew Kenny and me to Brewster. Now I firmly believe that it was more than the convenient highway access. I think God planted us in a community that would take care of us. That would welcome Kenny, the boys and me into their organizations. That would help develop our knowledge, skills, and talents. It is a witness to the strength of this community to see the outpouring of support and love over the years. Especially these last two difficult years. I don't know how we could have physically managed without the meals, rides, and genuine love you have shown us. And what a testament to the friendships that Colin and Tim are developing: so many teenagers paying their respects to them at Beechers Funeral Home over the last two days and sitting dressed up, respectfully, supporting our sons. I can only hope that these bonds will develop into the unbreakable Astoria-type. How can I possibly thank all of you?

Danbury Baseball—Last year Colin started playing summer baseball for a Danbury League. He was one of the few non-Danbury players on the team, but you welcomed him as one of your own. Those boys had been playing together since tee-ball, but he never felt like an outsider. This summer has been the most challenging of Colin's life, but the coaches, boys, and parents have been both an important distraction and a support at this critical time. Last night, we had a long row of young men standing in line for Colin. I can't help but notice the resemblance to the honor guard standing for Kenny. May you grow to have that same pride and bonded brotherhood that Kenny shared with his FDNY brothers.

St. Lawrence O'Toole Parish—Several years ago, Father Doughty told us that we should pray to the patron saint of our parish. That Saint Lawrence O'Toole has been chosen to intercede for us and that God may have called us to our parish. I can't help but believe that to be true. The St. Lawrence Community has grown to be an essential, life-giving source of support to our family. As we have tried to make sense out of a challenging life and terrible suffering, Father Richard, staff, and fellow parishioners have rallied around us to give us the physical, emotional, and spiritual support that we need and yearn for. Without this opportunity to grow in faith, to learn more deeply of Christ's suffering for us, we could never have begun to understand the suffering that Kenny has endured. Never have been able to see the value and the connection between Christ suffering, because of his love for us, and Kenny suffering, because of his love for the boys and me. This realization has brought all of us closer to our faith and I hope that you will ponder that reality and come to the same understanding.

281

My Cornerstone Sisters—The Cornerstone Ministry that began four years ago at St. Lawrence has changed my life forever. The bonds that I have formed with you faith-filled women can never be broken. We have all prayed and supported each other through every possible type of challenge. It is a warm comfortable feeling to walk into church at any time and see several sisters, for them to ask me about Kenny, to know they are praying and sincerely wanting that glorious miracle as much as I do. When a crisis would hit, the first thing I would do is send out a prayer alert to my sisters. I knew they would join me in storming heaven with prayer. This year I was chosen to be Lay Director for the upcoming 2014 Cornerstone Retreat. That role caused me to take you women along on my journey. You shared my fear and sorrow and loss. You also shared your faith and have helped me to remember that God's timing is impeccable and that God has a bigger plan that we cannot begin to understand. You have helped me carry the cross, but also to better understand it. May God bless you.

Medical Professionals—As challenging as Kenny's health issues were, we were so blessed to have the very best doctors and medical professionals in the world taking care of him. Locally, as well as in Memorial Sloan Kettering, New York Presbyterian, and Yale New Haven Hospitals. If you were to name the ten top hospitals in the Northeast, these three would certainly be on that list. We had the brightest, most compassionate, and dedicated medical professionals trying to cure and heal Kenny. They recognized scientifically that Kenny was a unique case: his cancer grew differently, side effects were more debilitating, but that he was the strongest, most determined man they had ever seen. They rallied around him and wanted to help him; they wanted to help him succeed. The seventeenth floor at Sloan is the Head and Neck floor and Kenny has spent a lot of time there over these twenty-one years. We became very close to some of the nurses and doctors.

When he was transferred to NY Presbyterian, we had to start all over with new medical professionals that didn't know him. It wasn't long and they were enamored by Kenny too. And don't forget he couldn't talk by that time. His pain doctor, Dr. Adams, was so dedicated to helping Kenny that she would stay at his bedside massaging his shoulder and wait patiently while he struggled to write a simple note to her. She never rushed him. Before she was transferred to another assignment, she told me that Kenny made her and the other staff feel good to help him. I told her that I was not used to hearing that—that Kenny always wanted to help others, not take help. That didn't come naturally. But it seems that Kenny Holler had found a way to help others by allowing others to help him.

By the way, when I called the seventeenth floor at Sloan on Sunday to tell them that Kenny had died, even the receptionist that answered the phone knew him and was shocked. She turned and I heard her say, "Mr. Holler's wife is on the phone and he has died." I heard a big moan break out in the background and someone say, "No, not Mr. Holler. We were just talking about him yesterday!" She put me on hold and one of the nurses talked to me. Where ever would we have been if Kenny had not had this top medical care? I don't even want to think about it.

Family By Blood and By Choice—Sister, brothers, nieces, nephews, aunts, uncles, cousins, and other family members that have been our grounded support since the beginning. There are also those friends that over the years have become family, although they are born of different mothers. Together with our blood family you have laughed, cried, prayed, and just stayed with us for the twenty-one challenging years of this journey. Newer friends do not know what you know. Walking the path with us, wanting what is best for us, and hurting when our dreams are shattered has earned you a high rank in our cross-carrying army. You know us well, encourage our strengths, and compensate for our weaknesses. You take calls at all hours, drop everything to come help, and know what to say and when to say nothing at all. Thank you from the bottom of our hearts!

Prayer Family—I realize that this thank you would not be complete without a salute to our prayer family. This category overlaps all the others, because most certainly, the Astoria crowd, the firemen, the Brewster and Danbury Communities, St. Lawrence O'Toole parishioners, my Cornerstone sisters, our families, and even some medical professionals have been praying for us. But it hasn't stopped there. Friends are asking friends to pray and those friends are adding Kenny's name to other church bulletins, in other church services, and so forth and so on. Sometimes I really wonder how many people are praying for Kenny every day. I'll never be able to thank them, but hopefully someday they will know how much it has meant to us.

Over the years I have heard so many people say that it isn't fair that Kenny be so sick, that he suffer so much and that the challenges just go on and on, but although it doesn't take away the pain, I have seen great things come from Kenny Holler's suffering.

- We learned the value of accepting help. Admitting that we can't do it all and recognizing that we are helping others when we allow them to help us.
- Kenny has rallied people together for a common cause. Initially, the cause might be to help Kenny, the boys, and myself, but ultimately the lessons learned should be used to help others like us that need help with their crosses.
- Acknowledging that although Kenny died, the cancer didn't win. Kenny's job here was done. We couldn't have prayed more. We stormed the heavens with prayers, men, women, and children, here and far beyond, so I am convinced that God has a bigger plan and that Kenny has fulfilled his mission.
- I am not an outsider anymore. The amount of friends that I have acquired, thanks to that fireman in an FDNY hat, cannot be counted. The boys and I will be starting a new chapter, and I know we will be ok, because no matter how heavy our new cross will be, we will be able to carry it, with your help.

What I Learned

As you know by now, this book started as a thought. Since then I haven't stopped thinking about what I have learned and what it all means. I am a ponderer and these interviews have given me much to ponder. I'd like to share some of the thought trains that grew out of my work on this project and on my life with Kenny.

When I got started, I had no idea how many people I would ultimately interview. I was thinking maybe fifty. I expected each person to have their own unique perspective, but before I got started I envisioned that a certain amount of the messages would become redundant. I didn't want the reader to get half-way through the book and say, "Ya, ya, he was a nice guy." But the week that I interviewed the fifty-fourth and fifty-fifth contributors, I had an epiphany. I realized that I could interview hundreds of people that knew Kenny and they would all have something distinctive and meaningful to contribute. That is how uniquely each of us looks at our world.

That week was also very sobering, because it became clear to me that Kenny had no idea of the impact he was making on the people in his life. Friends and acquaintances don't generally tell us these things, right? He knew that he was living a good life of service, but he had no clue of the profound impact he was making and the life altering attitudes being formed. That led me to understand that none of us do. None of us are fully aware of the impressions we are making on the people around us.

Of course, there were many people that said Kenny was a nice guy, that was one thread that connected most of the people that contributed, but there were many other threads. I am sure you noticed them, but I was amazed to see people that didn't know each other, that were different ages, from different communities saying the same thing. Sometimes, in the exact same descriptive words. And sometimes in the same exact words that Kenny would have used to describe himself—although they wouldn't have known that. This illustrated how interconnected we are with people we don't know. We may appear to be individual human beings living individual lives, but our interconnected webs, though invisible, are very real and very influential.

Just as I know that the Holy Spirit inspired me with the ideas that led to this book, I often recognized the Holy Spirit speaking through these friends. Sometimes I noticed it during the interview, but many times it was later when I played back the recording or transcribed it into text.

For instance, Connor's comment on Tim's perseverance came out unexpectedly and was spoken so eloquently that no editing was needed. Other times people would suddenly say, "You know, I haven't thought of this for a long time, but ..." and would go on to share a very meaningful thought. Or I would think an interview was finished, turn off the recorder, then the interviewee would start to say something completely out of the blue that was very profound, like when Will told me about going home from the wake to change his clothes. Sometimes I would be inspired to ask a question that I hadn't thought to ask anyone else and it would stimulate an exceptional response. It was a beautiful process that revealed some very important truths on life.

I saw how God gave Kenny the talents that people admire, so that people would be drawn to him, come to love him, stay friends with him, and then be touched by him as his journey unfolded. Throughout the years, the people that knew him early on respect and admire him for the gifts and witness that he shared at that time. The people that knew him in Brewster didn't know that side of Kenny, so much had changed for him, but he was able to reinvent himself and share his evolved palette of gifts and witness. What is amazing is that the outcome was the same. Whether he was a prankster or a quiet presence, he still transmitted his humble spirit and people that knew him felt important and loved.

Did you notice how many people said that he made time for them? That when they were together he gave them his complete attention, that he really listened, and he made it seem that what they were saying was important? That he made them feel loved and valued? That response reveals how people long for meaningful, one-on-one interaction and how this attention is rare in our society today. How many times a week do you hear someone say, "I didn't have time to call you back…"

Or, "I was going to do this for her, but I didn't have time …"

Or, "Sorry that I didn't stop by, but I had to …"

It is natural for us to internalize that as, "I am not as important as the other things she is doing."

We are all so busy doing whatever, that we do not make enough time to really interact in sincere, loving ways. Through Kenny, I see that we influence the people in our lives in ways we could never anticipate. Not only did people walk away feeling better from their time with Kenny, but they walked away with distinct memories that they could recall years later. Sometimes very seemingly insignificant things.

I thought it was very interesting that Chief Jack from SOC worked with thousands of firefighters over his thirty-four years with the FDNY and acknowledged that it just isn't possible to remember that many of them. He only worked with Kenny for about three of those years and admitted that he wasn't good friends with him, but he not only remembered Kenny vividly enough to tell specific anecdotes of firehouse life, but remembered outside details like where Kenny grew up, that he played basketball and golf, and liked to fish. That is a significant amount of knowledge to remember about a man that he hadn't seen for fifteen years and didn't have a close personal relationship with.

Kenny invested his entire life, his energy, his talents, his service, and his resources into people. It was an investment that paid high dividends; when Kenny needed help, there was no shortage of friends lined up for him. And that means they were there for his wife and children too.

Out of all the observations that I made through this process, there is one that is truly illuminating and may be the culminating message from this project for me and my sons—one important truth that we will live by and hopefully pass down through words and actions. I think Nancy said it best: *"The interesting thing about suffering is that you never realize it at the time, but the experience usually allows you to learn something or see something you wouldn't have otherwise. While we are suffering, we can't see the good in it. It can be very hard to see anything."*

Were you surprised to hear some people say in their interviews that they thought I was lucky? That the boys were lucky? I was. They wouldn't have said that six years ago. None of it made sense then. Now they see that how Kenny lived his life impacted their lives and they recognize that he would have impacted us even more deeply. Two years after Kenny passed they see that the boys and I are happy, joyful, living our lives with hope and purpose, so they are able to recognize the good that grew out of the suffering.

Accepting our suffering and living it out the way it was meant to unfold was liberating. Rather than give suffering the satisfaction of directing our lives, we called the shots. Of course those directives had to change over the years, but rather than complain or avoid suffering, we searched for its value and embraced all that life had to offer. Even the hardships.

Kenny living out his life to its natural end empowers and inspires people to live better lives, to accept their own hardships with courage and humility. I have referred to Kenny's "small corner of the world;" now as you ponder the impact that this one simple man made, how small do you think his world was? Don't forget to include those people connected by those invisible threads.

Now, more importantly, ask yourself, "How big is my world?"

Consider too, the people that want to avoid suffering at all costs, even to the extent of suicide. The current phenomenon of support for assisted suicide belies the truth that life has value through both the joys and the sorrows. People became friends with Kenny because of his personality, his athleticism, or his service, but ultimately it was the way that Kenny handled his suffering that made the biggest impact and changed lives for the better.

I believe that the way that we die could be the culminating statement of each of our lives. Everything that we do from birth is building and developing to that final moment. If we have a life well lived no matter how long, if we have developed our spirituality so we are ready for the transition, if we are content with our relationships, if we have truly learned to love, we are teaching the rest of our world how to both live and how to die. What is more important, more powerful, and more purposeful than that?

Index

227, 232, 233, 240, 244, 246, 254, 259, 270, 274

September 11th: 89, 90, 91, 93, 96, 99, 104, 173, 240, 249

Sportsmanship/Coaching: 6, 9, 12, 14, 20, 38, 41, 61, 82, 88, 92, 131, 139, 140, 141, 142, 143, 144, 148, 151, 154, 156, 165, 166, 167, 168, 169

Talking/Oral Challenges: 6, 18, 30, 32, 38, 53, 56, 61, 71, 78, 80, 82, 92, 93, 96, 104, 112, 116, 121, 125, 127, 135, 148, 150, 154, 156, 180, 184, 197, 200, 203, 204, 208, 214, 223, 225, 227, 230, 232, 234, 244, 246, 249, 256, 261, 266, 270, 274

Tracheostomy: 38, 61, 71, 80, 108, 118, 184, 189, 190, 196, 197, 208, 270

Value of/Redemptive Suffering: 3, 6, 9, 30, 35, 38, 47, 56, 57, 58, 61, 66, 77, 87, 108, 116, 120, 135, 144, 156, 158, 177, 178, 183, 184, 188, 197, 206, 208, 210, 214, 218, 232, 233, 238, 240, 244, 246, 254, 255, 259, 261, 266, 270, 278, 285

Made in United States
North Haven, CT
27 October 2021